The Blossom
Which We Are

SUNY SERIES
LITERATURE...IN THEORY

SERIES EDITORS

David E. Johnson, *Comparative Literature, University at Buffalo*
Scott Michaelsen, *English, Michigan State University*

SERIES ADVISORY BOARD

Nahum D. Chandler, *African American Studies, University of California, Irvine*
Rebecca Comay, *Philosophy and Comparative Literature, University of Toronto*
Marc Crépon, *Philosophy, École Normale Supérieure, Paris*
Jonathan Culler, *Comparative Literature, Cornell University*
Johanna Drucker, *Design Media Arts and Information Studies, University of California, Los Angeles*
Christopher Fynsk, *Modern Thought, Aberdeen University*
Rodolphe Gasché, *Comparative Literature, University at Buffalo*
Martin Hägglund, *Comparative Literature, Yale University*
Carol Jacobs, *German and Comparative Literature, Yale University*
Peggy Kamuf, *French and Comparative Literature, University of Southern California*
David Marriott, *History of Consciousness, University of California, Santa Cruz*
Steven Miller, *English, University at Buffalo*
Alberto Moreiras, *Hispanic Studies, Texas A&M University*
Patrick O'Donnell, *English, Michigan State University*
Pablo Oyarzún, *Teoría del Arte, Universidad de Chile*
Scott Cutler Shershow, *English, University of California, Davis*
Henry Sussman, *German and Comparative Literature, Yale University*
Samuel Weber, *Comparative Literature, Northwestern University*
Ewa Ziarek, *Comparative Literature, University at Buffalo*

The Blossom Which We Are

The Novel and the Transience of Cultural Worlds

Nir Evron

Cover image: *Hummingbird and Apple Blossoms*, by Martin Johnson Heade, 1875. Courtesy of the Met.

Published by State University of New York Press, Albany

© 2020 State University of New York

All rights reserved

No part of this book may be used or reproduced in any manner without written permission. No part of this book may be stored in a retrieval system or transmitted in any form or by any means including electronic, electrostatic, magnetic tape, mechanical, photocopying, recording, or otherwise without the prior permission in writing of the publisher.

For information, contact State University of New York Press, Albany, NY
www.sunypress.edu

Library of Congress Cataloging-in-Publication Data

Names: Evron, Nir, 1976– author.
Title: The blossom which we are : the novel and the transience of cultural worlds / Nir Evron.
Description: Albany : State University of New York Press, 2020. | Series: SUNY series, literature . . . in theory | Includes bibliographical references and index.
Identifiers: LCCN 2019058377 | ISBN 9781438480671 (hardcover : alk. paper) | ISBN 9781438480688 (pbk. : alk. paper) | ISBN 9781438480695 (ebook)
Subjects: LCSH: Fiction—20th century—History and criticism. | Fiction—Social aspects. | Literature and society—History—20th century. | Social change in literature. | Culture in literature.
Classification: LCC PN3344 .E97 2020 | DDC 809.3/9358—dc23
LC record available at https://lccn.loc.gov/2019058377

10 9 8 7 6 5 4 3 2 1

Contents

ACKNOWLEDGMENTS	vii
INTRODUCTION	1
CHAPTER 1 Culturalism, Vulnerability, and Transience	29
CHAPTER 2 An Ironist's Elegy: Edith Wharton's *The Age of Innocence*	75
CHAPTER 3 "Und siehe da: Es gab also fremde Länder!": Joseph Roth's Parochializing of Empire	109
CHAPTER 4 The Culturalization of Zionism: Yaakov Shabtai's *Past Continuous*	147
CHAPTER 5 Culturalism and Historicism in Contemporary Intellectual Life	185
WORKS CITED	205
INDEX	217

Acknowledgments

This book has had a long gestation period, during which I have accrued many debts to mentors, friends, and colleagues. I would like to thank Amir Eshel, Russell Berman, and Sepp Gumbrecht for their belief in this project when it was still in its infancy, as well as to Marton Dornbach for introducing me to Joseph Roth. I was fortunate to find an academic home in the most nurturing of departments. My thanks go out to my colleagues Noam Reisner, Shirley Sharon-Zisser, Yael Sternhell, Roi Tartakovsky, Dara Barnat, Jonathan Stavsky, Elana Gomel, and Sonia Weiner for their friendship and support, as well as to Ilana Etgar and Sigalit Shual for their professionalism and kindness. Anat Karolin has read every word of the manuscript and saved me from countless errors and embarrassments. Harris Feinsod, Yael Shapira, Leona Toker, and Irene Tucker have each provided valuable comments at crucial junctures. I owe particular debts of gratitude to Hana Wirth-Nesher, for her unflagging encouragement and advocacy, and, finally, to Milette Shamir who has been everything one could hope for in a colleague, and so much more.

My daughters, Talila and Nina, have been a constant source of pride and happiness, especially during the last few intensive years. What I owe to my wife, Galia Evron, can hardly be expressed here. I dedicate this book to her.

Early versions of parts of chapters 2 and 4 have been published under the following titles:

"Realism, Irony and Morality in Edith Wharton's *The Age of Innocence*," *Journal of Modern Literature* 35, no. 2 (2012): 37–51.

"Against Philosophy: Yaakov Shabtai's *Past Continuous* as Therapeutic Literature," *Partial Answers: Journal of Literature and the History of Ideas* 14, no. 1 (2016): 35–55.

Introduction

"The greatest creations in world literature," remarked the late Amos Oz, "have generally been produced in the twilight, or in relation to a period of twilight."¹ Twilight stands here for the unraveling of a cultural world, as its customs, beliefs, and linguistic patterns are overtaken by new regimes of meaning and power. "Periods of flourishing success . . . when things are getting bigger and stronger are not propitious to storytellers," states Oz. It is when a civilization begins to fall apart, when established institutions and ideologies lose their purchase on the minds of their inheritors, that the literary imagination comes into its own:

> And so, in the twilight between a great sunset and the vague glimmering of a new dawn, someone like Dante stands poised between the Middle Ages and the Renaissance. Or Cervantes and Shakespeare on the threshold of the modern age. Or the great Russian literature of Gogol, Tolstoy, Dostoevsky, Chekhov, written to the accompaniment of the death-knell of Orthodox, tsarist Russia. . . . Similarly Thomas Mann, and in a different way Kafka too, [writing] in the period of the decline of comfortable bourgeois Europe, heavy with years and old ways and manners and patterns of behavior and speech and mentalities, and in their differing ways knowing that this world was doomed.²

---

1. Amos Oz, *Under This Blazing Sun*, trans. Nicholas de Lange (Cambridge: Cambridge University Press, 1979), 22.
2. Oz, *Under This Blazing Sun*, 23–24.

This rough-and-ready sketch is open to criticism on several fronts.[3] But Oz is surely right that "twilight"—the ending of a Golden Age or passing of an era—has been one of Western literature's earliest and most enduring preoccupations. How early? Another well-known survey—this one by Raymond Williams—wryly traces the trope from twentieth-century invocations (by F.R. Leavis and others) back to nineteenth-century elegies to the pre-industrial English countryside (in Thomas Hardy and George Eliot), eighteenth-century paeans to pre-enclosure rural virtues (Oliver Goldsmith), early Elizabethan responses to commercialism (Philip Massinger), Thomas More's *Utopia*, the Magna Carte, Virgil, and eventually all the way back to the Garden of Eden, the *terminus post quem* of the Western canon.[4]

The present study will not stretch quite that far, nor will it cover the range of literary modes evoked by Oz's and Williams's sweeping genealogies. For reasons that will soon become evident, it will restrict itself to a single type, which I call the novel of cultural extinction, and offer close readings in the works of three of its most accomplished twentieth-century practitioners: American Edith Wharton, Austro-Hungarian Joseph Roth, and Israeli Yaakov Shabtai. Contextualizing the book's argument, however, will require reaching back beyond the Great War to the beginning of the long nineteenth century, when the form acquires its trademark historicist view of culture and culturalist view of the self. For it is then, in the seminal works of Maria Edgeworth and Walter Scott, that the theme of *cultural* extinction, by which I mean the terminal disappearance of distinct, geographically locatable, and culturally identifiable ways of life, begins to assume its recognizable modern shape.

As this book will show, underlying the striking similarities in concern and method among Wharton, Roth, and Shabtai is a durable, fertile, and highly appropriable repository of tropes and representational strategies, which, after being first assembled and reworked into narrative prose fiction by Edgeworth, Scott, and their peers, radiated out of England's Anglo-Celtic periphery to become, by the middle of the twentieth century, a truly global genre. Indeed, the preoccupation with cultural vanishing not only

---

3. A critical reader of Oz's essay might point out, for instance, that great works of literature have been known to appear in times of prosperous stability, not just of crisis. Besides, any critical statement that overlooks the vast differences in culture, circumstance, and outlook that distinguish a late-Medieval Florentine poet from a German-speaking Czech modernist must seem, at least by today's critical standards, deeply problematic.

4. Raymond Williams, *The Country and the City* (New York: Oxford University Press, 1973), 9–12.

links the exemplary figures at the center of this study; it is the thread that ties James Fenimore Cooper to Edward Bulwer-Lytton, Ippolito Nievo to Thomas Hardy, Theodor Fontane to Willa Cather, S.Y. Agnon to Chinua Achebe, Ahmed Ali to Evelyn Waugh, and Tomasi di Lampedusa to Mario Vargas Llosa—a provisional list that would expand significantly were we to include the scores of mid- and late-nineteenth-century regionalist writers in Europe and America who sought to record in fiction their nations' vanishing pockets of traditional life.

Why does the specter of cultural extinction loom so large in the history of realist fiction? How do we account for the fact that the literary genre famously credited by Benedict Anderson with imagining communities into existence seems to have dwelled, as insistently, on their dispossession and collapse? What distinguishes twentieth-century renditions of the cultural-extinction trope from its earlier invocations? And what, finally, might this enduring thematic preoccupation have to teach us about what philosopher Samuel Scheffler has described as the "elusive influence of time in our thinking about ourselves"?[5] These are the questions at the heart of *The Blossom Which We Are*. Its main objectives are, first, to make a case for cultural extinction as a theme that grounds a genre; and, second, to argue that this genre, far from incidental or marginal to the realist enterprise, offers a privileged site for exploring key aspects of the history and development of this literary mode. If the theme of cultural transience warrants our attention today, I claim, it is because, like the more closely studied marriage and Bildungs masterplots, it opens an invaluable window onto what Georg Lukács called the ideology of realism,[6] while also illuminating how the novel has negotiated the pressures and challenges of modernity. Insofar as many of these challenges are still ongoing, the novel of cultural extinction, I claim, also has a timely lesson to teach.

In maintaining that the novels I shall be examining impart a common lesson, I do not mean to suggest that they converge on a single moral viewpoint or that their authors espoused a similar set of political "positions" or "values." Indeed, comparing Wharton, Roth, and Shabtai on such a basis would yield only superficial similarities. Their biographies, the milieus in which they moved, and the sociopolitical contexts to which they

---

5. Samuel Scheffler, *Death and the Afterlife* (New York: Oxford, 2013), 16.
6. Georg Lukács, "The Ideology of Modernism," in *Marxist Literary Theory: A Reader*, ed. Terry Eagleton and Frew Milne (Oxford: Wiley-Blackwell, 1996), 141–162.

responded were simply too different to repay such comparisons. What these twentieth-century realist writers did significantly share, I want to claim, is not a set of moral or political convictions exactly, but a common *attitude*, a similar way of relating to their respective values and beliefs.

I take my cue here from the way Louis Menand describes the intellectual temperament shared by the founding fathers of the American pragmatist tradition: Oliver Wendell Holmes, William James, Charles M. Peirce, and John Dewey: "If we strain out the differences, personal and philosophical, they had with one another, we can say that what these four thinkers had in common was not a group of ideas, but a single idea—an idea about ideas."[7] That meta-idea, writes Menand, was that the concepts we use are not representations of the world "out there" but tools invented by human groups in order to deal with themselves and their environments.[8] This idea could take root in late-nineteenth-century America, he goes on to claim, because of the cultural climate that set in during the post–Civil War years. To come of age in the wake of that national catastrophe was to assume a new and decidedly more skeptical relation to accepted truths and received ideas, an attitude born of the recent experience of the fragility and ephemerality of social and political institutions.[9]

A similar awareness, I claim, ties together the figures at the center of my study. Their different social backgrounds and political commitments notwithstanding, Wharton, Roth, and Shabtai all believed they had experienced what Wharton described as the "sudden and total extinction" of the worlds of their youth: Old New York (in the case of Wharton), the Habsburg Empire (in Roth), and so-called Little Tel Aviv [*Tel Aviv ha'ktana*], the urban hub of the historical Zionist labor movement (Shabtai).[10] All three then narrated this experience from the presumptive standpoint of survivor-witnesses in major works: *The Age of Innocence* (1920), *The Radetzky March* (1932), and *Past Continuous* (1977). While the cultural formations whose demise these novels chronicle could scarcely have been more different, the manner in which they are depicted is the same. Culture, as represented in Wharton's, Roth's, and

---

7. Louis Menand, *The Metaphysical Club* (New York: Farrar, Straus and Giroux, 2001), x.

8. Menand, *Metaphysical Club*, xii.

9. This disposition, it should be noted, is equally conducive to pragmatist skepticism and xenophobia and self-isolationism, which was the other face of that era.

10. Edith Wharton, *A Backward Glance* (New York & London: D. Appleton-Century Company, 1934), 7.

Shabtai's works, is *both* a world-structuring and identity-sustaining power *and* an ungrounded, vulnerable, and ultimately transient episode.

Richard Rorty, in one of his essays on Heidegger, captures the picture of culture projected by Wharton's, Roth's, and Shabtai's novels of cultural extinction. On Rorty's interpretation, one of Heidegger's aims, in his revisionary rewriting of the history of Western philosophy, was to get us to think of our culture neither "as the place where human beings finally got clear on what is really going on," nor as an expression of some deep spiritual substance or *Geist*, but rather "as just one cherry blossom alongside actual and possible others, one cluster of 'understandings of Being' alongside other clusters. But we also have to think of it as the blossom which *we* are. We can neither leap out of our blossom into the next one down the bough, nor rise above the tree and look down at a cloud of blossoms (in the way in which we imagine God looking down on a cloud of galaxies)."[11] Rorty's choice of the cherry blossom, long a symbol of transience, as the focus of his metaphor is, of course, no accident. For coming to terms with what he elsewhere calls "[our] lonely provincialism" (the idea that we are nothing but our cultural and historical moment) entails accepting that no part of our way of life, from its mundane practices to its most revered values and institutions, is immune to time and change.[12] Culture thus emerges from Rorty's sketch, as from the novels examined below, simultaneously as the constitutive stuff of the self—"the blossom which *we* are"—and as a human artifact, consigned like all human things to pass. To read Wharton's, Roth's, and Shabtai's representative works in this light, I want to suggest, is to see them as offering searching explorations of the precariousness of identity and the transience of value under conditions of modern acceleration and change. As such, these novels speak in powerful and provocative ways to concerns that are as pressing today as they were at the time they were written.

If, as Menand suggests, the experience of the Civil War and its aftershocks impressed upon Holmes, James, Peirce, and Dewey that values and ideas must constantly adapt to the changing cultural environment if they are to survive,[13] the belief that they had witnessed the extinction of their native

---

11. Richard Rorty, "Heidegger, Contingency, and Pragmatism," in *Essays on Heidegger and Others* (Cambridge: Cambridge University Press, 1991), 27–49, 37.

12. Richard Rorty, "Solidarity or Objectivity," in *Objectivity, Relativism, and Truth* (Cambridge: Cambridge University Press, 1991), 21–34, 30.

13. Menand, *Metaphysical Club*, xi.

worlds left Wharton, Roth, and Shabtai with the conviction that adaptability has its limits: that some sociohistorical transitions open chasms too wide to bridge. And so, while they shared the early pragmatists' view of values and beliefs as mutable social constructs, they were far less sanguine about the individual's capacity for readjustment. On the view their novels advance, while human life can and does appear in a bewildering array of cultural expressions, individual human beings do not evince such suppleness. The two beliefs are not incompatible. To say with Margaret Mead that human nature "is almost unbelievably malleable" is not to extend the same flexibility to the already-formed personality.[14] Wharton, Roth, and Shabtai thought that we are less elastic than we would perhaps like to think. The self that their fictions project is a creature tethered to the matrix of practices and beliefs that produced and sustains it. Once the clay of personality has hardened, their novels suggest, it can be tweaked but not refashioned.

This view is likely to meet with considerable resistance today. The culture of capitalism, in the course of its long reign, has elevated flexibility and adaptability to the status of cardinal virtues, while casting the failure or reluctance to adjust as signs of blimpish conservatism or debility. "We have encouraged an identity," observes Charles Taylor, "of which the core is the ability to 'reinvent' ourselves," so as to become "free, self-reliant, creative, imaginative, resourceful . . . the highest stage of human development."[15] This moral vocabulary, adds Slavoj Žižek, is now routinely deployed to legitimize the gradual erosion of job security under global neoliberalism: "I am no longer just a cog in the complex enterprise but an entrepreneur-of-the-self, who freely manages my employment, free to choose new options, to explore different aspects of my creative potential, to choose my priorities."[16] If Taylor and Žižek look askance at this rhetoric of reinvention and self-reliance, it is not because they think that freedom, creativity, or resourcefulness are bad things. The point of their critiques, rather, is that the hyperbolic and often cynical neoliberal veneration of self-invention and personal adaptability has conspired to occlude other and equally pressing needs and desires. These include the individual's intimate reliance on a relatively stable cultural

---

14. Margaret Mead, *Sex and Temperament in Three Primitive Societies* (New York: Morrow, 1963), 280.

15. Charles Taylor, "A Different Kind of Courage," *New York Review of Books*, April 26, 2007, 6.

16. Slavoj Žižek, *The Courage of Hopelessness: Chronicles of a Year of Acting Dangerously* (Brooklyn, NY: Melville House, 2017), 30.

environment for familiarity and moral orientation (not least when he or she is in open revolt against it) as well as the limits imposed on the desire for self-transformation by the need to maintain a sense of continuity and coherence with one's prior self. Different people will of course negotiate the competing desires for self-invention and self-maintenance differently. But it is doubtful that anyone can be so malleable so as to meet the requirements of the contemporary protean ideal while retaining a functioning personality.

Nor is the overestimation of malleability and adaptability characteristic solely of free-market ideology. Contemporary intellectual discourse in the human and social sciences has produced its own variant of the protean ideal.[17] The poststructuralist polemics against closure; Judith Butler's and Walter Benn Michaels's attacks on identity; the critiques leveled by progressive anthropologists such as Renato Rosaldo, Arjun Appadurai, and Lila Abu-Lughod against the allegedly homogenizing and anti-individualist implications of the anthropological concept of culture—these and similar arguments are motivated (at least in part), I want to suggest, by the often-unstated desire for the kind of unencumbered existence and free-floating selfhood that comport with the ideal of absolute autonomy. As Susan Hegeman sums up her critical reading of Walter Benn Michaels: "Ultimately, Michaels may well be a kind of existentialist, whose ideal is a space of radical freedom from externally imposed identity."[18] And if *that* is what human life can and should be, then the thing to do is to liberate the authentic self by ruthlessly deconstructing, denaturalizing, or otherwise undermining the allegedly repressive conceptual and political constructs that hem it in. And again, the problem here is neither with the ideal of self-invention or free choice as such, let alone with the anti-metaphysical stance common to the aforementioned critics.

---

17. These two apparently antagonistic discourses—of capitalism and of high theory—may be, as Marxist critics have long argued, two faces of a single ideology. As Terry Eagleton puts it, the high premium that both place on "plurality, plasticity, dismantling, destabilizing, the power of endless self-invention . . . smacks of a distinctively Western culture and an advanced capitalist world." But then, as Franz Boas has pointed out, similar effects often spring from dissimilar causes. The fact that that the protean ideal looms large in both discourses does not prove that they are similarly motivated, that they are collapsible into a single agenda, or that poststructuralism has unwittingly served as capitalism's dupe and handmaiden. See Terry Eagleton, *Sweet Violence* (Malden, MA: Blackwell, 2003), xi.

18. Susan Hegeman, *The Cultural Return* (Berkeley: University of California Press, 2012), 31.

It is, first, with the tendency of this critical discourse to overemphasize the individual's capacity for radical change, while underestimating the persistent need for collective identity, self-coherence, and continuity; and second, with the manner in which, in spite of its proclaimed antiessentialism, it tends to lapse into arguing for the existence of a radically free, pre-cultural "real self," which it then becomes the theorist's mission to liberate.

Against this background, the insistence common to Wharton, Roth, and Shabtai that the range of individual adaptability is limited (not only for the harried masses who lack the leisure and opportunity necessary for self-fashioning, but also for the relatively privileged and educated protagonists of their novels) seems to court charges of conservatism. These charges, it should be said, would not be unfounded. Though often unsparing in their critiques of their native societies, Wharton, Roth, and Shabtai all looked on with profound dismay at the social and political regimes that had displaced them. Yet pointing to the reactionary aspect of their writings is easy work. The more challenging question that their novels raise is to what extent, when it comes to the core practices and institutions that give shape and meaning to our lives, can we avoid being conservative. When put in these terms, the issue of conservatism invites an examination of the dynamics of value and valuing that extends beyond what we conventionally refer to as "political positions." These issues will be addressed concretely in the readings that follow. For now, suffice it to suggest that our celebration of fluidity, variability, and indeterminacy may be due for some tempering—not because the past enjoys some special privilege over the future, but because the protean ideal, while important and even vital in certain contexts, may well be obstructive in others. A bit of "intractability," as Terry Eagleton quips, "is sometimes just what we need."[19]

The latter remark is drawn from *Sweet Violence* (2002), Eagleton's polemical study of tragedy, a literary form, he argues, that offers some much-needed correctives to some of the least helpful tendencies of the intellectual Left. Like Eagleton's book, *The Blossom Which We Are*, too, is concerned with highlighting "what is perishable, constricted, fragile and slow-moving about us."[20] The emphasis on human vulnerability, which Eagleton sees as the moral core of tragedy, I want to show, is also a feature of the novel of cultural extinction. More specifically, what the plays of Aeschylus, Sophocles,

---

19. Eagleton, *Sweet Violence*, xv.

20. Eagleton, Sweet *Violence*, xvi.

and Euripides were for the ancients, prose narratives of cultural passing have been for us moderns: namely, a way to acknowledge, via vicarious identification, the finitude and vulnerability of our own private and collective lives. "The pitier," as Martha Nussbaum claims in connection with the range of responses that Greek tragedy drew from its audiences, "trembles for his or her own possibilities."[21]

Novels of cultural extinction in general and *The Age of Innocence*, *The Radetzky March*, and *Past Continuous* in particular have frequently been read as escapes into fabled pasts or as expressions of elite ennui in the face of sociopolitical change. And while I do not want to deny that nostalgia and political despair figure centrally in these works, I do want to contest the idea that such readings exhaust the interpretative uses to which these particular novels (and their kind) can be put. We would do better, I believe, to read Wharton's, Roth's, and Shabtai's cultural elegies—or, for that matter, Ahmed Ali's *Twilight in Delhi* (1940), Achebe's *Things fall Apart* (1958), and Lampedusa's *The Leopard* (1958)—not (only) as nostalgic escapes from a troubled political present to a vanished past, but also as modern meditations on the transience and vulnerability of cultural values and institutions. For reading these novels in this way may help us (to quote Rorty again) "recapture a sense of contingency, of the fragility and riskiness of any human project."[22]

Fostering such a sense is, I believe, a particularly urgent task today. We live in precarious times, in which the future of longstanding social and political institutions suddenly seems to have been thrown into question. The deepening crisis of liberal democracy and resurgence of ethnic populism, the rising inequality between the global North and South, the looming threat of environmental catastrophe and, most recently, the severely destabilizing worldwide outbreak of the COVID-19 virus—these threats combine to generate a widespread sense of unease that cuts across conventional party lines and divisions. For while each of these crises poses distinct challenges and threats, to which different people react in different ways, they all confront us jointly with the unsettling probability that the world that we will leave behind us will be radically different, not only from the one we inherited but also from the one we currently inhabit. We are situated, in this respect, in a position not unlike that of the post–Civil War intellectuals

---

21. Martha Nussbaum, "Tragedy and Self-sufficiency: Plato and Aristotle on Fear and Pity," in *Essays on Aristotle's Poetics*, ed. Amélie Rorty (Princeton, NJ: Princeton University Press, 1992), 261–290, 267.

22. Rorty, "Heidegger," 34.

that Menand describes, or indeed of the novelists discussed later. For like them, we will probably live to see much of what we today take for granted become obsolete or simply nonexistent, including our own social, political, and professional identities. Can anyone reading this book speak confidently about the long-term prospects of the cultural world we call the humanities? In this fraught context, the novels at the center of this study have, I maintain, a lot to say to us. For each, in its way, explores the breakable, fragile, and transient nature of the socially constructed and culturally maintained frameworks that we inhabit. And even if they hold out no solutions to this quintessentially modern predicament, they may help us acknowledge and perhaps come to terms with it.

To accept that our familiar and everyday reality is a precarious, consensually produced narrative—a fragile fiction—is difficult to do, not least because our ability to pursue personal projects and assign value to our lives in the present depends on an implicit trust in the (relative) solidity and endurance of the values and institutions that make up our "world." Having long prided ourselves, as cultural critics, on our power to demystify and denaturalize conventional patterns of thought and action, we tend to forget that a certain degree of reification is not only an inevitable part of social life, but is also vital for keeping the enterprise going. Reification, understood as "the apprehension of the products of human activity *as if* they were something other than human products" is what enables us to "forget" the exceedingly tenuous nature of the social world in which we move, and thus to engage with it in an assured and deliberate way.[23] Without such active forgetting and the illusion of security and durability that it encourages, it is doubtful we would be able to get much done, either individually or collectively. Still, "the decisive question," as Peter Berger and Thomas Luckmann write in their classic study, is whether when we are not caught up in our pragmatic engagements we succeed in retaining the awareness "that, however objectivated, the social world was made by men—and, therefore, can be remade by them."[24] Keeping this awareness alive is hard even under the best of circumstances. But when the familiar order of things is threatened by radical disruption—as, for instance, in the case of the ongoing environmental emergency—the tendency is often to

---

23. Peter Berger and Thomas Luckmann, *The Social Construction of Reality: A Treatise in the Sociology of Knowledge* (London: Penguin, 1991), 106.

24. Berger and Luckmann, *Social Construction*, 106.

disavow it altogether. As Roy Scranton puts this point in his *Learning to Die in the Anthropocene* (2015), "It is hard work for us to remember that this way of life, this present moment, this order of things is not stable and permanent. Across the world today, our actions testify to our belief that we can go on like we are forever."[25] Powerful economic interests have of course been diligently at work to encourage the general complacency and lassitude with which the world's industrialized nations have hitherto responded to what everyone more or less agrees is a clear and immediate danger to the continued existence of our species. But these economical and political factors cooperate with deep-set cultural and psychological impulses of the kind that Scranton discusses. The more precarious the established order becomes, the more inclined we are to disown its historicity and malleability.

If the novel of cultural extinction matters today it is because it acknowledges *both* the necessarily conventional dimensions of social life *and* their endemic frailty and impermanence. From Walter Scott's *Waverley* to Yaakov Shabtai's *Past Continuous*, each of the novels examined below aspires to the world-making totality of vision and density of detail characteristic of the realist genre, while also giving the lie to the reassuring belief that the represented cultural world—any cultural world—can go on forever. "Giving the lie" is perhaps the wrong phrase here, because fiction never really "proves" or "demonstrates" the truth-value of propositions; rather, it mobilizes its rhetorical resources to coax its readers into a certain view of themselves and their worlds. That view, in the case of the novel of cultural extinction, is one that works out from the ambiguous recognition of the structuring power of cultural institutions, on the one hand, and their fragile and episodic nature, on the other. As such, this narrative form can help us to think in fuller and more meaningful ways about what it means to live as finite cultural beings who thrive and perish within perishable worlds of our own making. If Scranton is right that effective response to our current predicament requires taking a long hard look at our private and collective vulnerability, if "our future . . . [depends] on our ability to confront it not with panic, outrage, or denial, but with patience, reflection, and love,"[26] then, I submit, we have something to learn from the novel's most concentrated attempt to find meaning in the face of inevitable loss.

---

25. Roy Scranton, *Learning to Die in the Anthropocene: Reflections on the End of a Civilization* (San Francisco: City Lights, 2015), 16.

26. Scranton, *Learning to Die*, 27.

Culturalism, Historicism, Realism

These then are the topical concerns that I bring to this study. However, in framing them in the particular way I've done, I have been taking a broad range of assumptions for granted. For instance, I have assumed that history flows in a linear rather than cyclical manner, such that loss, once incurred, is irreversible; I have assumed that our individual lives transpire within the socially concrete yet metaphysically ungrounded structures we call "cultures"; and I have assumed that these complex meshes of language and practice not only shape our subjectivities but also constitute them, so that our individual selves are wholly continuous with the webs of beliefs and practices into which we are socialized. Some of these postulates (for instance, that history moves forward like an arrow) are today broadly assumed; others, like the anti-Cartesian idea that we are cultural-linguistic creatures all the way down, are still fiercely contested. In combination, however, they comprise an immediately recognizable and prevalent (though by no means exclusive) modern self-image, and one whose historical emergence, consolidation, and dissemination dovetails with that of the realist novel.

In this book, then, I try to link the rise of the latter self-image (here called *culturalism*) with the emergence of a certain temporal imaginary (often called *historicism*), and to locate both in the literary tradition we call *realism*. Mine is hardly the first study to draw such connections. Thanks to the enormous sway of realism's greatest mid-twentieth-century champions, Georg Lukács and Erich Auerbach, we have long been accustomed to associate the appearance of the nineteenth-century realist novel with the post-1789 discovery of history in the fully historicist sense. More recently, a number of powerful studies have established the role of realist fiction in the emergence of the modern, holistic and relativistic, concept of culture.[27] Though I will gratefully draw on these studies in what follows, my aim is not to repeat them, but to chart an as-yet under-theorized part of the

---

27. See Katie Trumpener, *Bardic Nationalism* (Princeton, NJ: Princeton University Press, 1997); Ian Duncan, *In Scott's Shadow: The Novel in Romantic Edinburgh* (Princeton, NJ: Princeton University Press, 2016); James Buzard, *Disorienting Fiction: The Autoethnographic Work of Nineteenth-Century British Novels* (Princeton, NJ: Princeton University Press, 2005); Susan Hegeman, *The Cultural Return* (Berkeley: University of California Press, 2011); Michael Elliott, *The Culture Concept* (Minneapolis: University of Minnesota Press, 2002); Brad Evans, *Before Cultures* (Chicago: University of Chicago Press, 2005); and Nancy Bentley, *The Ethnography of Manners: Hawthorne, James, Wharton* (Cambridge: Cambridge University Press, 1995).

critical terrain they explore. Specifically, I want to show that realist fiction (a category whose use in this book will be defined momentarily) encodes a view of the human situation, in which cultural vulnerability, fragility, and finitude are built-in features. My claim, in other words, is that insofar as literary realism historicizes and culturalizes social reality (as Katie Trumpener, James Buzard, Michael Elliott, Brad Evans, and Nancy Bentley have variously argued), it also ephemeralizes it. Indeed, it is a telling and, in my view, still insufficiently appreciated fact, that the texts most often credited with launching literary realism proper—Edgeworth's *Castle Rackrent* and Scott's *Waverley*—are both also novels of cultural extinction, written in the express purpose of chronicling the final disappearance of geographically localized and ethnographically realized lifeworlds. Part of the aim of this book is to demonstrate what happens to our understanding of literary realism when it is keyed to its nineteenth-century founders' preoccupation with the friability of social customs and institutions.

To jumpstart an argument about the connections between culturalism, historicism, and realism requires providing some preliminary definitions. These terms have simply been used for too long, by too many people, and in too many contexts to be of any critical use before one takes the risk of more narrowly demarcating them. And it is a risk, for any definition of such contested concepts involves exposing oneself to charges of one-sidedness or oversimplification. The following then is a series of working definitions, which I will use to get the argument going, on the understanding that a fuller and more nuanced account will have to emerge in the course of the subsequent discussions.

Culturalism, as I shall be using this term, refers to a structure of thought and feeling that begins to take shape toward the end of the eighteenth century in reaction to Enlightenment thought and policy. My choice of culturalism to refer to this discourse is meant to distinguish it from its later disciplinary expressions (in twentieth-century anthropology, pragmatist philosophy, hermeneutics, new historicism, cultural studies, and so on), but also in order to imply its diffused and attitudinal, as opposed to strictly doctrinal, quality. In its most basic sense, culturalism is founded on the idea that the individual self—whatever else it might be—is "so entangled with where [it] is, who [it] is, and what [it] believes that it is inseparable from them."[28] This idea appears for the first time in the years leading up to the

---

28. Clifford Geertz, "The Impact of the Concept of Culture on the Concept of Man," in *The Interpretation of Cultures* (New York: Basic Books, 1973), 35.

French Revolution, and it was its gradual acceptance in the decades that followed that gave rise sometime on or about 1900 to the modern, holistic and relativistic, concept of culture and its dedicated disciplinary matrices.

When culturalism first appeared on the scene, the reigning assumption among the leading intellectual lights of Europe was that the springs of human feeling, action, and thought remain constant across languages, places, and times. Over and above their various disagreements, Spinoza, Voltaire, John Locke, David Hume, Immanuel Kant, and Samuel Johnson all believed that in spite of the ostensible differences among and within social groups, all human beings are at bottom cast from a single, unchanging mold. None of these intellectuals, it should be said, doubted that different societies organize human life differently, or that human beings are profoundly modified by the contingencies of their time and place. But they shared the conviction that local particularities are a superficial veneer draped over a more fundamental human essence or core that is knowable, general, and unchanging. For some (Spinoza and Kant), that essential humanity was rational in nature; for others (Hume and perhaps Johnson), it was passional. But thinkers on both sides of this internal divide agreed that the most vital part of the individual—the part that makes her human—is also the part that remains untouched by the contingent specificities of her social environment. In order to become more fully human, this dominant view maintained, one must overcome, transcend, or otherwise purify oneself of these contingencies, so as to draw closer to the universal and immutable core of one's being. This self-image, as Arthur O. Lovejoy remarked in his celebrated intellectual history, "was the central and dominating fact in the intellectual history of Europe from the late sixteenth to the late eighteenth century."[29] Culturalism was its rejection.

Setting themselves expressly against Enlightenment uniformitarianism, the early exponents of the culturalist view—Giambattista Vico, Johann Gottfried Herder, and Edmund Burke, later followed by the Romantic poets and the German Idealists—argued that local and individual differences mattered more than similarities; that diversity was to be cultivated rather than overcome; that abstract reasoning was a dangerous lure rather than a panacea; and that there is no single model of human perfection, either moral or aesthetic, that all human groups should strive to attain. On a deeper level, however, what set Vico against Descartes, Herder against Kant, Burke against the French

---

29. Arthur O. Lovejoy, *The Great Chain of Being: A Study of the History of an Idea* (Cambridge, MA: Harvard University Press, 2001), 293.

philosophes, and Wordsworth and Coleridge against the neoclassical poets, was the question of which self-image the West should adopt. If the Enlightenment thinkers insisted that the most genuinely real part of the individual is also the most antithetical to its immediate sociohistorical environment, the early culturalists maintained that the self was wholly *coextensive* with and *expressive* of its culture. If the eighteenth-century uniformitarians believed that the true self was to be sought above or beyond its inherited customs and beliefs, the culturalists held, as Clifford Geertz would later assert, "that men unmodified by the customs of particular places do not in fact exist, have never existed, and most important, could not in the very nature of the case exist."[30] To repeat, what made this late eighteenth-century reorientation so revolutionary was not the truism, as apparent to Plato and Herodotus as it was to Locke and Kant, that human identities arise from and reflect the social arrangements of their time and place. Rather it was the early culturalists' bold *transvaluation* of these contingencies. To say, with Burke and Herder, that human beings are constituted by the habits of thought, practice, and speech of their respective communities was to invest these local and transitory circumstances with unprecedented significance, while also changing the definition of what it means to be a person. From mere impediments that had to be cleared away so that the essential self—however conceived—could come into view, factors like language, manners, folk traditions, and inherited morals suddenly became the very fabric from which a human subject is woven. To strip a person of her cultural "trappings," on this view, was not to reveal some underlying universal template or core, but to deny that person of her humanity.

The importance of this movement of ideas for the subsequent development of the modern concept of culture is too well known to require extensive comment here.[31] I will be briefly reconstructing parts of this story in the next chapter, but only in order to spotlight one implication of the shift in self-image that late eighteenth-century culturalism had set into motion. On the view I will develop, culturalism did more than give rise to a novel form of self-recognition; it also introduced new anxieties and

---

30. Geertz, "Impact," 35.

31. Isaiah Berlin's *Vico and Herder: Two Studies in the History of Ideas* (1976) remains the authoritative intellectual history of the period. For an account of Herder's significance as the "source of cultural pluralism and anthropological relativism" (20), see George Stocking, *Victorian Anthropology* (New York: Free Press, 1987). For Burke's influence on the emergence of the modern culture concept, see Williams, *The Country and the City*.

vulnerabilities into the human repertoire (or at least brought them into much sharper relief than ever before). For the more reconciled individuals became to viewing themselves as cultural creatures, wholly entangled in the contingent network of social relations and institutions that make up their sociohistorical habitat, the more they perceived their personal fates as inextricably linked with how this particular habitat fares. Should that precarious constellation of practices and beliefs be violently disrupted or destroyed, they stand to lose the only meaning-making context in which their individual identities make sense. In other words, insofar as being able to locate oneself within a culturally demarcated space has become "a hallmark of what it means to be a subject in modernity," as Hegeman writes, then so has living with the heightened awareness of the brittle and time-bound nature of one's social identity.[32] Much of the labor in the subsequent chapters will be to flesh out the historical and conceptual link between the rise of the culturalist view and the emergence of this peculiarly human and distinctly modern vulnerability.

If culturalism (as I shall be using this term) refers to a self-image organized around an awareness of our constitutive entanglement in the web of practices and institutions that we inherit, historicism will refer to the equally modern consciousness of the temporality and mutability of these arrangements. Like culturalism, historicism is a product of the turn of the nineteenth century. Lukács's *The Historical Novel* (1937) remains an indispensable account of the birth of historicism out of the spirit of the French Revolution. On his famous argument, the unprecedented nature of the events of 1789–1815 compelled Europeans and other observers to comprehend for the first time "their own existence as something historically conditioned [and to] see in history something which deeply affects their daily lives and immediately concerns them."[33] The way history itself was configured also changed in the wake of the Revolution. The decades following 1789 witnessed the decisive retreat of the cyclical and providential conceptions of time, which had defined the historical consciousness of the medieval and early-modern mind, and the advent of a linear and secular view of history as a sequence of unrepeatable events, scored by periodic ruptures and transformations that affected whole societies (as opposed to just their

---

32. Hegeman, *The Cultural Return*, 25.

33. Georg Lukács, *The Historical Novel*, trans. Hannah and Stanley Mitchell (Boston, MA: Beacon Press, 1963), 24.

ruling classes) in profound and irreversible ways.³⁴ As Peter Fritzsche sums up this point in his more recent *Stranded in the Present* (2004), "[It] was during the revolutionary epoch that the new appeared to contemporaries as an unmistakable if unknowable force, which upended, uplifted, and destroyed. Inconstancy was the new constant."³⁵ History, in the wake of 1789, became not only more visible, but also more forbidding.

Thus, if culturalism had inserted fundamental—sometimes irreconcilable—differences between contemporary forms of life, historicism introduced a consciousness of separation between present and past. If culturalism emphasized commonalities based in language, tradition, and custom, historicism generated affinities among strangers who inhabit the same historical generation (giving rise to what Fritzsche calls that "modern species 'contemporaries' ").³⁶ The changing meaning of the term "revolution" serves as a useful index of this shift in perception. Before 1789 the word was typically used to refer to the cyclical patterns of nature, as in the revolution of the stars. From the French Revolution onward, however, it came to signify drastic, often violent, change—the most extreme version of which being, of course, extinction. And indeed, starting in the early decades of the nineteenth century it is possible to discern a growing interest in disappearing races, cultures, and species: from the Romantics' fascination with relics, ruins, and last-of-the-race figures (think of Wordsworth's "Michael" or "The Old Cumberland Beggar")³⁷ to the emerging scientific preoccupation with the fossil record, culminating in Georges Cuvier's conclusive demonstration of the reality and prevalence of species extinction.³⁸ The idea of local and relative extinction

---

34. For a well-known but still provocative study of the late-eighteenth-century transition from cyclical and providential views of history to a linear one, see Mircea Eliade, *Cosmos and History: The Myth of the Eternal Return*, trans. Willard R. Trask (New York: Harper, 1954), in particular 49–137.

35. Peter Fritzsche, *Stranded in the Present: Modern Time and the Melancholy of History* (Cambridge, MA: Harvard University Press, 2004), 30.

36. Fritzsche, *Stranded in the Present*, 53.

37. For a ranging and engrossing account of the modern myth of the belated survival, see Fiona Stafford, *The Last of the Race* (Oxford: Clarendon, 1994).

38. When Cuvier came on the scene in the early 1800s, the accepted view among the proponents of extinction (most notably Comte de Buffon) was still that only a single species in earth's history had actually suffered this ignominious fate: the so-called "American *incognitum*" (mastodon), discovered in Big Bone Lick, near the Ohio River, in 1739.

events, of the kind that spells the terminal ending of a single race, species, or community while leaving the rest of creation untouched—an idea that had been unthinkable from within a worldview organized around the metaphor of the Great Chain of Being—becomes in the early nineteenth century both a scientific fact and a recurring literary trope. From within the emerging historical awareness urged on by these developments, writes Zygmunt Bauman, the world began to appear "ever more human [in] form . . . [revealing] the temporality of all worldly arrangements, [for] temporality is a feature of human, not divine, existence."[39] Put simply, by humanizing the world, historicism also infected its components—institutions, practices, moralities—with the canker of mortality.

What the emergent historicist awareness had in common with its coeval counterpart, the culturalist self-image, was their secularist thrust. By this I do not mean that either culturalism or historicism *refuted* (or had really anything to say about) God's existence. Nor do I hold that either was (or is) incompatible with religious belief. Instead, the secular dimension of the historicist and culturalist orientations consisted of the manner in which they reshaped the nineteenth-century's horizon of expectation. Historicism redirected people's attention from the possibility of postmortem rewards and punishments to the immanent and mundane realm of experience, newly conceived as the principal arena in which human destinies are concretely determined.[40] Culturalism's secular aspect, meanwhile, consisted in its suggestion that the self is not an entity apart from the contingent world of inherited customs and transient conventions but is continuous with it, thus effectively substituting the otherworldliness common to Descartes's and St. Augustine's conceptions of the self with an earthly, rooted alternative.[41] Similarly, just as historicism insisted on the self-sufficiency of history, such that "[its] apprehension," as Reinhart Koselleck writes, "no longer required recourse to God or nature,"[42] so did culturalism insist on the self-supporting and autotelic nature of cultural formations. Already in Burke, and even more so in Herder, there is the idea that while a form of life exists *in relation* to its counterparts, it is not

---

39. Zygmunt Bauman, *Culture as Praxis* (London: Sage, 1999), xi.

40. See Reinhart Koselleck, *Futures Past: On the Semantics of Historical Time*, trans. Keith Tribe (New York: Columbia University Press, 2004), 255–276 and in passim.

41. For a suggestive exploration of rootedness as a modern metaphor, see Christy Wampole's *Rootedness: The Ramifications of a Metaphor* (Chicago: University of Chicago Press, 2016).

42. Kosellek, *Futures Past*, 196.

grounded in anything beyond itself. A culture, in the pluralized sense of the term that these thinkers were among the first to propound, acts as its own foundation: it does not express or reflect a source of value that is deeper, higher, or otherwise external to the assembled wills of its constituents.

Literary realism, to turn to the last of the three framing categories of my argument, is the artistic genre chiefly responsible for narrativizing and thus concretizing the transformative energies of culturalism and historicism, as well as for disseminating them to broad nineteenth- and twentieth-century audiences on both sides of the Atlantic. As nearly a century of literary criticism has amply borne out, our modern conceptions of nation, society, and culture are indebted in many and complex ways to the forms of realist representation that began to take shape in the wake of the French Revolution, and which dominated the literary field until the early decades of the twentieth century. We can think in this connection of Lukács's and Raymond Williams's overlapping descriptions of the novel as a form of holistic social analysis; or of Benedict Anderson's and Homi Bhabha's complementary reflections on realism's key role in the production of national consciousness; or of Franco Moretti's and Fredric Jameson's shared emphasis on the allegorical dimensions of realist representation.[43] On the view forcefully articulated in these and similar accounts, realist fiction was not, as it often proclaimed itself to be, merely a reflection of the way people and things independently are. George Eliot's self-ascribed mission, "to give no more than a faithful account of men and things as they have mirrored themselves in my mind,"[44] though in keeping with the genre's vaunted mandate, was never a good description of what it actually did. Hardly a passive mirror to society, realist fiction was an active social agent that helped to shape the intellectual sensibilities and moral identities of its readers. Nancy Armstrong's claim, that "the history of the novel and the history of the modern subject are, quite literally, one and the same,"[45] while no doubt overstated, is justified to the extent that

---

43. See, Lukács, *The Historical Novel*; Williams, *The Country and the City*; Benedict Anderson, *Imagined Communities: Reflections on the Origin and Spread of Nationalism*, Revised Edition (London: Verso, 2006); Homi Bhabha, ed., *Nation and Narration* (London: Routledge, 1990); Franco Moretti, *The Way of the World* (London: Verso, 1988); and Fredric Jameson, *The Political Unconscious* (Ithaca, NY: Cornell University Press, 1981).

44. George Eliot, *Adam Bede*, ed. Carol A. Martin (Oxford: Oxford University Press, 2008), 221.

45. Nancy Armstrong, *How Novels Think: The Limits of Individualism from 1719–1900* (New York: Columbia University Press, 2005), 3.

in the course of the previous two centuries realist fiction did indeed replace both religion and philosophy as the site to which literate women and men went in search of a self-image. That self-image, thanks to the culturalist and historicist grammar underwriting the form, became increasingly more *this-worldly*, more cognizant of its historical underpinnings, and more tolerant to what Milan Kundera called "the essential relativity of human things."[46] Realist fiction, as I understand this multifaceted cultural phenomenon, was one of the great engines of modern secularization.

I have been referring to realist "fiction" rather than to the realist "novel" advisedly. For in this book, I want to describe as realist not only the kind of text exemplified by Balzac's *Le Père Goriot* (1835) Dickens's *Bleak House* (1852–1853), and Henry James's *The Portrait of a Lady* (1880–1881), but also the works produced by these metropolitan novelists' so-called "regionalist" or "local-color" contemporaries: writers such as Swiss-German Berthold Auerbach, French George Sand, Russian Ivan Turgenev, and American Sarah Orne Jewett. As will become evident in greater detail in the next chapter, the reason for this expanded definition is that each of these closely related genres—metropolitan and regionalist realism—took up and developed different aspects of the culturalist and historicist outlook that began to coalesce at the turn of the nineteenth century. Schematically speaking, while metropolitan realism adopted the holistic and historicist view of society, and employed it to produce nation-building narratives of social integration at the hegemonic center, its regionalist counterpart, which specialized in the depiction of fading lifeworlds on the national or imperial periphery, gave expression to the post-1789 awareness of the precarity and vulnerability of social institutions.

The latter distinction, I hasten to emphasize, should not be taken as absolute. In the first place, it is possible to read the novel's desire for the real, the urgency with which it strove to naturalize and normalize middle-class identities and institutions, as a reaction to the newly perceived fragility and tenuousness of the social bond. "Despite its appearance of solidity," as George Levine observes, "[metropolitan] realism implies a fundamental uneasiness about self, society, and art";[47] or, as Hilary Schor put it more recently, "to be in a realist novel is at once to be in a world of plentitude and certainty,

---

46. Milan Kundera, *Art of the Novel*, trans. Linda Asher (New York: Harper & Row, 1988), 7.

47. George Levine, *The Realistic Imagination: English Fiction from Frankenstein to Lady Chatterley* (Chicago: University of Chicago Press, 1981), 12.

and another world of potential loss and chaos."[48] In the second place, as Amy Kaplan, Richard Brodhead, and others have pointed out, in spite of regionalism's trademark focus on vanishing natives and dying out traditions—indeed partly through that very preoccupation—its local-color fiction also served to further the nineteenth-century projects of national consolidation and middle-class self-affirmation.[49] But despite this confluence of motives and functions, only to be expected given the congenital origin of these two realist forms (likewise to be discussed later in this book), the novel and the regionalist tale served to articulate and manage different aspects of the modern self-image to which they administered. Whereas the novel affirmed its evermore culturalist and historicist readers in the stability and perdurability of their nation- or class-based identities, the regionalist text, via its traditional gesture of pushing the prospect of cultural extinction away from the metropolitan center and toward its peripheral or premodern "others," reassured these same middle class readers in their immunity to that unsettling possibility.

Demonstrating these assertions will put me in a position to stake a claim for the distinctiveness of the novels examined later in the book. On the basis of close readings in the careers and works of Wharton, Roth, and Shabtai, I will argue that what distinguishes the twentieth-century novel of cultural extinction from its precursors is its transposition of the cultural-extinction trope from periphery to center. That is, what a novel like Wharton's *The Age of Innocence* has in common with Roth's *The Radetzky March* and Shabtai's *Past Continuous* (and with other similarly configured twentieth-century works of elegiac realism) is not only that they are all indebted in similar ways to the tradition that begins with Edgeworth and Scott, but also, and more pointedly, that each does to a self-conscious metropolitan elite what earlier texts and discourses had done to outlying, nonurban communities: depict it as a time-bound and ultimately perishable human creation. In thus parochializing the center and ephemeralizing its social types, these twentieth-century novels—so goes my argument—close the realist/regionalist divide that opened in the early nineteenth century, while also facing up to the full implications of the culturalist and historicist paradigm implicit in the grammar of their form.

---

48. Schor, Hilary M. *Curious Subjects: Women and the Trial of Realism* (New York: Oxford University Press, 2012), 43–44.

49. See Amy Kaplan, "Nation, Region, Empire," in *The Columbia History of the American Novel*, ed. Emory Elliott (New York: Columbia University Press, 1991), 240–266; Richard Brodhead, *Cultures of Letters* (Chicago: University of Chicago Press, 1993).

Telling this story, as my selection of proof texts already suggests, will require me to range more broadly and more eclectically than is often done in contemporary critical studies. *The Blossom Which We Are* deals in a large historical and cultural landscape, linking figures and modes of writing from diverse linguistic and cultural backgrounds, while also extending across more than two centuries of social, intellectual, and literary history. Whether the book succeeds in painting a compelling picture from its materials is a judgment that must be left to its reader, but I want to say a few words in defense of the scope (historical, linguistic, cultural) of my canvas. For while there once was a time—in the heroic age of literary studies, when the titanic figures of Lukács and Auerbach, Lionel Trilling and Irving Howe, René Wellek and George Steiner still roamed the field—in which such a procedure required no special justification, this is no longer the case. The preference, common to new historicism and cultural studies, for relatively narrow frames of temporal and cultural reference, coupled with the pressures of specialization, which lead scholars to fashion themselves as experts in neatly demarcated periods or national traditions, have made microhistory and synchronic discourse-analysis the typical approaches of choice. To historicize, under this still-prevailing critical regime, as Wai Chee Dimock argues, has come to mean "[imputing] meanings to a text by situating it among events in the same slice of time. . . . The object of inquiry is dated. Its reference points are events that began and ended in its original context."[50] Cleaving close to this context (typically a decade, two or three at most) enables the critic, in turn, to claim a kind of immediacy and specificity to her speculations, while also indemnifying herself against accusations of overgeneralization or—horror of horrors—essentialism.

Now, the disciplinary orientation toward the proximate and the political, which began in the 1980s, has had a resoundingly positive overall effect on both pedagogy and research, producing highly sophisticated explorations of the ways texts interact with the discourses of their day and facilitating the recovery of marginalized writers and groups. But it also had less salutary consequences, including the cultivation (in some cases) of a finicky mindset that outlaws any large-order historical or moral claims about the way we live now, by encouraging us to assume, wrongly, that an analysis that does not restrict itself to what Dimock calls "relations of simultaneity between

---

50. Wai Chee Dimock, "A Theory of Resonance," *PMLA* 112, no. 5 (1997): 1060–1071, 1061.

concurrent events,"⁵¹ or that fails to parse its subject down to demographic or gender determinates (the famous gender-class-race shuffle), is either naively pretheoretical or politically regressive. In this connection, Matti Bunzl's reflections on the path traveled by his own discipline, anthropology, are relevant to the realm of literary studies as well. "What is truly disastrous," he writes, "is our failure to recognize that we have wandered from one trap into another. . . . Having conditioned ourselves to pounce on any and all generalities, we spend more and more time worrying about smaller and smaller things [that] often tell us very little about what really matters in the world."⁵² What had started from the commendable desire to overcome essentialism has all too often metastasized into an unworkable will to "total deconstruction and absolute empirical specificity," which is to say, to a new form of positivism.⁵³

The point of these critical observations, it should be clear, is not to deny the value of high-resolution explorations of the ways texts interact with their immediate sociohistorical environments. Even less am I suggesting that we should (or could) dispense with periodization. What I am claiming, rather, is that the critical emphasis on temporal concurrency and cultural proximity, while valuable and even indispensable, may often obscure continuities and affinities that outstrip such framings. Why, we might ask, despite the growing interest in "transnationalism," "critical internationalism," and "globalism," is it still far more common to find Wharton discussed in connection with William Dean Howells or Henry James than with, say, Walter Scott, or, for that matter, Joseph Roth—even though she is in important respects closer to the latter two than to the former? And similarly, why is it that one practically never sees Yaakov Shabtai, arguably the boldest and most influential Israeli realist writer, placed in a literary-intellectual trajectory that extends beyond the historical boundaries of Israeli culture or modern Hebrew literature, and this despite the fact that his canonical *Past Continuous* demonstrably owes much more to developments that took place in early

---

51. Dimock, "A Theory of Resonance," 1061.

52. Matti Bunzl, "The Quest for Anthropological Relevance: Borgesian Maps and Epistemological Pitfalls," *American Anthropologist* 110, no. 1 (2008): 53–60, 58. For Bunzl's concise discussion of the "conceptual upheaval that has characterized the development of American anthropology in the course of the last forty years," see his, "Anthropology Beyond Crisis: Toward an Intellectual History of the Extended Present," *Anthropology and Humanism* 30, no. 2 (2005): 187–195, 187.

53. Bunzl, "The Quest," 57.

nineteenth-century Ireland or Scotland than to any of its more immediate Hebrew-language antecedents. Indeed, one of the goals of this book is to make historical sense of the fact that writers such as Wharton, Roth, and Shabtai, who neither met socially nor (to the best of my knowledge) ever read each other's works, could produce novels that so clearly belong on a single shelf. The historical reach and multilingual diversity of this study's archive, in short, was not only chosen out of a desire to extend the purview of its critical field;[54] it also forms a central part of its argument.

"History," as Eagleton notes, "is striated with respect to rates of change," featuring both the "speedy temporality of the 'conjuncture'" and the more glacial processes of cultural and generic change.[55] This means that any given text is both of its "moment" and of other (sometimes distant and often forgotten) places and times. To reconstruct the history of a genre, as Katie Trumpener writes, is thus an exercise in "[tracing] how specific intellectual-historical formations within which new genres are forged and flourish become subsumed, over the course of the genre, into its formal and tropic vocabulary."[56] What this kind of investigation seeks to reveal is the complex dialectic between inherited narrative tropes, whose origin is always particular and situated, and their appropriation and implementation in very different spaces and scenarios. Accordingly, throughout this book, I will be devoting equal space to the *longue durée* of generic change and to the specific exigencies that informed my novels' moments of production and reception. My aim in this endeavor is to reveal how a "formal and tropic vocabulary" developed around the turn of the nineteenth century in Britain's Anglo-Celtic periphery was taken up and reworked by twentieth-century writers oceans away.

Overview

The main section of this book consists of three chapters that are devoted in turn to the careers and major works of Edith Wharton, Joseph Roth,

---

54. Trumpener's, Buzard's, and Evans's aforementioned studies primarily examine nineteenth-century fiction. Hegeman's and Elliott's books, while concerned with twentieth-century literatures, make modernism their genre of choice. *The Blossom Which We Are*, with its focus on twentieth-century metropolitan realism thus fills a gap in this developing critical conversation.

55. Eagleton, *Sweet Violence*, xii.

56. Trumpener, *Bardic Nationalism*, 148.

and Yaakov Shabtai. This central interpretative section is framed by a preliminary chapter, which traces the vicissitudes of the cultural-extinction trope from its earliest appearance in the late eighteenth century until the end of the long nineteenth century, and a concluding chapter that brings the themes discussed in the previous chapters home, to the current crisis of the humanities—themselves a cultural form of life that many today believe may be tipping into extinction.

Chapter 1 argues for a connection between the late-eighteenth-century emergence of the culturalist view of the self and the emergence of the heightened modern awareness of mutability and transience. The chapter reviews the thought of Edmund Burke and Johann Gottfried Herder (arguably the two most influential early formulators of the culturalist view), before moving to a discussion of Edgeworth's and Scott's novels, focusing in particular on their association of extinction with peripherality. The chapter then traces the persistence of this association throughout the long nineteenth century. The discussion concludes with the twentieth-century transposition of the cultural-extinction trope from the periphery to the center.

Edith Wharton's dual status as one of her era's premier realists and as an accomplished regionalist writer makes her career a particularly useful example of the transposition of the extinction trope from periphery to center. Chapter 2 begins by describing Wharton's response to the Great War, which I set alongside comparable responses from the period (by Stefan Zweig, Paul Valéry, and others) to tease out the common culturalist and historicist assumptions that framed their generation's processing of that momentous event. The second part of the chapter brings this discussion to bear on Wharton's *The Age of Innocence*. I read the novel both as a meditation on the transience of cultural formation and as an instructive attempt by a card-carrying realist to hold on to the genre's representational strategies, while recognizing that the view of morality that had traditionally informed the realist novel has become difficult to sustain in the intellectual climate of the post–World War I years. My reading draws parallels between Wharton's formal "solution" to this impasse and her protagonist's process of maturation.

The third chapter opens with a discussion of the well-known shift in Joseph Roth's career, from his early engagement with the aesthetics of the *Neue Sachlichkeit* [New Objectivity] to his later "realist" phase, which began with *Job* (1930) and reached its acme in *The Radetzky March*, Roth's farewell to the Austro-Hungarian Empire and one of the great realist novels of the twentieth century. The chapter offers an account of Roth's transition from the objectivist, camera-eye depictions of the chaotic postwar present of his early novels to the increasing preoccupation with the irretrievable past that defines his later work. This transition, I argue, reflects Roth's increasing absorption and fluency in the culturalist and historicist idiom that he begins to hone in his reportages of the 1920s. The chapter then proceeds to read *The Radetzky March* as an application of what Andreas Kilcher usefully describes as Roth's ethnoliterary approach.[57] Like Wharton before him, Roth employs the vocabulary of cultural extinction to describe the fate of an entrenched hegemonic class, thus parochializing and ephemeralizing the center.

Chapter 4 is devoted to the work of Israeli writer Yaakov Shabtai, with special emphasis on *Past Continuous*, his 1977 elegy to Little Tel Aviv and the social milieu associated with it. Like his predecessors, Shabtai's literary project consists of provincializing and temporalizing the hegemonic ethnic-political class into which he was born—the uniformly Ashkenazi cadres of the Zionist labor movement—thus divesting it of its presumption to representative status and subverting the ideological legitimation it drew from this self-image. This he does on the eve of the 1977 election, which spelled a political end to the unbroken dominance of the Zionist Labor Party, and at a time when Israel had already become fatefully embroiled in its micro-imperialist venture of colonizing the Occupied Territories.

In anticipation of the book's next and final chapter, I then proceed to discuss *Past Continuous*' critical depiction of its protagonist's increasingly more desperate spiritual and philosophical attempts to transcend his time and culture. Shabtai, I show, shared Nietzsche's and John Dewey's suspicion of the metaphysical cast of mind and its quest for certainty. Like Wharton and Roth before him, he interprets the desire to transcend the cluster of contingencies we call culture as symptomatic of the inability to come to terms with the relative and time-bound nature of our values, institutions, and beliefs.

Those readers who will read the book's interpretative chapters in sequence will probably note that the chapter on Shabtai differs somewhat in presentation from the preceding ones. In the latter chapters, I could count on my intended readers' familiarity with at least some of Wharton's and Roth's works as well as with the now-voluminous scholarship on both authors. This, however, is not the case with Shabtai. Unlike more contemporary Israeli writers such as David Grossman, Amos Oz, or Etgar Keret,

---

57. Andreas Kilcher, "The Cold Order and the Eros of Storytelling," in *Writing Jewish Culture: Paradoxes in Ethnography*, ed. Gabriella Safran and Andreas Kilcher (Bloomington: Indiana University Press, 2016), 68–93.

whose translated works regularly feature in bestseller lists across the world, Shabtai, who died in 1981 at the age of forty-seven, has remained, despite his enormous influence within Israeli culture and the availability of excellent English translations of his novels and short stories, relatively unknown to international readerships. This state of affairs required me to do a lot more stage setting, cultural-linguistic mediation, and close reading, making the chapter dedicated to him read somewhat differently from those that come before it. One of my hopes for this part of the book is that it will encourage more readers to delve into the oeuvre of a writer whom Irving Howe described as the Israeli William Faulkner, and whose *Past Continuous* represents, in my estimation, one of the most innovative and stimulating works of prose fiction produced in the twentieth century.

Chapter 5 applies the discussion developed in the book as a whole to the current state of the humanities, which I describe (following Simon During) as a cultural way of life. We would do well, I argue there, to follow the examples of Wharton, Roth, and Shabtai and face the parochialism and contingency of the cultural world that sustains our social and professional identities, and that infuses our lives with purpose and meaning. To view ourselves in this way—as members of a fragile cultural formation of singular yet non-universal value—entails resisting the desire (still very much with us) to insist on the universal significance of the kind of work we do. The way forward for our profession, the book concludes by arguing, is not to roll back the culturalist and historicist turn but to consummate it. This means continuing to argue for the contingency of value and the situatedness of knowledge, while also extending these assumptions to our own practices and disciplinary identities. Accepting that the humanities are one cultural tribe among others will not prevent us from arguing for the significance of what we do. It would recommend, however, that we couch our defense of our way of life and the kinds of goods that it produces in more modest and hopefully more effective terms.

Chapter 1

Culturalism, Vulnerability, and Transience

A Shared Vulnerability

The novels at the focus of this book are all studies in a peculiarly human and, I will argue, distinctly modern vulnerability: our susceptibility to the kind of injury that occurs when the cultural structures that we rely upon for the ongoing maintenance of our identities as well as for moral and epistemological orientation break down or are superseded by others. The most detailed discussion so far of our shared susceptibility to this kind of loss is Jonathan Lear's *Radical Hope: Ethics in the Face of Cultural Devastation* (2006). I would like to begin this chapter by critically reviewing Lear's account (much of which I endorse), as doing so will help me to develop a theme common to his book and mine, while also explaining where and how my approach to thinking about our culturalist vulnerability differs from his. These differences, I want to show, are not merely "methodological" but go to the heart of the matter at hand.

Lear writes:

> We are familiar with the thought that as human creatures we are by nature vulnerable: to bodily injury, disease, aging, death—and all sorts of insults from the environment. But the vulnerability we are concerned with here is of a different order. We seem to acquire it as a result of the fact that we essentially inhabit a way of life. Humans are by nature cultural animals: we necessarily inhabit a way of life that is expressed in a culture. But our way

of life—whatever it is—is vulnerable in various ways. And we, as participants in that way of life, thereby inherit a vulnerability. Should that way of life break down, that is *our* problem.[1]

To illustrate this thesis, *Radical Hope* recounts the tragedy suffered by the Native American Crow nation following the tribe's confinement to a reservation in the late nineteenth century. As Lear describes it, the impact of this transition on the men and women who lived through it was debilitating in the extreme. While in one sense life did go on for the Crow, there is another sense—the one central to his project and mine—in which, with the onset of the reservation period, their world ended.

It ended because while the tribe's members could still identify themselves as "Crow," the meaning of that designation was no longer clear. Being a Crow subject had traditionally meant engaging in specific practices (buffalo hunting, intertribal warfare), maintaining certain rituals (the Sun Dance, coup planting), and pursuing role-specific ideals (bravery in battle, daring feats of horse stealing). These activities were in turn objectified in a host of institutions, status markers, and subject positions, which together made up the tribe's world. Once the Crow practices became impossible—the buffalo were eradicated; intertribal warfare was outlawed by the US government—its veteran members found themselves in an unprecedented situation. No longer able to perform their identities, they lost the ability to constitute themselves as persons in any sense familiar to them. From a thriving community, they turned into a baffled and disoriented group, strangers to themselves and increasingly alienated from the younger generations born to the reservation reality. In one poignant instance, a tribeswoman recounts how she once resorted to striking a wayward grandchild out of frustration (thrashing children was not traditionally part of Crow education). Failing to account for her actions, she says: "'I am trying to live a life I don't understand' . . . 'I feel like I am losing my children to this new world of life that I don't know.'"[2]

Lear makes far-reaching claims for the significance of the tragedy that his book describes and analyzes. The radical destitution suffered by the Crow in the wake of their confinement, he argues, is a possibility that "we *all* must live with—even when our culture is robust, even if we never have

---

1. Jonathan Lear, *Radical Hope: Ethics in the Face of Cultural Devastation* (Cambridge, MA: Harvard University Press, 2006), 6.

2. Lear, *Radical Hope*, 62.

to face its becoming actual."³ I agree with this claim, as I do with Lear's observation that "we live at a time of a heightened awareness that civilizations are themselves vulnerable," and that this uneasy awareness may help explain the "widespread intolerance that we see around us today."⁴ Where he and I disagree is on the question of how to account for our shared culturalist vulnerability. This question, *pace* Lear, is indissociable from the question of who "we" are, or more precisely, of how and when we came to view ourselves as cultural creatures in the first place. To ask such questions, as we shall see, is not to take away from the perspicacity of Lear's analysis, nor necessarily to gainsay its general—even universal—applicability. But it is to point to the limits (or, better yet, the blind spots) of the kind of philosophical inquiry that he undertakes in his book.

As I see the matter, the vulnerability that Lear's book brings into focus is indeed one "we *all* must live with," but only on the proviso that by "all" we mean the majority of the current inhabitants of the planet, regardless of nationality, race, gender, class, or religion (but perhaps excluding certain deep-jungle Amazonian tribes or other thoroughly isolated human communities—if any such still exist—whose modes of self-understanding employ categories completely foreign to our own). This is an empirical claim, and is susceptible to counter examples, but as a committed historicist, I see no problem in asserting that certain modes of thought or feeling are now "universal," or nearly so (in the sense of being held or felt by most people alive today). There is nothing essentialist about such a claim, provided of course that we insist in addition on the *contingency* of this universality: on the fact that it could have been otherwise; that there is no deep, ahistorical or transcultural, reason for why we presently think, feel, and act in the ways that we do.

Now, in the world as we know it today, where the reality of culture is not only assumed by most human beings (more on this below) but also actively shapes juridical and political realities, Lear's analysis of our cultural vulnerability does indeed have the widest possible relevance. Moreover, when read in this light, *Radical Hope* offers something that literary criticism has been failing to produce for a long time now: namely, the kind of forthright investigation into the way we live now that Matthew Arnold envisioned as the soul and chief social utility of cultural criticism. Lear, however, is not

---

3. Lear, *Radical Hope*, 9.
4. Lear, *Radical Hope*, 7.

content to be an Arnoldian cultural critic; he wants to be a *philosopher* of culture. That is, he wants to claim that his analysis of our contemporary sensibilities and susceptibilities reveals something deeper or more permanent than the way *we* live now. "The possibility that concerns me," he emphasizes, "is not the special province of [the Crow] or any other culture: it is a vulnerability that we all share simply in virtue of being human."[5] This claim is necessary for Lear's methodological self-positioning because it enables him to couch his philosophical reconstruction of the Crow tragedy in Kantian terms, as an inquiry into "the field of possibilities in which all human endeavors gain meaning."[6] What Lear is after, in other words, are the transcendental conditions that determine the range of human experience everywhere and always, and which thus make a fit object for a philosophical inquiry of the Kantian variety. For the idea of such an investigation makes sense only when one assumes the existence of a necessary, noncontingent template or context—something like "human nature" or the "human condition"—capable of uniting all cultures, past, present, and future, into a single human community. To touch ground on this assumed bedrock would be to arrive at our common essence: at that part of our species-being that remains inert and unchanging across culture and time.

That this vestigial Kantianism appears in a work devoted to the analysis of our culturalist vulnerability is both ironic and telling. Ironic, because, as noted in the previous chapter, when the culturalist view of the self emerges in the late eighteenth century, it is in the context of a broad reaction *against* the Enlightenment notion that human beings are so many instantiations of a single and unchanging prototype—the notion of which Kant's critical method was at once the culmination and *reductio ad absurdum*. Telling, because Lear's desire to ascend to a position from which to survey what he calls "the scope and limits of human possibilities" attests to the difficulty of coming to terms with the selfsame vulnerability that he himself describes so well.[7] For to accept (as Lear does) that we are "cultural animals" whose conceptual and moral horizons are shaped by the cultural-linguistic "worlds" that we inhabit entails denying ourselves (as he does not) of access to transcendental vantage points from which objective, universal, and necessary truths can come into view.[8]

---

5. Lear, *Radical Hope*, 8.
6. Lear, *Radical Hope*, 7.
7. Lear, *Radical Hope*, 10.
8. Lear, *Radical Hope*, 6.

Culture, in the plural and relativistic sense that Lear invokes in his book, is like Derrida's notion of the text: it has no outside (unless it is another culture). A culturalist world, by extension, is one whose human landscape is parceled out into different but ontologically equivalent cultural enclaves *without remainder*. Such a world order can still accommodate notions of cultural hybridity, mimicry, and appropriation, as well as the whole range of perspectives on self and other that such differential relations open up. What it cannot accommodate, however, is a standpoint (either within or without the subject) from which necessary and universal conditions of possibility might be grasped. For such a standpoint assumes what culturalism denies: namely, a subject that "[has] no biases, and hence no culture at all."[9] Hence, in claiming such a standpoint for his philosophical analysis, Lear is in effect denying his own cultural embeddedness, while also absolving himself (at least in part) of the vulnerability that it entails. For wherever it is that the transcendental philosopher presumes to travel in his quest for the permanently true, it is by definition a realm untouched by the vagaries of history and change, which make for our culturalist vulnerability.

On the anti-Platonist line of argument that I am invoking here, philosophy does not begin in wonder but in the desire to transcend the contingencies of one's time and place. Nietzsche introduced this idea when he wrote that human beings invented true knowledge so as "[to] *affirm another world* than the world of life, nature, and history."[10] John Dewey, the most important early twentieth-century proponent of this critique, concurred. Philosophy's quest for certainty, he argued, is an expression of the wish to rise above "the world of chance and change, and [into] the world of perfect and unchanging Being."[11] As Richard Rorty sums up this critical view of traditional philosophy's hankering after certain and immutable foundations:

> *To admit that mere spatiotemporal location, mere contingent circumstance, mattered would be to reduce us to the level of a dying animal.* To understand the context in which we necessarily live, by contrast . . . [would enable one] to die with satisfaction, having accomplished the only task laid upon humanity, *to know the truth,*

---

9. Roy Wagner, *The Invention of Culture* (Chicago: University of Chicago Press, 1981), 2.

10. Friedrich Nietzsche, *The Gay Science*, ed. Bernard Williams, trans. Josefine Nauckhoff (Cambridge: Cambridge University Press, 2001), 201.

11. John Dewey, *The Quest for Certainty*, vol. 4 of *John Dewey: The Later Works, 1925–1953*, ed. Jo Ann Boydston (Carbondale: Southern Illinois University Press, 2008), 233.

to be in touch with what is "out there." There would be nothing more to do, and thus no possible loss to be feared. Extinction would not matter, for one would have become identical with the truth, and truth, on this traditional view, is imperishable.[12]

Rorty's description of philosophy as an attempt to circumvent extinction helps to pinpoint the incoherence at the heart of Lear's project. For the culturalist self-image that Lear invokes when he claims that we are "cultural animals" takes its impetus from the insistence that "spatiotemporal location [and] contingent circumstance" matter—indeed, that they are the *only* determinants that matter when it comes to who and what we are. But coming to terms with the implication of this self-image involves giving up on the comfort offered by its metaphysical alternative. If we are the kind of decentered creatures in whom socialization goes all the way down, then there is no part of our selves that swings free of culture and time. To see oneself as a cultural animal, in short, involves coming to terms with being a "dying animal," too.

To sum up, my issue with Lear's account of our shared vulnerability is the allowance he makes for his own theoretical vocabulary and subject position. When describing the predicament of the Crow, he stresses the cultural basis of the beliefs and concepts that comprise their world. But when it comes to his own diagnostic discourse, he abandons his culturalism and goes Kantian. While the Crow are presented as fully submerged in and defined by their native practices and beliefs, Lear (in his capacity as philosopher) affects to transcend his cultural programming, and assume a vantage point from which he can detect general, nonlocal and operative, truths. His self-described project of "philosophical anthropology" thus adds up to an attempt to hold the stick at both ends: to honor the claims of cultural relativism *and* philosophical objectivism—to embrace value pluralism, on the one hand, while preserving the possibility of a universal human nature, on the other.[13]

Such inconsistencies, however, are benign enough. The more vexing issue that Lear's account raises stems from the uneven distribution of human possibilities that it implies. Lear depicts the Crow as locked into

---

12. Richard Rorty, *Contingency, Irony, and Solidarity* (Cambridge: Cambridge University Press, 1989), 27. First emphasis mine.

13. Lear, *Radical Hope*, 7.

the epistemological and moral parameters of their culture. Even when they eventually find creative ways to cope with the change that had been forced upon them, they do so from within the symbolic horizon of their language and traditions. The tribe's Chief, Plenty Coups, following ancient Crow custom, retreats to a secluded mountaintop to seek a dream-vision, which might point a way forward for the Crow. As Lear tells it, thanks to Plenty Coups's courageous leadership and vision, the Crow do indeed succeed in finding ways to preserve some aspects of their identity even in the midst of their catastrophe. But, significantly, they accomplish this remarkable feat of accommodation and (partial) self-preservation by employing the resources that their traditions place at their disposal. At no point do they transcend the limits of their cultural situatedness. When it comes to the tribe, in other words, the limit of their culture is always also the limit of their world.

Not so for Lear. His analysis, as we've seen, absolves at least one area of his culture the area we call philosophy, his own "indigenous" province—from such constraints. If the Crow, as Lear describes them, are defined and circumscribed by the parochialism of their culture, he, *qua* intellectual, grants himself access to a standpoint from which "the scope and limits of human possibilities" come into view.[14] Whereas the Crow can only ever move within, or creatively rearrange, the givens of their culture, he is able to transcend his socialization altogether (for only an observer who can stand apart from its cultural-linguistic conditioning can mark the "limits of human possibilities").[15] In the final analysis, then, Lear is culturalist about others and metaphysical about self.

If I have taken what might seem like an inordinate amount of space to spell all this out, it is because Lear's selective application of the culturalist premise is far from idiosyncratic. As we shall see later in this chapter, the rise of culturalist thought, from the late eighteenth century to the present, has been the story of a halting and reluctant centripetal movement from *periphery to center, region to metropole, other to self.* It took a long time before "we"—the denizens of the modern metropolitan West—were able to view

---

14. Lear, *Radical Hope*, 10.

15. In this respect, Lear's account is reminiscent of the traditional anthropological mode of representation, wherein the "natives" are presented as "confined by what they know, feel, and believe . . . prisoners of their 'mode of thought,'" whereas their metropolitan observers claim for themselves the unsituated position of "the movers, the seers, the knowers." Arjun Appadurai, "Putting Hierarchy in its Place," *Cultural Anthropology* 3, no. 1 (1988): 36–49, 37.

our values and institutions as ontologically on par with those of the various "savages" and "primitives" that Western civilization had conjured up as its foils. For much of the nineteenth century, as Ruth Benedict remarks in *Patterns of Culture* (1934), the idea that values were neither universal nor predetermined, but rather relative to the communities that produce them, "could not occur to the most enlightened person of Western civilization." And even today, she adds (speaking of the 1930s), "[we] are still preoccupied with the uniqueness, not of the institutions of the world at large, which no one has ever cared about anyway, but of our own institutions and achievements, our own civilization."[16] If twentieth-century Westerners are still reluctant to place their practices, beliefs, and conceptual schemes on equal footing with those of the pagans and barbarians, Benedict is saying, it is because to do so would be to subject the last bulwark of Western exceptionalism—the insistence that "our" practices and institutions are not just preferable to us, but are of an altogether "different order to those of lesser races"—to the kind of indignity that Copernicus and Darwin had inflicted upon the cherished beliefs of our predecessors.[17]

The latter insight is surely one of the highpoints of Benedict's essay, not least because of its ongoing relevance nearly a century after it was written. But, as the foregoing discussion has tried to make clear, there is, I think, a deeper reason behind our continued unwillingness to bite the culturalist bullet, one that has less to do with the desire to protect a prized sense of exceptionalism and more with what Ernest Becker famously dubbed "the denial of death."[18] For, to accept that we are just our cultural-historical moment is not only to give up on the legitimation that we would like to bestow upon our way of doing things—whoever we may be—by insisting that it is somehow closer to the essence of the Human; it is also to confront the vulnerability and mortality of the moral and conceptual frameworks that give meaning and substance to our lives.

Lear, I have argued, confronts this picture directly, but he goes only halfway in drawing its implications. A more consistent culturalist position would need to extend its relativizing premises to its own axiomatic foundations. By this I mean that taking such a position involves recognizing that

---

16. Ruth Benedict, *Patterns of Culture* (New York: The New American Library, 1934), 19–20.
17. Benedict, *Patterns of Culture*, 20.
18. Ernest Becker, *The Denial of Death* (New York: Simon & Schuster, 1973).

the culturalist self-image that Lear invokes when he writes that "humans are by nature cultural animals" *is itself a cultural artifact*, and therefore just as parochial and timebound as the Crow practices it is used to analyze. After all, a time may come (perhaps sooner than we think) when the culturalist paradigm that we assume as a matter of fact will be ousted by some other identity-explaining vocabulary, or perhaps by a discourse in which "identity" itself is no longer an organizing category of human experience. Should the day arrive when our biological descendants will cease to think of themselves as cultural creatures, the meaning of being human will change in ways we can neither foresee nor prepare for. What we may assume with a fair degree of certainty, however, is that this as-yet unimaginable future world would be as alien and unintelligible to us as the reservation reality was to the Crow.

Of course, it is tempting at this point to claim that these hypothetical descendants, with their bewildering beliefs and incomprehensible technologies, would simply be "culturally" different from us, as we are culturally different from our distant ancestors. But that is precisely the temptation we must resist. For to describe group-based differences using this term is to invoke an entire conceptual apparatus that our post-culturalist descendants would no longer see the point of using. Appealing to "culture" to explain human affairs is a feature of our, well, culture—a circularity that attests to the term's indispensability *for us*. But essential though "culture" is today, this concept, along with everything else about who and what we are, may well seem incoherent, ludicrous, or deplorable to future generations. Our conceptual and moral paradigms, alas, are just as transient as we are.

The methodological upshot of this preliminary discussion is that accounting for our culturalist vulnerability requires an approach different from Lear's—one that conceives of itself in historicist rather than ontological terms. This chapter will now go on to provide such a genealogy (or at least a necessarily abridged version of one). My aim in what follows is threefold: first, to point to the historical emergence of the modern culturalist view of the self by briefly examining the positions of its earliest exponents; second, to argue that culturalism was tinctured from its inception by a secular recognition of the fragility of human institutions and impermanence of value; and third, to trace the ambiguous role that realist fiction (broadly conceived) played in promoting and disseminating the culturalist self-image, even as it sought to ward "our" civilization against its more unsettling implications. Telling this historicist story will put me in a position to argue for the literary and cultural significance of the novels examined later in this book.

Culturalist Genealogies

If naturalization is the measure of an idea's success, the culture concept's career in the course of the twentieth century has been a resounding triumph. Given that "culture," in its modern, so-called "anthropological" sense, only entered popular usage at the turn of the twentieth century, it is remarkable just how indispensable it has become since then, both within and without academe. Writing as early as 1952, A.L. Kroeber and Clyde Kluckhohn were already confident enough to assert that the culture concept "in explanatory importance and in generality of application [has become] comparable to such categories as gravity in physics, disease in medicine, evolution in biology."[19] Kroeber and Kluckhohn's supreme confidence in the theoretical efficacy of culture, characteristic of the early days of their discipline, is no longer to be encountered among anthropologists. What Susan Hegeman aptly describes as the "panic over reification" that has swept over the human and social sciences in the final decades of the twentieth century has not left anthropology's flagship concept untouched.[20] Recent decades had seen a flurry of influential theoretical assaults on culture as an essentializing "tool for making other,"[21] a devious way to talk about race,[22] or simply as too general to be of any use.[23] The concept of culture, its critics say, flattens out internal social conflicts and inconsistencies, reifies and thus dehistoricizes ever-changing social realities, or is, otherwise, merely a fiction invented to justify the institutional practice of anthropology itself.[24] As Marshall Sahlins

---

19. A.L. Kroeber and Clyde Kluckhohn, *Culture: Critical Review of Concepts and Definitions* (Cambridge, MA: Peabody Museum of American Archaeology and Ethnology, Harvard University, 1952), 3.

20. Susan Hegeman, *The Cultural Return* (Berkeley: University of California Press), 24.

21. Lila Abu-Lughod. "Writing Against Culture," in *Recapturing Anthropology: Working in the Present*, ed. Richard G. Fox (Santa Fe, NM: School of American Research Press, 1991), 137–162, 143.

22. See for instance, Walter Benn Michaels, *Our America: Nativism, Modernism, and Pluralism* (Durham, NC: Duke University Press, 1995).

23. For this argument, see Adam Kuper, *Culture: The Anthropologist's Account* (Cambridge, MA: Harvard University Press, 1999).

24. For useful overviews and critical assessments of the range of arguments leveled against culture see Hegeman, *The Cultural Return*, 21–40 and Christoph Brumann, "Writing for Culture: Why a Successful Concept Should Not Be Discarded," *Current Anthropology* 40, suppl. 1 (1999): S1–S27.

describes the curious state of affairs in which the culture-concept's erstwhile advocates had become its most insistent critics, "pretty soon everyone will have a culture; only the anthropologists will doubt it."[25]

But anthropology's in-house worries about culture seem almost beside the point when we consider how ubiquitous and commonsensical the term has become in other social spheres. Cultures and subcultures confront us today on every side, all proclaiming their authenticity and clamoring for recognition. In this culture-saturated environment, each of us is seen as inhabiting several overlapping cultures at once, as per our national, ethnic, socioeconomic, institutional, and religious loyalties. So-called "subcultures" too are legion: LGBTQ culture, New Age culture, survivalists, woodworkers, the mafia. It is not the plurality of such modern tribes and subtribes, groups and communities that is modern, but rather their conscious self-presentation as cultures and the unprecedented value accorded to this term. As James Buzard sums up the omnipresence of this keyword, "it is scarcely an exaggeration to say that sustained conversation about human affairs could hardly be carried on without almost constant recourse to the idea that the world population is divisible into a number of discrete cultures."[26] For all of its recent devaluation by academic experts, culture's general utility and popular appeal are, it would seem, greater today than at any point in the past.

Nor is culturalism strictly a Western phenomenon. What had been a scientific term of art for Franz Boas and his students is today both a coveted badge and fixture of thought across linguistic and national boundaries, not least among the former objects of the West's scientific curiosity. Remarking on the twentieth-century rise of the culture-concept, Sahlins adds: "All of a sudden everyone got 'culture.' Australian Aboriginals, Inuit, Easter Islanders, Chambri, Ainu, Bushmen, Kayapo, Tibetans, Ojibway: even peoples whose ways of life were left for dead or dying a few decades ago now demand an indigenous space in a modernizing world under the banner of their 'culture.' They use that very word, or some near local equivalent. . . . 'If we didn't have *kastom*,' the New Guinean said to his anthropologist, 'we would be just like White Men.'"[27] Such is the appeal of this flexible idea that the very people

---

25. Marshall Sahlins, "Two or Three Things that I Know about Culture," *Journal of the Royal Anthropological Institute* 5, no. 3 (1999): 399–421, 402.

26. James Buzard, *Disorienting Fiction: The Autoethnographic Work of Nineteenth-Century British Novels* (Princeton, NJ: Princeton University Press, 2005), 3.

27. Sahlins, "Two or Three Things," 401.

whose customs and traditions once supplied the grist for the anthropological mill now seek to appropriate it for their own diverse economic, political, and psychological uses. People, as Christoph Brumann straightforwardly puts this point, seem to "*want* culture, and they often want it in the bounded, reified, essentialized, and timeless fashion that most of us [anthropologists] now reject."[28] This does not mean, as Brumann goes on to argue, that we intellectuals should applaud such *volksgeistlich* essentialism, but it does indicate just how universally accepted the idea of culture has become. Thinking of oneself as a member of a culture (to which, importantly, alternative cultures exist) is now a universal feature of our global modernity, and this regardless of how its contemporary intellectual custodians might feel about it. And like other paradigm-shifting ideas, once culture has installed itself in our collective imaginary, we find it very difficult to look at ourselves and our world—past, present, and future—in any other way. As James Clifford, who did more than most to underscore the provisional and aporetic nature of the culture concept, famously put this point, "culture is a deeply compromised idea I cannot yet do without."[29]

But as with other ideas that seem unavoidable to us today, "culture" is a relatively recent invention, a product of the revolutionary eighteenth century. Prior to that time, and for most of human history, social groups went about the business of life blithely unaware that they were the bearers of "culture" and ignorant of the assumptions that this term encodes. Of course, human beings always recognized, and were fascinated by, group-based differences rooted in ritual practices, styles of governance, culinary habits, and kinship structures. "These people all paint themselves red and eat monkeys," reported Herodotus, the Attic father of historiography and anthropology, of the Gyzantian people he encountered on his North-African tour.[30] But for all of Herodotus's proto-ethnographic interest in foreign peoples and customs, he, along with his many counterparts down the centuries, did not think of the self as consubstantial with or expressive of a complexly integrated and self-validating lifeworld that we today call culture.

When this modern idea is formulated for the first time, it is as part of a broad backlash against the leveling implications of Enlightenment rationalism

---

28. Brumann, "Writing for Culture," S11.

29. James Clifford, *The Predicament of Culture* (Cambridge, MA: Harvard University Press, 1988), 10.

30. Herodotus, quoted in James Redfield, "Herodotus the Tourist," *Classical Philology* 80, no. 2 (1985): 97–118, 99.

and cosmopolitanism. Its most prominent (though by no means exclusive) promulgators were the Irish statesman and man of letters Edmund Burke and his contemporary, the German Counter-Enlightenment thinker Johann Gottfried Herder. Neither Herder nor Burke, it should be said, was the inventor of this mode of thought and feeling: Vico and Montesquieu, for instance, had formulated important strands of the culturalist view before either came on the scene. And it is also possible to go much further back into history and trace the influence of Hebraic sources on Herder or the role that Aristotle's and Aquinas's ideas played in Burke's thought.[31] (The search for origins is an exercise in infinite regression.) But even if Burke and Herder were not strictly speaking the originators of the modern culture-concept, they were, as we shall see, pivotal in lending this keyword its recognizable modern sense.

On the now-familiar view that they helped make plausible, there is no self prior to its socialization, no pre-lingual "I," in the rich sense of individuality and interiority associated with the first-person singular before culture steps in and shapes the organism into full-fledged human being. Try to untangle the self by stripping it of its cultural inheritance, argued Burke in his celebrated invective against the French Revolution, and all you are left with is "naked, shivering nature"—hardly the robust rational subject of Locke's and Kant's philosophies.[32] Practical morality, he added, is a matter of inherited "prejudices," not abstract principles.[33] In fact, pure reason is not only an inadequate guide in human affairs; it can be positively harmful. For "in proportion as [its dictums] are metaphysically true, they are morally and politically false."[34] If individuals and societies wish to successfully navigate the complex and ambiguous realities of life, Burke insisted, they must avail themselves of the collected wisdom of the past, which, for that reason, should be venerated and preserved. To willingly discard the hard-won wisdom of the ages for "the shallow speculations of the petulant, assuming, shortsighted coxcombs of philosophy," he thought, was the very definition of folly.[35]

---

31. For the influence of Hebraic thought on Herder, see F.M. Barnard, *Herder on Nationality, Humanity, and Freedom* (Montreal: McGill-Queen's University Press, 2003), 17–37. On Aristotle and Aquinas, see for instance, Francis P. Canavan, *The Political Reason of Edmund Burke* (Durham, NC: Duke University Press, 1960).
32. Edmund Burke, *Reflections on the French Revolution* (London: J. M. Dent & Sons, 1951), 74.
33. Burke, *Reflections*, 84.
34. Burke, *Reflections*, 59.
35. Burke, *Reflections*, 49.

His contempt for abstract theorizing notwithstanding, Burke would have balked at the suggestion that he was any kind of relativist. His vehement condemnation of Warren Hastings's brutalities in India, for instance, was informed by a firm belief in the universality of moral truths: what is wrong in Britain, he held, is equally wrong elsewhere. At the same time, however, Burke confessed to being unable "[to] give praise or blame to anything which relates to human actions, and human concerns, on a simple view of the object, as it stands stripped of every relation, in all the nakedness and solitude of metaphysical abstraction."[36] To justly evaluate a political position or social institution requires placing it in its concrete context. As he saw it, while universal principles have their place (though what that place is, given his contempt of abstraction, is unclear), everything stands or falls on the particular circumstances of the case. For it is the latter that give to every human reality "its distinguishing color and discriminating effect."[37] Thus, according to Burke, any moral or political program that ignores the specific exigencies of its time and place will not only fatally undermine its own feasibility, but may also (as the events in France illustrated) lead its proponents down a disastrous political road. Human life transpires, root and branch, in the concreta of lived traditions and established institutions, not in the lofty precincts of philosophical abstraction.

Herder agreed. "Human nature," he claimed, "is not the vessel of an absolute, unchanging and independent happiness, as defined by the philosopher. . . . It is a pliant clay which assumes different shape under different needs and circumstances."[38] There is, he believed, no single moral *Weltanschauung* or set of beliefs that is more essentially human than others. Nor can one ascend to an external standpoint from which one might evaluate and rank the relative merits of different societies or historical epochs. In fact, we cannot speak of a human subject at all before it is socialized into one or another cultural formation: "to be human," as Bhikhu Parekh glosses this Herderian idea, "[is] to grow up within a particular cultural community and become a particular kind of person."[39] These theses put

---

36. Burke, *Reflections*, 6.

37. Burke, *Reflections*, 6.

38. Johann Gottfried Herder, *Herder on Social and Political Culture*, trans. and ed. F.M. Barnard (Cambridge: Cambridge University Press, 1969), 185.

39. Bhikhu Parekh, *Rethinking Multiculturalism: Cultural Diversity and Political Theory*

Herder immediately at odds with every form of rationalism, *a priorism*, moral monism, and political contractualism—in short, with each of the reigning philosophical notions of his day. Where most of his intellectual peers (with the exceptions of Montesquieu and Helvetius) took for granted Voltaire's dictum that "man in general has always been what it is,"[40] Herder argued to the contrary, that there are as many ways of being human as there are distinct cultural-linguistic communities to produce them. Culture is not a disposable garnish sprinkled atop what is essentially the same universal dish. It is constitutive and pervasive.

Thought, Herder famously maintained, does not precede language, but is coeval with it. "Not even the slightest action of [human] understanding," he writes in the *Treatise on the Origin of Language* (1772), "could occur without a characteristic word."[41] Human beings think *in* language rather than with it. Words, accordingly, are not vehicles for ostensibly language-independent meanings (be they Platonic ideas, physical referents, or internal mental images); they are the very constituents of meaning, so that where there is no language there is also no thought. This meant, among other things, that the human mind, upon which the Enlightenment *philosophes* had pinned their epistemological and cosmopolitan hopes, was itself a culturally constructed artifact. To exercise one's reason, on the view that Herder would bequeath to Saussure, Heidegger, and Wittgenstein, is not to rise above one's culture but to apply the linguistic resources of one's society in more or less creative ways. This did not preclude the possibility of choice or innovation; Herder, writes F.M. Barnard, firmly believed that humans are "creatures of *freedom* as well as of nature."[42] But it did mean that freedom and choice are always exercised within a culturally demarcated and historically determined horizon of meaning. "Even in philosophical probings," as Benedict would elaborate on this theme, "[the individual] cannot get behind [his culturally determined] stereotypes; his very concepts of the true and the false will still have reference to his particular traditional customs."[43] Culture, as Herder

---

(New York: Palgrave, 2006), 68.

40. Quoted in Barnard, *Social and Political Culture*, 35.

41. Herder, Johann Gottfried, *Herder: Philosophical Writings*, trans. and ed. by Michael N. Forster (Cambridge: Cambridge University Press, 2002), 128.

42. Barnard, *Herder on Nationality*, 9.

43. Benedict, *Patterns of Culture*, 18.

imagined it, could still be reformed, even revolutionized, but it could not be transcended.[44]

Like his Irish counterpart, Herder was a trenchant critic of imperialism and colonialism. In particular, he abhorred the subjugation and destruction of indigenous cultures in the name of progress. "The culture of *man* is not the culture of the *European*," he inveighed against his contemporaries, "it manifests itself according to place and time in *every* people."[45] True to this dictum, Herder rejected the stadial theory of history, according to which human history progressed through a sequence of discrete stages, from barbarism to enlightenment, each with its corresponding forms of manners, beliefs, and political regimes. This progression, on the view defended by the Scottish school of Adam Smith, Lord Kames, and Adam Ferguson, was both universal and ineluctable, affecting all societies in similar and predicable ways, thus enabling the historian to assign each nation to its appropriate pigeonhole in humanity's coming-of-age story. Herder emphatically rejected this universalist teleology. The attempt to set up a putatively objective and universal yardstick against which to measure the achievements and merits of the world's cultures, he believed, was merely a disguised attempt to impose one's standards on others. Doing justice to a foreign people requires suspending the assumptions of one's own culture and trying to see as they see and feel as they feel. Human realities, as opposed to the inert facts of nature, he claimed in proto-hermeneutical fashion, can be known only from the inside.

Between them, Herder and Burke articulated the basic premises of the culturalist view that would go on to have such far-ranging intellectual, scientific, and political implications in the centuries that followed. What was new and potentially disquieting about this incipient mode of thought when it first appeared was not just the weird suggestion, common to Herder and Burke, that non-Europeans have culture, too; it was their willingness to take the very elements that Christian doctrine and Enlightenment thought had dismissed as mere ephemera—language, manners, customs, traditions, local attachments—and turn them into the very stuff of the self. For implicit in this willingness is an entailment that Burke and Herder would

---

44. As Bhikhu Parekh writes, "Unlike Montesquieu, Herder did not assign much importance to great lawgivers. Their ability to rise above and give their society's culture a new direction was limited . . . because they were themselves profoundly shaped by it." See Parekh, *Rethinking Multiculturalism*, 67.

45. Quoted in Barnard, *Herder on Nationality*, 135.

not themselves have conceded, but to which their nascent culturalism had effectively opened the door. To describe the self as not only embedded *in* but also constituted *by* what Samuel Johnson dismissed as "the accidents of transient fashions and temporary opinions" was to dislodge it from its traditional metaphysical anchoring.[46] And so, though Burke's and Herder's rediscovery of the self in the concreta of social and political institutions of its time and place was intended to act as a *check* to what both thinkers viewed as the myopic and ultimately destructive intellectual currents of their day, what their reconceptualization of identity actually accomplished was to make access to traditional sources of metaphysical comfort more difficult. A self conceived in Burkean and Herderian terms is, at once, more conscious of its dependence on the cultural-historical frameworks that it inhabits and less secure in their stability and continuity.

If Burke and Herder were shielded from the revolutionary implications of their view it was, first, because both, as Raymond Williams notes, were speaking "from the relative stability of the eighteenth century against the first signs of the flux and confusion of the nineteenth century";[47] and, second, because of their strongly held religious views. However, the culturalist view of the self that they helped make credible would prove as inimical to the theistic conception that they endorsed as it was to the Enlightenment conception that they attacked.[48] On the assumption common to the philosophers and theologians of their day, the true self—however defined—is a thing utterly unlike anything that is to be found in its physical, historical, and cultural environment. Both the heirs of St. Augustine and the followers of Descartes agreed that the deepest, most essential part of the individual was also the most otherworldly. Burke and Herder, each in his way, repudiated this notion. And while neither ever seems to have doubted the existence of

---

46. Dr. Johnson is quoted in Clifford Geertz, "The Impact of the Concept of Culture on the Concept of Man," in *The Interpretation of Cultures* (New York: Basic Books), 33–54, 35.

47. Raymond Williams, *Culture and Society 1780–1950* (Garden City, NY: Anchor Books, 1960), 11.

48. Arthur O. Lovejoy's observation on the curious career of historical ideas is at point here: "It is one of the instructive ironies of the history of ideas that a principle introduced by one generation in the service of a tendency or philosophic mood congenial to it often proves to contain, unsuspected, the germ of a contrary tendency—to be, by virtue of its hidden implications, the destroyer of that Zeitgeist to which it was meant to minister." Arthur O. Lovejoy, *The Great Chain of Being: A Study of the History of an Idea* (Cambridge, MA: Harvard University Press, 2001), 288.

the soul or the sovereignty of God, both would have agreed with Talcott Parsons's later claim that "without culture neither human personalities nor human social systems would be possible."[49] It is acculturation, they held, that makes human beings human, not their possession of, relation to, or identity with some mysterious substance that transcends time and space.

One of the consequences of the gradual reconceptualization of identity that begins in the late eighteenth century, I am claiming, was the introduction of a new and uncanny sense of vulnerability. For once the idea that *what* human beings are is indistinguishable from *where* and *when* we find them begins to take root, a whole new range of susceptibilities and anxieties begins to make itself felt. First, as Geertz writes, "to entertain the idea that the diversity of custom across time and over space is not a mere matter of garb and appearance . . . is to entertain also the idea that humanity is as various in its essence as it is in its expression. And with that reflection some well-fastened philosophical moorings are loosed and uneasy drifting into perilous waters begins."[50] What made the culturalist line of thought common to writers like Herder and Burke so perilous, according to Geertz, was that it ushered in those two great scourges of modern thought, relativism and determinism: "Either [the individual] dissolves, without residue, into his time and place, a child and perfect captive of his age, or he becomes a conscripted soldier in a vast Tolstoian army, engulfed in one or another of the terrible historical determinisms with which we have been plagued from Hegel onwards."[51] This is certainly true as far as contemporary debates in philosophy and related disciplines are concerned. But relativism and determinism, while no doubt dreadful to contemplate, are precisely that: theoretical bugbears. Like their close relatives, skepticism, solipsism, and nihilism, they prey on the philosophically minded, while being safely ignored by most everybody else.

As I hope the foregoing discussion has made clear, the general discomfort that has attended to the deepening of the culturalist view was probably occasioned less by its problematic epistemological or metaethical implications than by the more visceral sense of groundlessness and precariousness that it produces. If culturalism unsettles, in other words, it is because its denial

---

49. Talcott Parsons quoted in Zygmunt Bauman, *Culture as Praxis* (London: Sage, 1999), xvii.
50. Geertz, "Impact," 37.
51. Geertz, "Impact," 37.

of a universal human nature takes away the sort of consolation that comes with believing that our values and beliefs are somehow also Humanity's own. The culturalist picture of the self as wholly the creature of its time and place removes this metaphysical crutch, leaving us with a heightened awareness of the contingency and ephemerality of our private and collective identities. It ushers us into the sort of consciousness that Jacob Burckhardt, one of Herder's most prominent nineteenth-century disciples, describes as follows: "As soon we rub our eyes, we clearly see that we are on a more or less fragile ship, borne along on one of the million waves that were put in motion by the revolution. We are ourselves these waves."[52]

And, indeed, as Burckhardt's reference to the French Revolution implies, the destabilizing implications of the culturalist ideas that had begun to circulate in intellectual circles in the years leading up to the events of 1789 became both more evident and more broadly felt in their wake. The twenty-five years separating the storming of the Bastille from the Congress of Vienna witnessed drastic and irreversible changes to the social, political, and intellectual fabric of Europe: killing off between one quarter and one third of its young men, reshaping most of its regimes, instigating the dissolution of the Holy Roman Empire and precipitating new styles of art and thought. The idea that humanity was progressing along a single trajectory, from savagery to civilization, began to lose its plausibility, as had the idea that morality issues from a set of universal norms. "Virtue as well as villainy," writes Thomas Pavel in his survey of the cultural impact of the revolution, "were now assumed to originate in the particular customs in force at a certain time, in a certain place, among people of a certain social class."[53] These transformations, for those who lived through them, were both exhilarating and profoundly disquieting.

In the first place, the post-1789 recognition that the social order was not a fixed entity to which one had to conform but a pliable medium that could be shaped according to human needs and desires inspired Europeans and others with new confidence in their capacity to take charge of their future and remake their worlds. This recognition, in turn, made radical politics and utopian schemes (from Robert Southey and Samuel Taylor Coleridge's

---

52. The quote is from the 1869 version of Burckhardt's *Einleitung in die Geschichte des Revolutionzeitalters*, quoted in Hans Blumenberg, *Shipwreck with Spectator: Paradigm of a Metaphor for Existence*, trans. Steven Rendall (Cambridge, MA: MIT Press, 1997), 69.
53. Thomas Pavel, *The Lives of the Novel: A History* (Princeton, NJ: Princeton University Press, 2013), 170.

short-lived pantisocratic venture to Bakunin's anarchism) into staple features of nineteenth-century thought and praxis. But the selfsame recognition also confronted Europeans with the tenuousness of human institutions. After all, if the *ancien régime*, a divinely sanctioned bastion of absolutism, could vanish so abruptly, if centuries-old customs and entrenched social forms could be discarded almost overnight, what might be said for the long-term prospects of the cultural and political regimes that replaced them? This, then, as Isaiah Berlin noted, was the great irony of the French Revolution: that while it set out to create "a static and harmonious society, founded on unalterable principles . . . its consequences threw into relief the precariousness of human institutions."[54] From within the new historical consciousness that emerged in the post-revolution era, writes Peter Fritzsche, "Europeans became more aware of the frailty of cultural and social formations. The world appeared to them more restless than it had in the past."[55] Contingency, it turned out, was the price of historical agency.

Yet it is important to recognize that while the events of 1789–1815 may have *prompted* in those who lived through them a sense of "inconstancy . . . that seemed to render the exterior world at hand superficial and fragile," it did not *supply* them with this particular interpretation.[56] The revolutionary era did not wear its meaning on its sleeve; no human affair does. "An event," writes Sahlins, "is not simply a phenomenal happening. . . . Only as it is appropriated in and through the cultural scheme does it acquire an historical *significance*."[57] If the epochal view of the French Revolution, as marking the unmaking of one "world" and the beginning of another, occurred to so many early nineteenth-century intellectuals, it was because they had already started to think of themselves and their social environs in increasingly secularist and culturalist terms. Seen this way, the events of 1789–1815 served to make salient implications that had hitherto been only dimly felt intuitions in the minds of those Europeans with sufficient wealth, security, and leisure to reflect on their experiences. Those Europeans, to borrow Lucien Febvre's words, "learned one thing which their

---

54. Isaiah Berlin, *Three Critics of the Enlightenment: Vico, Hamann, Herder*, 2nd ed. (Princeton, NJ: Princeton University Press, 2013), 299.

55. Peter Fritzsche, *Stranded in the Present: Modern Time and the Melancholy of History* (Cambridge, MA: Harvard University Press, 2004), 202–203.

56. Fritzsche, *Stranded*, 30.

57. Marshall Sahlins, *Islands of History* (Chicago: University of Chicago Press, 1987), xiv.

predecessors had not known when they brought the word *civilization* into circulation about the year 1770. They learned that civilization could die."[58]

For an instructive early expression of this new awareness, consider the case of François-René de Chateaubriand. Born in 1768, Chateaubriand lived through the revolutionary years, and like many of his fellow aristocrats never fully managed to reconcile himself to the post-1789 reality.[59] But Chateaubriand was more than a beleaguered nobleman. An astute historical observer, his reflections on the events he had lived through offer a usefully condensed statement of the new culturalist and historicist sensibility that set in during the early decades of the long nineteenth century. "A straggler in this life," he writes, "has witnessed the death, not only of men, but also of ideas: principles, customs, tastes, pleasures, sorrows, opinions, none of these resembles what he used to know. He belongs to a different race from the human species among which he ends his days."[60] Three metaphors are compressed into Chateaubriand's retrospective reflection: the culturalist image of the self as the product of its time, place, and milieu; the proto-anthropological idea that social practices and ideas ("principles, customs, tastes") are expressions of an underlying identity-sustaining entity, here denoted as "species" and "race"; and, finally, the assumption that this composite entity is as timebound and mortal as the individuals who inhabit it. Separately, each of these ideas predates the nineteenth century, but in combination they mark a new phase in the evolution of culturalist thought. For while the as-yet unnamed idea of culture would continue to retain its Burko-Herderian charge as a marker of stability, unity, and continuity well into the twentieth century, starting in the early 1800s it also becomes suffused with a countervailing consciousness of disruption and transience.

Cultural Extinction: From Periphery to Center

Having provided an outline of the contours of the culturalist outlook that began to take shape around the turn of the nineteenth century, I would

---

58. Lucien Febvre, "Civilisation: Evolution of a Word and a Group of Ideas," in *Classical Readings in Culture and Civilisation*, ed. John Rundell and Stephen Mennell (London: Routledge, 1998), 160–190, 176.
59. See Fritzsche, *Stranded*, 56.
60. Quoted in Fritzsche, *Stranded*, 55.

now like to turn to the textual medium that served as this discourse's primary vehicle: realist fiction. For it was the novel and its related form, the regionalist tale, rather than the philosophical treatise or the political pamphlet, that served as the primary sites in which the culturalist view of the self and its attendant anxieties were expressed and disseminated. As I will show, examining the diverging but complementary trajectories of these two central nineteenth-century fictional modes—metropolitan and regionalist realism—offers us a useful vantage point from which to assess how the societies in which they flourished related to the unsettling implications of the culturalist self-image, particularly to the recognition, to recall Febvre, "that civilization could die."

My aim here, it should be clear, is not to provide any kind of detailed historical survey of the Victorian novel or of nineteenth-century regionalism, nor to offer a full account of their role in the rise of the concept of culture. My goal is to show how each of these nineteenth-century realist modes adopted different aspects of the culturalist and historicist outlook that began to coalesce at the beginning of the century. While metropolitan realism, I will claim, arrogated to itself this outlook's proto-functionalist holism, regionalism took up its post-1789 attunement to the fragility and transience of social forms and institutions.

My point of entry into this discussion will be Maria Edgeworth and Walter Scott, who conveniently stand at the beginning of both the realist and regionalist genres. But here, too, a bit of preliminary stage setting is required. For by the time Edgeworth and Scott began publishing, the theme of cultural extinction had already been around for several decades in the form of popular poems, such as Thomas Gray's "Elegy Written at a Country Churchyard" (1751), James Macpherson's "translations" of Ossian (1760–1765), and Oliver Goldsmith's *The Deserted Village* (1770). These elegiac poems described the disappearance not of humanity as a whole, in the manner of biblical or millenarian accounts of the End, but of socially and geographically identifiable forms of life: pre-enclosure rural England and Ireland (in the cases of Gray and Goldsmith) and the Gaelic Highlands (in Macpherson). In an era marked by accelerating social and economic change, as well as by a "growing interest in disappearing families, tribes, and communities," Gray's, Macpherson's, and Goldsmith's poems offered their readers a symbolic means to channel their nostalgic yearnings for simpler and more stable times.[61]

---

61. Fiona Stafford, *The Last of the Race* (Oxford: Clarendon, 1994), 83.

The significance of these widely circulated works for the subsequent development of the poetics of cultural extinction is twofold. First, as Earl Miner has claimed, by demonstrating "that an elegy could lament the passing of a society or of a way of life as poetically as the death of a single individual," Gray, Macpherson, and Goldsmith expanded the purview of this ancient form,[62] licensing subsequent writers to employ its wistful tone and backward-looking perspective not only to keen over the loss of a person—either mythological (as in Theocritus's elegy for Adonis) or real (Milton's Lycidas/Edward King or Shelley's Adonais/John Keats)—but also of a community. Second, by setting their poems in locales that were perceived, already in their time, as peripheral to the main currents of British life, Gray, Macpherson, and Goldsmith helped establish a highly resilient association of extinction with peripherality. In each of the poems, the fate of the dying community is relayed to the reader by an isolated speaker who is either a surviving member of the vanished world or an emotionally invested witness, but whose perspective in either case is more cosmopolitan, and thus closer to the reader's, than the provincial order whose passing he describes.

Thus Goldsmith's *The Deserted Village* laments the passing of "Sweet Auburn" with its rural simplicity, its quaint village preacher and schoolmaster, in the voice of an urbane and well-traveled speaker who has firsthand knowledge of the city, "[where] wealth accumulates, and men decay." Similarly, in Gray's "Elegy," the speaker standing over the lichen-covered graves in which "the rude forefathers of the hamlet sleep" wonders whether they might contain "some mute inglorious Milton" or a "Cromwell guileless of country's blood," and indicates—by these learned references—his affinity to the cultural perspective of the implied reader and distance from the rural world described in the poem. Establishing such a distance, Susan Stewart has argued, is crucial for sparking nostalgic desire,[63] as well as for rendering tragic circumstances amenable to cathartic aestheticization. If this is so then the popularity of these prototypical decline-on-the-periphery narratives was occasioned by their ability to supply their eighteenth-century audiences with nostalgia-inducing points of reference, while also aiding those readers in processing the anxieties that attended to the accelerating pace of modern change which they perceived all around them. Be that as it may, it would be the set-up introduced by Gray, Macpherson, and

---

62. Earl Miner, "The Making of 'The Deserted Village,'" *Huntington Library Quarterly* 22, no. 2 (1959): 125–141, 140.

63. See Susan Stewart, *On Longing: Narratives of the Miniature, the Gigantic, the Souvenir, the Collection* (Durham, NC: Duke University Press, 1993), 146–151.

Goldsmith, wherein the disappearance of a marginal community is articulated from the standpoint of the metropolitan center, that would prove to be the most enduring aspect of their legacy. From the time of the poems' publication until the early decades of the twentieth century, cultural extinction would be depicted consistently as a fate exclusive to regional communities, premodern "races," and other peripheral folk.

Such is the case in Maria Edgeworth's *Castle Rackrent* (1800) and Walter Scott's *Waverley* (1814), the works that brought not only history but also the post-1789 recognition of the endemic vulnerability of culture to the novel. Edgeworth's and Scott's innovation consisted of combining the elegiac localism of Gray, Macpherson, and Goldsmith with the techniques derived from Defoe, Richardson, and Fielding, to produce historically sensitive depictions of vanishing social formations on the margins of the expanding British Empire.[64] Like their poetic forebears, Edgeworth and Scott positioned themselves as mediators between the English or Anglicized metropolitan reader and a fast disappearing regional order. But with the already considerable resources of the novel at their disposal, Edgeworth and Scott could give a much fuller rendering of the specificity and distinctiveness of the cultures at the centers of their novels, and therefore also a keener sense for what had been lost with their disappearance.

Whereas their poetic predecessors had to rely on the power of symbol and allegory to activate their reader's sensibilities, Edgeworth and Scott could take advantage of the breadth and flexibility of the novel to supply a more prolonged and immersive readerly experience. To read *Castle Rackrent* or *Waverley* and identify with their characters was to undergo the process that Gray's, Macpherson's, and Goldsmith's poems of cultural decline could only retrospectively frame. It was to enter into the regional world and witness its dissolution as experienced by the characters, while also maintaining the more distanced, backward-looking perspective from which the represented world can be grasped in its entirety.

Edgeworth and Scott thus stand at the beginning of a long textual tradition in which, as James Clifford writes, "whole cultures (knowable worlds) [are described] from a specific temporal distance and with a presumption of their transience."[65] In establishing the literary medium whereby this specific

---

64. Ian Watt, *The Rise of the Novel* (Berkeley: University of California Press, 2001), 32 and passim.

65. James Clifford, "On Ethnographic Allegory," in *Writing Culture: The Poetics and Politics of Ethnography*, ed. James Clifford and George Marcus (Berkeley: University of

vision of history and culture could be produced and transmitted, they cleared the path down which all subsequent cultural elegists, up to and including Wharton, Roth, and Shabtai, would travel.

Maria Edgeworth and the Birth of the Novel of Peripheral Decline

In Edgeworth's tale of familial decline on Britain's Anglo-Irish periphery, the allegory of cultural salvage is established early on. "These are 'tales of other times,'" she informs her reader in the Preface, "the race of the Rackrents has long since been extinct in Ireland."[66] This framing casts a distinctly elegiac hue over the book's tragicomic account of the progressive disintegration of the Rackrent line, while also alerting the reader of its synecdochal relationship to Irish history more broadly. The decline and fall of the Rackrents, we are invited to recognize, is the story not merely of a single family but of an entire social class associated with Ireland's past. "When Ireland loses her identity by an union with Great Britain," writes Edgeworth, "she will look back with a smile of good-humoured complacency on the Sir Kits and Sir Condys of her former existence."[67] As this remark implies, in *Castle Rackrent* Edgeworth set herself the task of bringing Irishness into view as a distinct collective national identity, at a moment in which its future was felt to be threatened by the imminent absorption into its more powerful neighbor. Written during the years separating the failure of the 1798 Rebellion and the 1801 Act of Union, *Castle Rackrent* seeks to define the nature of this impending loss as well as to negotiate conditions under which it might be mitigated. It is a complicated performance that attempts to uphold the independent dignity and value of Ireland and the Irish against the prejudice of the "*ignorant* English reader," while also criticizing the backwardness of its semi-feudal social order so as to make a case for the desirability of union with England.[68]

Edgeworth's pro-Union politics was largely a function of her upbringing. Though born in Ireland, she passed her early years in London, only returning to her family estate at Longford when she was fourteen. Her

---

California Press, 1986), 114.

66. Maria Edgeworth, Preface to *Castle Rackrent*, in *Castle Rackrent and Ennui*, ed. Marilyn Butler (London: Penguin, 1992), 61–63, 63.

67. Edgeworth, *Castle Rackrent*, 63.

68. Edgeworth, *Castle Rackrent*, 63.

father, the progressive Anglo-Irish intellectual and estate-owner Richard Lovell Edgeworth, made sure that young Maria would imbibe the best of what had been thought and said by the French, Scottish and Anglo-Irish luminaries of the day. An enthusiastic reader of the fictions of Richardson, Fielding and Frances Burney, Edgeworth was also acquainted with Diderot's *Encyclopédie* (1751–1772) and Adam Smith's *The Wealth of Nations* (1776). Her satirical portrayal of the "follies and absurdities" of Ireland's landowning class leave little doubt as to her Whig views.[69] Insofar as union with England meant a movement toward modernization, cosmopolitanism, and reform, Edgeworth supported it. The way forward for Ireland, her book tacitly argues, is to memorialize its precious but ultimately unfit past, while accepting the inevitability of union with England.

At the same time, however, Edgeworth was evidently distressed by the vicious portrayals of Ireland and the Irish that prevailed in the English press and travel literature of the time. "Many foreign pictures of Irishmen," she writes in one of her essays, "are as grotesque and absurd as the Chinese pictures of lions: having never seen the animal."[70] One of her expressed hopes for *Castle Rackrent* was that it might serve as a corrective to such caricatures, presenting English audiences with a more accurate and generous description of their "sister country."[71] The subtitle of the book, which begins with *An Hybernian Tale Taken from Facts*, as well Edgeworth's assurance to her reader that "all the features in the foregoing sketch were taken from . . . life," both draw on the already established authority of realist representation to capture and faithfully reproduce social reality. But the underlying motivation behind the novel's representation of Irish life was likely more pragmatic than mimetic. Edgeworth, as Ina Ferris notes, was probably less concerned with producing an accurate representation of "Ireland"—an identity formation that she herself approached (at least partly) as an outsider—than with "[mobilizing] the affective resources available to fictional . . . language in order to generate sympathy for Ireland in English readers."[72] But again, the reason it was important to her to foster

---

69. Edgeworth, *Castle Rackrent and Ennui*, ed. Marilyn Butler (London: Penguin, 1992), 63.

70. Maria Edgeworth, "Essay on Irish Bulls," in *Tales and Novels* (London: Henry G. Bohn, 1874), 81–188, 185.

71. Edgeworth, *Castle Rackrent*, 121.

72. Ina Ferris, *The Romantic National Rale and the Question of Ireland* (Cambridge: Cambridge University Press, 2004), 13.

such sympathy in the first place was that, like Scott after her, she regarded union with England as the best outcome for her native land.

These ambiguities explain the mixed tone of Edgeworth's narrative, which, while relentlessly poking fun at the foibles and inadequacies of traditional Irish customs and institutions, also keens over their impending disappearance. Though Edgeworth was emphatic on the need to refute the prejudiced view of the Irish, her book persistently caters to the selfsame stereotypes she condemns. Celebrating Irish dialect against its detractors one moment, it steps in to rationalize or correct its ostensible deficiencies the next; insisting on inherent dignity of Irish hospitality and loyalty, it also continually foregrounds its excesses and absurdities. The constant oscillation between sympathy and criticism, immersion and reflection, one may assume, reflects Edgeworth's own complicated position vis-à-vis her native "culture." But whatever its psychological or biographical causes, this internal rhythm is what enabled her "inventive and bizarre study of a localized system in terminal decay" to appeal to the sensibilities of its English audiences, while also lending an air of tragic dignity to a way of life about to exit the world stage.[73]

While Edgeworth seemed not to have shared Burke's conservative anxieties about reform, her view of national identity was very much of a piece with his.[74] The soul or spirit of a nation, Burke held, was to be sought in "the peculiar circumstances, occasions, tempers, dispositions, and moral, civil, and social habitudes of [its] people."[75] But this hodgepodge of local peculiarities and particularities, he cautioned, must not be construed as a "momentary aggregation," a loose collocation of inert elements, but as a complexly integrated totality—a culture—which extends horizontally, to bind contemporaries, as well as temporally across generations.[76] The problem facing Edgeworth was how to render this newfangled object into narrative form. How was one to represent Irish identity as both a composite of disparate elements and as a discrete and self-contained unit?

Edgeworth's inventive solution to this problem consisted of juxtaposing two narrative voices, each presenting the reader with a different perspective

---

73. Marilyn Butler, "Introduction," in *Castle Rackrent and Ennui*, ed. Marilyn Butler (London: Penguin, 1992), 1–54, 8.

74. Edgeworth's father Richard was personally acquainted with Burke, and Maria herself greatly admired his writing. She once contemplated writing an essay on the fellow Irishman's thought and style, but then thought better of it.

75. Burke, quoted in Williams, *Culture and Society*, 12.

76. Burke, quoted in Williams, *Culture and Society*, 12.

on the represented world. The first, which dominates most of the narrative, is personified in the figure of the family's loyal retainer, Thady Quirk, who delivers a highly engaged but unreliable first-person account of the Rackrents' diminishing fortunes, as each of the family's increasingly more inept heirs drives its estate deeper into the ground. Though Thady is, as Liz Bellamy argues, far from "a transparent device to convey an authorial line,"[77] his dialect-rich narrative provides the kind of insider's on-the-ground perspective that would go on to become one of the hallmarks of realist representation. We may not trust everything he tells us, but his colorful authenticity, often conveyed through Edgeworth's pioneering use of local colloquialisms, is made to seem irreproachable. Thady's narrative, the reader soon recognizes, delivers a markedly partisan history of the events, but it does so in a manner that conveys the distinctive habits of mind and speech that Edgeworth sought to establish as the folkish baseline of Irish "culture."

To bring this putative object into view as a whole, however, required Edgeworth to include a perspective external to it. This viewpoint is embodied in the knowledgeable and urbane (which is to say, Anglicized) persona of the Editor. The ostensible purpose of this second narrator, who speaks in the novel's Preface, Glossary, and footnotes, is to "translate" the characters' Irish vernacular and explain their local references for the benefit of the uncomprehending English reader. So, for example, when Thady exclaims "'Oh, boo! boo!" in response to his master's claim that he does not care whether he marry Judy, a local girl, in place of the rich Miss Isabella, the Editor chimes in to explain that "Boo! boo! [is] an exclamation equivalent to *pshaw* or *nonsense*."[78] The more significant role of the second narrative voice, however, is to locate the events, facts, and circumstances that Thady relates within the larger framework of *Irishness*, thus turning them from mere incidents into tokens of culture. What seems obvious or humdrum from the standpoint of Thady, the internal narrator, becomes, when seen from the generalizing perspective of the framing narrator, a clue to the inner workings of the Irish way of life. Thus, when Thady offers up some unexpectedly astute commentary on Sir Condy's carelessness with his legal affairs, the reader is directed to the Glossary, where she finds the following:

---

77. Liz Bellamy, "Regionalism and Nationalism: Maria Edgeworth, Walter Scott and the Definition of Britishness," in *The Regional Novel in Britain and Ireland: 1800–1990*, ed. K.D.M. Snell (Cambridge: Cambridge University Press, 1998), 54–77, 62.

78. Edgeworth, *Castle Rackrent*, 89.

> The English reader may perhaps be surprised at the extent of Thady's legal knowledge, and at the fluency with which he pours forth law-terms; but almost every poor man in Ireland, be he farmer, weaver, shopkeeper, ox steward, is, besides his other occupations, occasionally a lawyer. The nature of processes, ejectments, custodians, injunctions, replevins, &c. is perfectly known to them, and the terms as familiar to them as to any attorney. They all love law. It is a kind of lottery, in which every man, staking his own wit or cunning against his neighbour's property, feels that he has little to lose, and much to gain.[79]

We can see here a very early version of what Benedict Anderson would describe as the novel's capacity "[to fuse] the world inside the novel with the world outside."[80] No longer an incidental detail or individual idiosyncrasy, Thady's "fluency" in legal affairs is transformed, via the Editor's knowing gloss, into a representative cultural trait that binds diverse levels of Irish society (from peasants to shopkeepers) into a single national community. Loving the law becomes a distinctly Irish characteristic, which, expressing itself even in the most untutored, can henceforth be used to distinguish this cultural group from others (say, the avaricious Jews represented in the novel by Sir Kit's wife). The passage's recourse to inventories of occupations and legal procedures is also significant here. For, as Anderson writes, nothing provides a sense of "sociological solidity" more effectively than a "succession of plurals."[81]

By playing off the tension between Thady's emotionally invested yet limited insider's perspective and the learned but disengaged viewpoint of the Editor, Edgeworth was able to produce a compelling version of Irishness that was both "authentic" and comprehensible, subjective and objective, exotic yet accessible. This Edgeworth did at a precarious juncture in her nation's history—suspended as it was between a disastrous near-past of the Rebellion and an uncertain future following the Union—but also at a moment in which a new conception of human identity was gaining ground, not least thanks to writers like Burke and Herder, who like her hailed from peripheral corners of the European world. If, as Walter Allen

---

79. Edgeworth, *Castle Rackrent*, 132–133.
80. Benedict Anderson, *Imagined Communities: Reflections on the Origin and Spread of Nationalism*, rev. ed. (London: Verso, 2006), 30.
81. Anderson, *Imagined Communities*, 30.

claims, the publication of *Castle Rackrent* in 1800 was "a date of the first importance in the history of English fiction, indeed of world fiction,"[82] it is because of Edgeworth's brilliant adaptation of post-1789 culturalist ideas and sensibilities into narrative form. To read her experimental novel is to enter into a clearly bounded and richly realized social order, whose sense of solidity and *thereness* is produced by a constant oscillation between two narratorial perspectives.

Walter Scott: Historicizing the Decline-on-the-Periphery Motif

Edgeworth's project of harnessing the novel's formal resources to the depiction of a discrete lifeworld at the moment of its passing would be emulated and developed by later practitioners of the Irish National Tale—most notably Sidney Owenson (better known by her married name, Lady Morgan) and Charles Maturin. But it was a Scotsman, Walter Scott, who perfected it.[83] While acknowledging his debt to Edgeworth, Scott went beyond his predecessor by more fully working out the literary possibilities inherent in the elegiac framing of the genre that she inaugurated. His breakout novel, *Waverley*, not only explores the tensions between the perspectives of the colonial insider and metropolitan outsider, but also constantly toggles between two historical standpoints: the time of the story's events (the 1745–1746 Jacobite Rebellion) and a position beyond their conclusion, whence their historical meaning can, presumably, be objectively determined and authoritatively evaluated. Thus what appears like a bewildering succession of events, locales, objects, and practices from the perspective of Edward Waverley, the novel's young English protagonist, as he moves across Scotland's war-torn landscapes, becomes legible, when viewed from the always-available retrospective standpoint of the knowing narrator, as the final episode in the life of a discrete and culturally marked world.[84]

---

82. Walter Allen, *The English Novel: A Short Critical History* (Harmondsworth: Penguin, 1986), 103.

83. The most complete discussion of this short but decisive period of creative effluence in Britain's internal colonies is Katie Trumpener's *Bardic Nationalism* (Princeton, NJ: Princeton University Press, 1997), 130.

84. In so doing, his historical novel, as Katie Trumpener argues, "reiterate[s] and transform[s] the national tale's generic premises by historicizing its allegorical framework" (141).

Like the London-educated Edgeworth, Scott was particularly well placed to take on the role of cultural explicator. A Lowlander with one foot in the culture of the colonized and another in that of the colonizer, he capitalized on his ability to render "Scotland" in terms that appealed to his audience's taste for the exotic, while also subverting some well-entrenched English notions regarding Scottish inferiority. "I felt that something might be attempted for my own country, of the same kind with that which Miss Edgeworth so fortunately achieved for Ireland," he writes in the General Preface of *Waverley*, "something which might . . . procure sympathy for their virtues and indulgence for their foibles."[85] Accordingly, the Scotland he invents in the Waverley novels is both bracingly heroic and hopelessly outdated, a repository of iconic national symbols and a body of outdated social structures and institutions that must be left behind if Scotland is to move into the nineteenth century.[86]

Making that move, Scott thought, required acknowledging Scotland's traumatic history and accepting its subaltern position as part of the United Kingdom, but without thereby wholly giving up on its relative cultural distinctiveness. In his Waverley novels, he sought to strike a careful balance between honoring Scotland's heroic past and critically evaluating this history from the allegedly more "modern" and "rational" English viewpoint. The destruction of Highland society in the wake of the Jacobite Rebellion, he writes in this vein, rid Scotland of "much absurd political prejudice," but it also deprived Europe of "living examples of singular and disinterested attachment to the principles of loyalty which they received from their fathers, and of old Scottish faith, hospitality, worth, and honour."[87] *Waverley*, which presents itself as a testament and elegy to this extinct form of life (represented by the doomed figures of the Highland chieftain Fergus Mac-Ivor and his arresting sister Flora) is thus equally determined to celebrate that lost world and to showcase its inadequacies and absurdities, so as to rationalize and legitimize the only course of action open to Scotland: union with the British Crown. This necessary but unequal union is represented at the conclusion of the novel by Waverley's marriage to Rose, the daughter of

---

85. Walter Scott, *Waverley; or 'Tis Sixty Years Since*, ed. Claire Lamont (Oxford: Oxford UP, 2005), 388.

86. The Highlander clan system is one example of the Highland culture's obsoleteness; the tradition of "blackmail," which Rose Bradwardine explains in detail to the bewildered Waverley (and through him to the reader), is another.

87. Scott, *Waverley*, 376.

a dispossessed Lowlander baron. Thus, the "death" of one form of life turns in Scott's historical novel into the condition of possibility for the "birth" of another, symbolized by the future offspring that would presumably issue from the conjugal union between Edward and Rose.

This compensatory ideological framework, wherein life issues from death, national unity from political disharmony, and modern enlightenment from premodern barbarism, not only reflects Scott's pragmatic pro-British politics but also echoes the philosophical view of history that he had imbibed during his student years at Edinburgh University.[88] This, to recall, was the teleological view of history that Smith and Ferguson developed—and Herder rejected—according to which all human societies progressed through necessary stages on their way to rational civilization. Scott, whose historical novel derives much of its emotional force from the conceit of giving the reader access into an alternative and now extinct form of life, evidently felt it necessary to curb the relativistic implications of this set-up, and thus protect the possibility of extracting a general "human" lesson from events and characters he imaginatively reconstructs. Early in *Waverley*, after he had laid out his plan of recounting the 1745 Rebellion from a position "Sixty Years Since," Scott turns to assure his audience of the ongoing moral relevance of his tale. "Mine," he tells the reader, "is more a description of men than manners," by which he means that it centers on "those passions common to men in all stages of society, and which have alike agitated the human heart, whether it throbbed under the steel corslet of the fifteenth century, the brocaded coat of the eighteenth, or the blue frock and white dimity waistcoat of the present day."[89] Human nature remains constant, Scott is insisting here, even while the historical and cultural scenery in which it appears changes. "It is from the great book of Nature . . . that I have venturously essayed to read a chapter to the public," he writes, so as to drive home the point that it is the eternal verities of "the human heart" rather than the contingencies of time and place that explain the fates of individuals and nations.[90] Scott, in other words, takes advantage of the

---

88. On the influence of the Scottish school of "philosophical" history on Scott's outlook and writing, see David Brown, *Walter Scott and the Historical Imagination* (London: Routledge, 1979), 195–205.

89. Scott, *Waverley*, 4–5.

90. Scott, *Waverley*, 4–5.

retrospective view to imbue a temporal succession of events with historical necessity, as per the stadial view of history, thus justifying the present state of affairs, while also affirming his English and Anglicized readers in their metropolitan identities by telling them that *their* moral outlook is somehow more in line with that of the "great book of Nature" than those of the Highlanders whose demise they are invited to observe.

What makes the latter passage so striking, however, is its markedly anomalous relation to the rest of *Waverley*. For so much of this novel seems geared toward denying in practice the very ideas that Scott here affirms in word. For all of his declared allegiance to the progressive view of history and universality of human nature, his first novel could be described as an extended demonstration that human beings are not cut from a single mold; that historical cultures do not flow together into a single "human" narrative, but form holistic and incommensurable individual entities; and that when one of these entities dies out, the loss is both absolute and irrevocable. In short, despite its author's stated allegiance to the teleological theory of history expounded by his erstwhile professors, *Waverley* in fact contests the underlying premises of this view.

When Edward travels from Baron Bradwardine's Tully-Veolan to Fergus Mac-Ivor's Highland residence of Glennaquoich, he enters into a region whose moral landscape is as alien and inscrutable as its geographical one. Indeed, Scott's description of this foreign locale could be taken as an illustration of Edward Sapir's claim that "the worlds in which different societies live are distinct worlds, not merely the same world with different labels attached."[91] The scene of the banquet that Mac-Ivor holds in Waverley's honor after his arrival furnishes us with an objective correlative of this culturalist vision:

> The hall, in which the feast was prepared, occupied all the first story of Ian nan Chaistel's original erection, and a huge oaken table extended through its whole length. The apparatus for dinner was simple, even to rudeness, and the company numerous, even to crowding. At the head of the table was the Chief himself, with Edward, and two or three Highland visitors of

---

91. Edward Sapir, "The Status of Linguistics as a Science," in *Culture, Language and Personality: Selected Essays*, ed. David G. Mandelbaum (Berkeley: University of California Press, 1949), 160–166, 162.

> neighbouring clans; the elders of his own tribe, wadsetters and tacksmen, as they were called, who occupied portions of his estate as mortgagers or lessees, sat next in rank; beneath them, their sons and nephews and foster-brethren; then the officers of the Chief's household, according to their order; and lowest of all, the tenants who actually cultivated the ground. . . . The liquor was supplied in the same proportion, and under similar regulations. Excellent claret and champagne were liberally distributed among the Chief's immediate neighbours; whisky, plain or diluted, and strong beer refreshed those who sat near the lower end. Nor did this inequality of distribution appear to give the least offence. Every one present understood that his taste was to be formed according to the rank which he held at table.[92]

Here, laid out before the reader (via his or her avatar, Waverley) is the Highland clan system as a "knowable community," with all its characteristic types and social relations in open display.[93] It is a scene meant to impress upon its reader the kind of unforced yet rule-governed regularity that twentieth-century ethnography would turn into one of the distinguishing marks of culture, with all the relativistic implications of the term's modern usage implies. For an instructive comparison, consider Bronislaw Malinowski's description of his initial experience among the Trobrianders: "Some of the natives—very frequently those of the finer looking type—are treated with most marked deference by others, and in return, these chiefs and persons of rank behave in quite a different way towards the strangers. In fact, they show *excellent manners* in the full meaning of this word."[94] Prefiguring Malinowski's relativistic realism, Scott is strongly invested in illustrating that the Highlanders are not savages but possess "excellent manners," in the sense of internalized codes of behavior and decorum that are appropriate to a stratified and complex social organization. Far from representing an inferior or "barbaric" stage of development, the world of the Highland clans, this

---

92. Scott, *Waverley*, 106–107.

93. Raymond Williams, *The Country and the City* (New York: Oxford University Press, 1973), 165.

94. Bronislaw Malinowski, *Argonauts of the Western Pacific* (London: Routledge, 1961), 40. Emphases added.

scene implies, is a self-standing and autotelic cultural reality—one whose value and meaning must be experienced from the inside to be appreciated and understood.

Waverley, as Buzard writes in his magisterial reading of Scott's historical novel, "translates Scotland into *culture* . . . forecasting as it does so the entangled meanings and fuzzy nondefinitions of culture in the century and more to follow."[95] During the banquet scene and throughout the episodes that follow, Waverley functions as an ethnographic participant-observer *avant la lettre*, moving ever deeper into the world of the Highlands, to the point of becoming an honorary member of it. At one moment, we even find Fergus dressing his young English recruit in a plaid tartan and sash so as to complete his transformation into "a complete son of Ivor."[96] Waverley, however, never goes fully native. Scott is careful to maintain a quotient of cultural strangeness and incomprehensibility between his protagonist and the foreign world through which he sojourns. This Scott does partly for reasons of plot: so as to save Waverley from Fergus's fate and thus make the compensatory, comedic conclusion of the novel possible. But the decision to maintain a measure of incommensurability between English and Highlander should also be read as part of the novel's culturalist and elegiac agenda. Scott's project, as Harry Shaw writes, is "to bring to living representation cultures and mentalities that are interesting precisely because they elude our own cultural norms."[97] But Scott's insistence on the ultimate foreignness of Highland culture was also a way of alerting his readers that the likes of Fergus's world will never again be seen. That is to say, the incommensurability of the Highlander world is the very marker of its unrepeatable singularity.

Scott established a model of representing historical traditions and institutions in culturalist terms: as a bounded and integrated "world," which is, at once, both totalistic and vulnerable. Culture, as Scott depicts it, is an order of loyalties that constructs the identities of its members down to their inmost core of their moral character—a fact made salient to the reader by Evan Dhu Maccombich's stunning proposal to the English court

---

95. Buzard, *Disorienting Fiction*, 70.

96. Scott, *Waverley*, 218.

97. Harry E. Shaw, *Narrating Reality: Austen, Scott, Eliot* (Ithaca, NY: Cornell University Press, 1999), 169.

that it take his own life in lieu of Fergus's.[98] But while insisting on the identity-constituting power of culture, on its capacity to terminally shape identities and lives, Scott's novel also foregrounds its fragility and transience. By the end of the novel, Fergus and Evan are dead, Flora has retreated to a French convent, and what remains of the Pretender's armies is being routed by Cumberland. Whatever is left of the myriad human types, inherited traditions, and shared habits that composed the culture of the Highlands, Scott's novel closes by announcing, is in the process of conclusively vanishing from the earth. Scott, to be sure, sought to rationalize and hence mitigate this fate by depicting it as a necessary phase in a progressive historical movement. But his compensatory framing leaves open the discomforting question of who history's next victims might be. By making the traumatic fate of the Highlands the mark of historical change, Scott (as Ann Rigney writes) "incorporated transience into the very principle of historicization," instilling in his readers and literary followers an amplified awareness of the violence of history and the fragility of culture.[99]

Realist and Regionalist Trajectories

The seminal role played by Edgeworth and Scott in the development of the nineteenth-century novel is, thankfully, a case that no longer needs to be made. After long decades in which Georg Lukács's *The Historical Novel* (1937) stood virtually alone in proclaiming the significance of Scott (while ignoring Edgeworth), recent years have seen a series of major critical statements that conclusively demonstrate how Scott's and Edgeworth's experimental texts effectively transformed the novel from a rambling mode of didactic entertainment into a tool for cross-cultural translation and national identity-formation. Thanks to studies such as Ian Duncan's *Modern Romance and Transformations of the Novel* (1992), Katie Trumpener's *Bardic Nationalism* (1997), Shaw's *Narrating Reality* (1999), and Buzard's *Disorienting Fiction* (2005) we've now come to regard Scott and Edgeworth as the literary forerunners, not only of obvious epigones such as James Fenimore Cooper or Edward Bulwer-Lytton, but also of Dickens and George Eliot, Balzac

---

98. For Buzard's compelling reading of Evan Dhu's gesture as the "*ne plus ultra* of cultural foreignness, its 'culture-proving' effect," see Buzard, *Disorienting Fiction*, 77.
99. Ann Rigney, *The Afterlives of Walter Scott: Memory on the Move* (Oxford: Oxford University Press, 2012), 4.

and Flaubert, Turgenev and Tolstoy—indeed of nineteenth-century realism *tout court*. For it is in *Castle Rackrent* and *Waverley* (not *Moll Flanders* or *Tom Jones*) that the culturalist and historicist conception of social life that would go on to become the defining feature of realism[100] achieves literary expression and unprecedented worldwide success for the first time.[101]

What the latter accounts of realism's colonial roots fail to take into account, however, is that while Edgeworth's and Scott's holism and historicism were indeed adopted by their realist successors, their shared preoccupation with the fragility of social institutions and elegiac regard for vanishing cultures was not. When Dickens and Balzac employed the methods developed in Britain's internal colonies in their descriptions of mid-century London and Restoration Paris, they did so as historians of the present,[102] not as salvage anthropologists seeking to record the death throes of a defeated cultural world. What the British and Continental realists took from Edgeworth and Scott was their culturalist holism, their conception of history as struggle, and their use of representative characters as indices of larger social forces—all of which they then applied to their explorations of their present-day metropolitan realities. But the ideological work to which these literary strategies were put was the reverse of the entropic logic guiding

---

100. Referring to the differences between the eighteenth- and nineteenth-century novel, John Richetti observes that "'society' as [a] supervising totality . . . did not fully exist for the eighteenth century, and society appears in its fiction as a constellation of distinct spheres of influence, a loosely federated collection of interests and smaller units." It was only in the wake of Edgeworth and Scott that novelists begin to claim the kind of comprehensive perspective that allows for "society" (or what I have been referring to as culture) to emerge as an integrated "supervising totality." Richetti, *The English Novel in History: 1700–1780* (London: Routledge, 1999), 5–6.

101. In the decade following the publication of *Waverley*, Scott's novels sold more copies in England than all other novels combined, shaping public taste and literary production for decades to come. The rapid appearance of French, German, Italian, Russian, Hungarian, Spanish, Czech, Polish, Slovene, Danish, Norwegian, and Swedish translations of voluminous historical novels that tumbled in improbably rapid succession from the desk of the author of *Waverley* between 1814 and 1832, ensured, moreover, that Scott's impact was not restricted to the British scene. For a survey of European impact of the Waverley novels see Murray Pittock, ed., *The Reception of Sir Walter Scott in Europe* (London: Continuum, 2006). On Scott's unprecedented sales see Ian Duncan, *Scott's Shadow: The Novel in Romantic Edinburgh* (Princeton, NJ: Princeton University Press, 2016), xi.

102. Georg Lukács, *The Historical Novel*, trans. Hannah and Stanley Mitchell (Boston, MA: Beacon Press, 1963), 83–85.

Castle Rackrent and *Waverley*. Whereas the fictions of Edgeworth and Scott highlighted the tenuous and episodic nature of social formations, the novels of their realist successors tended to encourage a sense of their (relative) fixity and stability. If the former underscored the parochial nature of the values and norms they describe, the latter wavered unsteadily between the demands of culturalist specificity and the more reassuring cadences of moral universalism. The classic nineteenth-century novel, I am suggesting, was neither the proto-ethnographic, historicist genre that Lukács and Buzard describe, nor an aggressive organ of imperialist self-universalization, as claimed by Edward Said and others—it was both.

What the novel emphatically was *not*, however, was an expression of some fabled Victorian self-assurance, epistemological naiveté, or uncritical belief in progress. To describe the genre and its era in such terms is to garble history and caricature the achievements of Balzac, Thackeray, Turgenev, Eliot, and Dickens—to name but a few of the writers whose works display an acute consciousness of social conflict and historical change. Far from a triumphalist celebration of bourgeois values, the novel, on both sides of the Atlantic, is better described using Amy Kaplan's terms, as an "anxious and contradictory mode which both articulate[d] and combat[ed] the growing sense of unreality at the heart of middle-class life."[103] To view the novel in this way is to see the vaunted thickness of its descriptions and the overt moralism of its narrators, not as an expression of confidence, but as an improvised response to mounting anxieties regarding the coherence of the self and the integrity of its world. Faced with a reality that seemed increasingly more fragmented and elusive, more resistant to traditional modes of representation, nineteenth-century writers reached for the resources that their traditions placed at their disposal to create that flexible hodgepodge of culturalism and Enlightenment universalism that we know as the classic realist novel.

The sense of "unreality" to which nineteenth-century metropolitan realism formed a response is often explained as a consequence of the rapid erosion of the religious underpinnings of nineteenth-century society under the combined pressures of socioeconomic transformation and scientific development—which it certainly also was. However, an equally decisive factor in the widening sense of fragmentation and existential hollowness, to which Matthew Arnold's 1867 "Dover Beach" offers eloquent testimony, was the

---

103. Amy Kaplan, *The Social Construction of American Realism* (Chicago: University of Chicago Press, 1988), 7.

trans-Atlantic consciousness of social contingency and impermanence that had begun to set in the wake of the French Revolution and which would go on to become a defining mark of the sensibility we call modern.[104] To say with Kaplan that the realist novel simultaneously articulated and combatted this emerging sensibility is to see it *both* as the fruit of the post-1789 culturalist-historicist turn *and* as a reaction formation against some of its more disconcerting implications. A creature of the post-revolution era, the novel, in Franco Moretti's words, became an instrument for narrating "'how the French Revolution could have been avoided."[105]

This reactionary imperative helps explain the genre's characteristic striving after total formal integration and architectonic stability. If the events of 1789–1815 had revealed the brittle nature of social and political institutions, the novel, with its panoramic scope and density of detail, conveyed a sense of their dependable solidity. If the revolution raised the specter of irreconcilable social antagonisms, the novel's staple Bildungs and marriage plots—via their comedic unity-in-difference narrative logic—"demonstrated" the stability of the social bond over and against differences of breeding and class.[106] The genre's massive effort (most conspicuous in the novels of George Eliot and Dickens but characteristic of the genre as a whole), to reveal the subtle tissue of correspondences and relationships that binds together what initially seem like unrelated people and things into a single palpitating whole, was, among other things, an attempt to reassert the essential unity and stability of the familiar world over and against its revealed precarity. The realist novel, as Terry Eagleton writes, "portrays a world so substantial—so richly, irresistibly *there*—that the idea that it could ever be radically altered becomes almost unthinkable."[107]

All this is not to deny that the nineteenth-century novel in Europe and America engaged in relentless and often bitter social critique. However, even Dickens's increasingly darker and more pessimistic novels of the 1850s

---

104. On the trans-Atlantic reverberations of the 1789–1814 period, see Fritzsche, *Stranded in the Present*, 160–200. Fiona J. Stafford's *The Last of the Race* (Oxford: Clarendon, 1994), which traces the migration of its titular trope across the English-speaking world, likewise disputes (albeit implicitly) American exceptionalism.

105. Moretti, *The Way of the World*, 64.

106. For a compelling reading of the nineteenth-century novel as a cultural response to the French Revolution, see Franco Moretti, *The Way of the World* (London: Verso, 2000).

107. Terry Eagleton, *The English Novel: An Introduction* (Malden, MA: Blackwell, 2005), 99.

and 1860s (to take an author who enjoyed immense popularity across the English-speaking world) were written from an essentially anti-revolutionary and reformist political position. One need only read the mob scenes in *A Tale of Two Cities* (1859), Dickens's retelling of the events of 1789, to get a sense of his visceral horror of collective political action and the anomic disorder that it signified. Indeed, as George Orwell once pointed out, Dickens's constant moral proselytizing was motivated (at least partly) by the wish to inspire in his middle-class audience the kind of change of heart that he believed was necessary if England was to be spared the fate of France. But on the formal level, too, the Dickensian project of recasting English society as a self-contained cosmos, a synthetic totality so solid and integrated that its stability seems unimpeachable, needs to be read as part of a prolonged cultural reaction to the specter of social disintegration. Almost a century after the attack on the Bastille, and a decade after the events of 1848, the stalking threat of revolution was still haunting the novel.

To write in the decades following 1789, Erich Auerbach observes, inevitably involved being "continually conscious that the social base upon which [one] lives is not constant for a moment but is perpetually changing through convulsions of the most various kinds."[108] This remark occurs in Auerbach's reading of Stendhal's *The Red and the Black* (1830), which he credits with introducing a new form of "modern tragic realism" to the novel.[109] But the task of representing the most radical and tragic kind of convulsion that may befall a way of life—its final and irreversible ending—would become the office not of the realist novel, as practiced by Stendhal, Balzac, and Flaubert (Auerbach's examples), but of another and equally influential nineteenth-century realist genre, which likewise claimed Edgeworth and Scott as its progenitors: local-color or regionalist fiction.

Thanks to the studies by Liz Bellamy, Judith Fetterley, Marjorie Pryse, and Josephine Donovan, among others, we now know how decisive Edgeworth and Scott were for the nineteenth-century explosion of Anglophone regionalist writing.[110] The novels and sketches of Washington Irving, Elizabeth Gaskell,

---

108. Erich Auerbach, *Mimesis: The Representation of Reality in Western Literature*, trans. Willard R. Trask (Princeton, NJ: Princeton University Press, 2003), 459.

109. Auerbach, *Mimesis*, 458.

110. See Liz Bellamy, "Regionalism and Nationalism: Maria Edgeworth, Walter Scott and the Definition of Britishness," in *The Regional Novel in Britain and Ireland: 1800–1990*, ed. K.D.M. Snell (Cambridge: Cambridge University Press, 1998), 54–77; Judith Fetterley and Marjorie Pryse, *Writing out of Place: Regionalism, Women, and American Literary*

Harriet Beecher Stowe, Thomas Hardy, and Sarah Orne Jewett (to name but a few) would have been impossible without the examples of their Irish and Scottish predecessors. Moreover, the almost immediate translations of *Castle Rackrent* and the Waverley novels into a host of European languages ensured their influence would not be restricted to the English-speaking world. By the middle decades of the nineteenth century, local-color traditions could be spotted across Europe. These included the German *Dorfgeschichten* [village tales], which flourished in what is today Germany, Austria, and Switzerland, as well as the French provincial novel. Scandinavian, Spanish, Italian, and Russian offshoots soon followed.[111] Writers such as the Swiss German Berthold Auerbach (sometimes dubbed *"[der] Walter Scott seines Heimatsdorf"*) and George Sand ("The Walter Scott of Berry") produced works centering on premodern communities and spotlighting the role of local geographies, inherited customs, and traditional forms of labor in the formation of collective identities.[112] The regionalists employed many of the same devices applied by their realist peers: the representation of class-specific dialect, for instance, or the use of frequent narratorial interjections for purposes of clarification and contextualization. What gave their intimate portrayals of provincial life their distinctive emotional valence was the framing supposition (always implied if not explicitly stated) that the communities being described are either endangered by or have already succumbed to the encroachment of modernity.

Like Edgeworth and Scott, the regionalist writers often accounted for their literary preoccupation with vanishing cultures in preservationist terms. American regionalist Mary Wilkins Freeman's self-ascribed mission, to "preserve in literature . . . this old and probably disappearing type of New England character," and Thomas Hardy's stated desire "to preserve for my own satisfaction a fairly true record of a vanishing form of life," are both typical in this regard.[113] As Josephine Donovan describes the trajectory

---

Culture (Urbana: University of Illinois Press, 2003); Josephine Donovan, *European Local-Color Literature: National Tales, Dorfgeschichten, Romans Champetres* (New York: Continuum, 2010).

111. For an instructive survey of regionalism as a European genre, see Donovan, *Local-Color Literature*.

112. Quoted in Donovan, *Local-Color Literature*, 97, 138.

113. Mary Wilkins Freeman, "Author's Preface," in *A Far-Away Melody: and Other Stories* (Edinburgh: D. Douglas, 1897), 5; Thomas Hardy, "General Preface to the Novels and Poems," in *Thomas Hardy's Personal Writings*, ed. Harold Orel (London: Macmillan, 1967), 46.

and motivations of this literary genre, "beginning in Ireland with Maria Edgeworth's *Castle Rackrent*, continuing in Scotland, Germany, and France, spreading eventually throughout the Western world, writers—themselves for the most part of the educated elite— . . . sought . . . to preserve ancient customs and traditions that were threatened with erasure and assimilation."[114] And it was this formally encoded awareness of historical vulnerability and finitude, over and above matters of style and representation, that set regionalist realism apart from its metropolitan counterpart.

Thus, a kind of division of labor was set up in the middle decades of the nineteenth century. The metropolitan realist novel, taking on Edgeworth's and Scott's historicist realism, set itself up as the representer and moral tutor of the rising middle-classes, while regionalist realism, adopting those same originators' localism and elegaism, tasked itself with mediating to those selfsame metropolitan readers the distinctive cultural rhythms and customs of fading lifeworlds located on the national or imperial periphery.[115]

The nineteenth-century association of extinction with peripherality, first introduced by Gray's, Goldsmith's, and Macpherson's eighteenth-century poems and carried forward by Edgeworth, Scott, and their realist and regionalist heirs, would receive significant reinforcement toward the end of the nineteenth century from yet another emergent genre similarly predicated on the center-periphery distinction: namely, modern ethnography. James Clifford has shown how modern anthropology had adopted the age-old contrast between the country and the city and mapped it unto the distinction between the Western self and the ethnographic Other: "ethnography's disappearing object is, then, in significant degree a rhetorical construct legitimating a representational practice: 'salvage' ethnography in its widest

---

114. Donovan, *Local-Color Literature*, 177–178.

115. The categories of "periphery," "center," "regionalism," and "realism" should not, of course, be taken as absolute. Not only do many writers trouble their stability (was George Eliot a realist or regionalist? What about Ivan Turgenev?), but the very division of national and imperial spaces into clearly demarcated "centers" and "peripheries" is fraught with complications (where does *Middlemarch* fall? How about Dickens's Tom-All-Alone's?). But to admit such complications is not necessarily to strike a point against the utility of these terms (after all, *all* our theoretical classifications and definitions are susceptible to deconstruction and counterexample). What these complexities recommend, rather, is that the specificities of the center-periphery relationship have to be worked out on a case-by-case basis and in reference to the particular cultural and historical circumstances that obtain in each.

sense."¹¹⁶ What is common to regionalism's tales of decline on the periphery and ethnography's elegiac accounts of vanishing natives is that both discourses trafficked in stories of dying cultures "over there" for the benefit of readers "over here" (in London, Paris, Berlin, and New York). Seen in this light, Bronislaw Malinowski's record of a Trobriand culture "[dying] away under our very eyes" is not so very different from James Fenimore Cooper's tales of the twilight of America's indigenous races or from Jewett's sketches of New England's "fast waning" country life.¹¹⁷ What these iconic cultures had in common (aside from their putative "extinction," that is) was their felt *remoteness*—both real and symbolic—from the metropolitan base with which the typical consumers of the era's literary and scientific journals identified.

Far from incidental, this remoteness was key to the cultural-extinction narrative's ideological work, which consisted of articulating this unsettling (yet captivating) possibility while keeping it at a safe distance. On the perception such texts encouraged, cultural death was the lot of History's losers, to be observed with wistfulness but also with a significant measure of reassurance from a secure position on the right side of Humanity, Civilization, and Progress. In other words, Cooper's Indians, Theodor Fontane's Junkers, or E.E. Evans-Pritchard Nuer were there (at least in part) to confirm by their inevitable decline the ascendant identity of the middle-class urbanites who consumed their stories. As Richard Brodhead argues in connection with American regionalism, the public function of the genre's stories of cultural extinction "was not just to mourn lost cultures but to purvey a certain story of contemporary cultures and the relations among them: to tell local cultures into a history of their supersession by modern order now risen to national dominance."¹¹⁸ To put this point more bluntly still: the death of eccentric cultures was needed, not merely to "prove" the hegemony of the metropole—a fact too obvious, one would think, to require demonstration—but to affirm the essential *rightness* of the values and institutions that centered in it. Nineteenth-century accounts of cultural extinction on the periphery thus played into what Ruth Benedict has identified as the deep-

---

116. Clifford, "On Ethnographic Allegory," 112.

117. Malinowski, *Argonauts*, xi; Sarah Orne Jewett, "Preface" to *Deephaven* (1893), in *Deephaven and Other Stories*, ed. Richard Cary (Albany, NY: New College and University Press, 1966), 32.

118. Richard Brodhead, *Cultures of Letters: Scenes of Reading and Writing in Nineteenth-Century America* (Chicago: University of Chicago Press, 1993), 121.

seated need to believe that "*our* achievements, *our* institutions are unique."[119] They assured "us" that while we share a basic humanity with the disappearing natives and obsolete rural folk, our way of life is grounded in something less contingent and more enduring than mere tradition or convention, and is thus immune to the vagaries of history and chance in a way theirs were not. In the post-Darwinian and increasingly more secular intellectual climate of the late nineteenth and early twentieth centuries, there was consolation in believing that, though we are mortal, our community's beliefs and institutions are rooted in something that transcends this condition.

Yet despite the ideological and metaphysical comforts it provided, the nineteenth century's asymmetrical distribution of human potentialities—between disintegrating "cultures" on modernity's periphery and a progressing "civilization" at its presumptive core—begins to break down in the 1920s and 1930s, when, reeling from the shattering impact of the Great War and chastened by the incipient diffusion of imperialist power, writers across national and linguistic boundaries begin to employ the semantics of cultural extinction to describe the fate, not of outlying communities, but of groups associated with the metropolitan base. "The tropes and modes of colonial knowledge," writes Jed Esty in his study of English modernism, "came home to roost."[120] Among the implications of this transition is the transposition of the cultural-extinction trope from the periphery to the center, as Western intellectuals begin to think of their societies using metaphors and narratives patterns hitherto reserved for modernity's designated others.

The early-twentieth-century blurring of the previously sacrosanct boundary separating the Western-metropolitan-modern "us" from the peripheral-rural-premodern "them" manifested as an increase of linguistic traffic between what had hitherto been quarantined spheres of representation. Terms and assumptions traditionally used to make sense of cultural strangers were turned back upon the Western self, who, as a consequence, began to see its own nature and fate in that of groups and communities formerly viewed as qualitatively other. Examples abound: Thorsten Veblen's "savaging" of genteel society in *The Theory of the Leisure Class* (1899); Freud's attempt to establish psychological continuities between neurotic behavior and various animistic practices in *Totem and Taboo* (1913); Oswald Spengler's anti-Eurocentric insistence in 1918 that all civilizations—the West included—follow a pattern of organic growth and decay; and Marlow's similar insistence, in Conrad's

---

119. Benedict, *Patterns of Culture*, 20.

120. Jed Esty, *A Shrinking Island: Modernism and National Culture in England* (Princeton, NJ: Princeton University Press, 2004), 9.

Heart of Darkness (1899), that London, too, was once (and remains) "one of the dark places of the earth"—these are some of the better known expressions of the increasing tendency to view the Western self using terms and assumptions originally devised for making sense of others.[121]

The increased tendency among early twentieth-century intellectuals to view their own societies in culturalist and relativistic terms is another facet of this shift. As Esty suggests, "by transferring the holistic ethos (writing about 'an entire way of life') from small-scale colonized societies to their own shrinking nation, English intellectuals found a distinctive way to respond to the imminent collapse of British hegemony."[122] That is, faced with the prospect of imperial contraction, English writers sought to redefine Englishness along culturalist, rather than universalist-imperialist lines, as a discrete and insular way of life. However, as the following chapters devoted to Wharton, Roth, and Shabtai will show, the culturalist turn that Esty's book isolates and analyzes was not strictly an English phenomenon, nor is it explainable solely as a function of post-imperialist nationalist retrenchment. The use of "ethnographic devices acquired in the colonies to the task of representing the home culture" is a much broader postwar phenomenon, and one that involved more than the casting of one's own society—be it a nation, an ethnic group, or an economic class—in functionalist terms. It also encouraged viewing it as a vulnerable and transient episode.[123]

We thus find a writer like Edith Wharton, who could claim a US president as a personal friend, describing her privileged milieu as the "vanishing denizens of the American continent doomed to rapid extinction"; or Joseph Roth likening his ill-fated Habsburgian elites to "baffling followers of some remote and cruel godhead" (a clear allusion to the fast-disappearing Eastern-European Jewish communities he had portrayed in his reportages of the 1920s).[124] And the same pattern recurs in the work of Yaakov Shabtai. Though written in a very different cultural and historical context, his requiem to Israel's founding generation similarly casts a hegemonic milieu in terms that nineteenth- and early-twentieth-century discourses had reserved for cultural aliens: as a vanishing tribe.

---

121. Joseph Conrad, *Heart of Darkness*, ed. Paul B. Armstrong (New York: W. W. Norton, 2006), 5.
122. Esty, *A Shrinking Island*, 10.
123. Esty, *A Shrinking Island*, 93.
124. Joseph Roth, *The Radetzky March*, trans. Michael Hofmann (London: Granta, 2002), 121.

Chapter 2

An Ironist's Elegy

Edith Wharton's *The Age of Innocence*

> In art, as in morals, what ought to be done does not depend on our personal judgment; we have to accept the imperative imposed by the time.
>
> —José Ortega y Gasset, *The Dehumanization of Art and Other Essays on Art, Culture, and Literature*

> Whenever, in conversation with younger friends, I relate some episode of the time before the first war, I notice from their astonished questions how much that is still obvious reality to me has already become historical and incomprehensible to them.
>
> —Stefan Zweig, *The World of Yesterday*

Postwar

Setting Edith Wharton's post–World War I novel of cultural extinction, *The Age of Innocence* (1920), against the backdrop of the long tradition in which it participates affords us not only with an instructive lesson in generic change over time, but also with a vantage point from which to assess more diffuse shifts in sensibility that accompanied the deepening hold of the culturalist view on the self-image of twentieth-century intellectuals. On the story that I have been telling in the previous chapters, the structure of thought and feeling that I am calling culturalism, along with its attendant anxieties and susceptibilities, had been gradually percolating into the consciousness of Europeans and Americans for well over a century before the outbreak of the Great War. But it was only in the wake of that "gigantic transformation . . . [of which] everyone was forced to be a witness," as Stefan Zweig described the war, that these implications finally hit home.[1]

Perhaps no single text captures this shift more succinctly than Paul Valéry's 1919 speech "Disillusionment," which I reproduce here almost in full:

> We modern civilizations have learned to recognize that we are mortal like the others.
>
> We had heard tell of whole worlds vanished, of empires foundered with all their men and all their engines, sunk to the inexplorable depths of the centuries with their gods and laws, their academies and their pure and applied sciences, their grammars, dictionaries, classics, romantics, symbolists, their critics and the critics of their critics. We knew that all the apparent earth is made of ashes, and that ashes have a meaning. We perceived, through the misty bulk of history, the phantoms of huge vessels once laden with riches and learning. We could not count them. But these wrecks, after all, were no concern of ours. . . . And now we see that the abyss of history is deep enough to bury all the world. We feel that a civilization is fragile as a life.[2]

The vanished "others," which Valéry goes on to cite, are the ancient civilizations of Elam, Nineveh, and Babylon, the "total ruin" of which, he writes, "meant as little [to us] as did their existence."[3] But, as we have already seen, Valéry could just as well have invoked Western modernity's more proximate others: say, James Macpherson's and Walter Scott's Highlanders, or James Fenimore Cooper's Indians, or any number of the numerous indigenous peoples whose customs and religious rituals E.B. Tylor and James Frazer catalogued in their classic nineteenth-century compendiums of anthropological lore, *Primitive Culture* (1871) and *The Golden Bough* (1890). After

---

1. Stefan Zweig, *The World of Yesterday* (Lincoln: Nebraska University Press, 1964), xxi.
2. Paul Valéry, "Disillusionment," in *Sources of European History Since 1900*, ed. Marvin Perry, Matthew Bera, and James Krukones (Boston, MA: Cengage, 2011), 78.
3. Valéry, "Disillusionment," 78.

all, those fading cultures were likewise "no concern of ours," in the sense that their sad fate was viewed as somehow irrelevant to or surpassed by our "modern civilizations."

Nineteenth-century fiction, I have been arguing, had variously contributed to the maintenance of this sense of metropolitan immunity by managing, containing, and redirecting the debilitating post–French Revolution consciousness of fragility and impermanence. The realist novel mobilized the world-making, totalizing vision that it inherited from Maria Edgeworth and Scott to impart a reassuring sense of fixity and integrity (structural as well as moral) to the frameworks of everyday life, while regionalism's stories of cultural decline, though seeming to confront the possibilities of historical rupture and cultural extinction more directly, in fact served to further shield its predominantly urban audiences from these tragic potentialities by projecting them away from the metropolitan center and unto its putative others. In so doing, the nineteenth-century regionalist text (later followed by its close relative, the ethnographic report) supplied its intended consumers with a cultural counterpoint against which to define themselves, while also placing them in the reassuring position of History's chosen people.[4] Its message to its contemporary readers was: "though we share a common humanity with these country yokels and exotic savages, the tragic ending of their history was necessary for the emergence of our own more enlightened civilization." Regionalist accounts of cultural extinction thus joined hands with metropolitan narratives of social integration to assure their middle-class audiences that *their* civilization was somehow immune to the ravages of time and chance in a way that those other cultures were not.

As Valéry's speech indicates, it took the global conflagration of 1914–1918 to crack this self-protective shell. If the French Revolution compelled those who lived through it to tarry for the first time with what Mircea Eliade memorably called "the terror of history"—its violence and apparent aimlessness—the Great War dismantled the emotional and conceptual

---

4. For an influential reading of how (American) regionalism helped to consolidate its metropolitan readership "into an imagined community by [providing it with] images of rural 'others' as both a nostalgic point of origin and a measure of cosmopolitan development" (251), see Amy Kaplan, "Nation, Region, and Empire," in *The Columbia History of the American Novel*, ed. Emory Elliott (New York: Columbia University Press, 1991), 240–266.

defenses that Victorian culture had erected to ward itself against it.[5] Those defenses, we now know, were poised to collapse regardless of the war, due to the pressures exerted by the era's intellectual, social, and technological developments. By the turn of the century, Darwin's view of natural history as a violent and undirected series of local extinction events had already seeped into every corner of intellectual life, as had the entropic picture of the universe contained in Lord Kelvin's second law of thermodynamics.[6] Whatever unity we find in the natural world, these paradigm-shifting scientific theories maintained, is but a momentary confluence of matter and energy eventually to be dispersed. Life was not a process of progress and growth but the forestallment of an inevitable breakup. This discomforting image of the natural world dovetailed with Nietzsche's widely circulating ideas and the cumulative impact of more diffused processes of secularization to inspire widespread worries of cultural enervation and atrophy among the educated classes. As T.J. Jackson Lears has shown, middle-class Americans at the turn of the century were beset by a range of affective malaises, from neurasthenia (famously diagnosed by George Miller Beard in his 1881 *American Nervousness*) to a more indefinite sense of spiritual "weightlessness," occasioned by

---

5. Mircea Eliade, *Cosmos and History: The Myth of the Eternal Return*, trans. Willard R. Trask (New York: Harper, 1954), 141–162 and *passim*. Eliade locates the full flowering of historicist thought in the decades separating Nietzsche from Heidegger, when the ideological battlements (religious, Marxist, and other) that had comforted earlier generations finally fell away, leaving modern women and men exposed to the terror-inspiring consciousness of humanity's cosmic loneliness and defenselessness. In a suggestive footnote, Eliade (now writing as a Romanian exile), offers the following reflection on the origins of Western historicist thought:

> We take the liberty of emphasizing that "historicism" was created and professed above all by thinkers belonging to nations for which history has never been a continuous terror. These thinkers would perhaps have adopted another viewpoint had they belonged to nations marked by the "fatality of history." It would certainly be interesting, in any case, to know if the theory according to which everything that happens is "good," simply because it has happened, would have been accepted without qualms by the thinkers of the Baltic countries, of the Balkans, or of colonial territories. (152)

Be that as it may, it seems that in the wake of 1914–1918, the idea that "everything that happens is 'good,'" lost most of its adherents.

6. For an overview of the cultural impact of the idea of entropy, see Eric Zencey, "Some Brief Speculations on the Popularity of Entropy as Metaphor," *North American Review* 271, no. 3 (1986): 7–10.

worries that their identities were becoming "fragmented, diffuse, perhaps even unreal."⁷ And a comparable set of anxieties, often condensed into that fin-de-siècle catchall, "degeneration," was similarly oppressing their European counterparts.⁸ Max Nordau's mildly hysterical attack on the culture of his day, *Entartung* [*Degeneration*] (1892), Gustave Le Bon's description of the modern crowd "as the place of inevitable regression" in *The Crowd* (1895),⁹ and Brooks Adams's gloomy historiographical prognostications in *The Law of Civilization and Decay* (1895) are useful indices for the cultural mood of the time.

Additional factors, including the changing urban environment, the late-nineteenth-century waves of mass migrations and immigrations (from country to city, South to North, Old World to New) and the ever-increasing rate of technological change, all contributed to the sense of disorientation and loss characteristic of the period. To live in the world that took shape during Wharton's lifetime, in Philip Fisher's words, was to inhabit a reality in which "all that now exists is half-real, half-unreal because it exists under the threat that it might soon become obsolete or be discarded."¹⁰ Under these conditions, the official belief in progress as an unabated good became increasingly hard to sustain. And while the quintessentially Victorian assumption that future meant better continued to command a kind of perfunctory assent into the 1900s, the long nineteenth century, as an epoch and a mindset, could be said to have expired well before Gavrilo Prinzip shot Duke Franz Ferdinand in Sarajevo.

Still it was only in the wake of the Great War that novels begin to appear which explicitly explore the possibility that *our* way of life was a fragile, merely human creation—that "we modern civilizations," as Valéry put it, "are mortal like the others." Edith Wharton's *The Age of Innocence* is exemplary of this postwar pivot from peripheral to metropolitan narratives of cultural extinction. Not only is Wharton the first major twentieth-century

---

7. T.J. Jackson Lears, *No Place of Grace: Antimodernism and the Transformation of American Culture 1880–1920* (Chicago: University of Chicago Press, 1983), 32.

8. See, for instance, Daniel Pick, *Faces of Degeneration: A European Disorder, C.1848–1918* (Cambridge: Cambridge University Press, 1993); William Greenslade, *Degeneration, Culture and the Novel: 1880–1940* (Cambridge: Cambridge University Press, 1994); and Stephen Arata, *Fictions of Loss in the Victorian Fin de Siècle: Identity and Empire* (Cambridge: Cambridge University Press, 1996).

9. Daniel Pick, *Faces of Degeneration*, 91.

10. Philip Fisher, *Still the New World* (Cambridge, MA: Harvard University Press, 1999), 13.

realist novelist to subject a still-hegemonic, economically prosperous, and racially unmarked urban milieu to the kind of fate that earlier fictional and scientific discourses had reserved for outlying rural communities and premodern tribes, she does this consciously and deliberately. Arguably the most intellectual of the Progressive Era writers, Wharton had a sure grasp of the literary history of the novel as well as a close acquaintance with the work of contemporary social scientists (Bronislaw Malinowski was a social acquaintance). In *The Age of Innocence* she brings this broad intellectual reach to bear, knowingly incorporating the same relativizing and ephemeralizing gaze that Scott had trained on the Highland clans, Thomas Hardy on the rustic farmhands of Wessex, and Malinowski on the Trobriand Islanders. However, unlike these authors, Wharton applied this perspective not to a vanishing peripheral society, but to a community located at the very heart of the burgeoning American empire.

To be sure, Old New York's "little tribe," as Wharton describes her native milieu, may have seemed quaint to her original readers. But its Mingotts, Wellands, and Lefferts were infinitely closer (geographically, culturally, genealogically, racially) to those readers' sense of who and what they were than the ethnographic "savages" to which Wharton repeatedly likens them.[11] Like her contemporaries, Veblen, Freud, and Max Weber, Wharton deliberately presents polite society using terms and metaphors drawn from discourses devised to mark and make sense of others, knowing full well that in so doing she was challenging entrenched assumptions of Western and metropolitan exceptionalism.[12] For instance, when Wharton describes the Old New York practice of "[concealing] the spot in which the bridal night was to be spent" as one of that society's "most sacred taboos,"[13] she is purposefully trespassing against the age-old "distinctions between ourselves and the primitive, ourselves and the barbarian," which Ruth Benedict has described as the biggest obstacle to the emergence of a fully-fledged, modern and relativistic, anthropological science.[14] But this willingness to reimagine

---

11. Edith Wharton, *The Age of Innocence*, Norton Critical Edition, ed. Candace Waid (New York: W. W. Norton, 2003), 111.

12. On the similarity between Wharton's representational strategies and those of contemporary social scientists, see Nancy Bentley, "'Hunting for the Real': Wharton and the Science of Manners," in *The Cambridge Companion to Edith Wharton*, ed. Millicent Bell (Cambridge: Cambridge University Press, 1995), 47–67, 48–49.

13. Wharton, *Age of Innocence*, 110.

14. Ruth Benedict, *Patterns of Culture* (New York: The New American Library, 1934), 19.

the universal subject of modernity through an ethnographic lens also meant subjecting it to the susceptibilities from which (thanks to the long-sustained distinction between "ourselves" and the "primitive") it was hitherto shielded. Thus, in Wharton's hands, the culturalist vulnerability that earlier poets, novelists, travel writers, and ethnographers had limited to modernity's others becomes for the first time an intimate prospect for the metropolitan self.

Wharton's conscious dismantling of the protective divide between metropolitan and provincial representation does not begin with *The Age of Innocence*, but can be detected earlier in her career. Unlike her prominent American peers (W.D. Howells, Theodore Dreiser, and Henry James), she did not confine herself to metropolitan or cosmopolitan settings, then considered the quarry of the serious, which is to say, male novelist. Alongside a string of bestselling novels of social realism in the grand nineteenth-century style, she also produced two starkly powerful novellas set in the backwaters of New England the preeminent locale of American regionalist writing, then construed as the province of women writers. *Ethan Frome* (1911), which Hermione Lee aptly describes as a "highly controlled, spare, short masterpiece," was the first of these regionalist works;[15] the controversial *Summer* (1917), which bears close affinity to another regionalist landmark, Hardy's *Tess*, is the second. But what makes Wharton's eclectic career exemplary, for my purposes, is not so much her ambidextrous mastery of both forms—the social realist novel and regionalist tale; rather, it is the manner in which she traverses the traditional aesthetic and ideological barriers between them.

In her memoir, Wharton explains that she was prompted to write her New England novellas by a desire to correct her predecessors' falsifications of that forbidding region: "I had wanted to draw life as it really was in the derelict mountain villages of New England," she writes, "a life even in my own time, and a thousandfold more a generation earlier, utterly unlike that seen through the rose-coloured spectacles of . . . Mary Wilkins and Sarah Orne Jewett."[16] Let us leave aside Wharton's mildly misogynistic description of the writings of Jewett and Wilkins Freeman, her questionable acquaintance with the "derelict" communities that she presumes to describe, as well as her epistemologically problematic claim to paint rural life "as it really was." Let us focus instead on her expressed desire to bring the hardnosed realism

---

15. Hermione Lee, *Edith Wharton* (London: Vintage, 2008), 375.

16. Edith Wharton, *A Backward Glance* (New York & London: D. Appleton-Century Company, 1934), 293.

then associated with the urban novel to territories that had hitherto lain beyond its purview. For while it is common to hear Wharton spoken of as a transitional figure between the nineteenth and twentieth centuries, the latter passage alerts us to the fact that her writing also bridged the divide (generic as well as conceptual) between the two main branches of the realist mode that has come down to us from Edgeworth and Scott: metropolitan and regionalist realism.

American regionalist Mary Austin's provocative claim in her "Regionalism in American Fiction" (1932) that Wharton's first New York novel, *The House of Mirth* (1905), should be regarded as a regionalist work, is apropos here. According to Austin, if a text is to count as regionalist, it is not enough that it be set in a recognizable national region. Geographical setting is not, in fact, a deciding factor at all. After all, *Uncle Tom's Cabin* mostly takes place in the South, but it can hardly be called a Southern novel, as its "moral and intellectual outlook is New England from the ground up."[17] If a text is to be properly regionalist—a term that Austin uses in a normative as well as descriptive sense—it must faithfully capture and represent the region's particular "moral and intellectual outlook" (or what we would call its culture). This criterion enables Austin to claim that although *The House of Mirth* takes place in an urban setting it should be considered a regionalist work, whereas Sinclair Lewis's *Main Street* (1920), despite being set in a small Midwestern town, should not. For while Lewis's satirical send-up of small-town life merely supplies its readers with a "generalized surface reflection of the . . . American character,"[18] Wharton's novel delves deep into the cultural outlook of its urban "region."

Whatever its merits as a theory of regionalism, Austin's 1932 essay usefully conveys how frayed and permeable the partition between metropolitan and regional representation had become by the early decades of the twentieth century. As I have argued in the previous chapter, the destabilization of the boundaries between categories that Victorian culture had labored to keep apart—human/animal, man/woman, savage/civilized, and country/city—manifested in an increase of traffic between these formerly polarized realms. By the time Wharton began her writing career, it was already common to find assumptions and tropes belonging to one side of

---

17. Mary Austin, "Regionalism in American Fiction," *English Journal* 21, no. 2 (1932): 97–107, 106.

18. Austin, "Regionalism," 100.

these divides being applied to social realities associated with the other. This large-order realignment of moral, epistemological, and aesthetic categories explains why Wharton felt licensed to bring a more "realist" sensibility to geographical locations and human types traditionally associated with realism's sister genre. But, by the same token, this process also enabled her to imagine the preeminent setting of the realist novel—the modern city—through the localizing and ephemeralizing lens of regionalist representation. Such a reverse metaphorical drift, I am claiming, helps explain *The Age of Innocence*. For what Wharton does in this Pulitzer Prize–winning elegy to her native New York is to fuse the backward-looking elegaism of the regionalist mode with the urban setting of the realist novel, thus effectively regionalizing the metropole or parochializing the center.

In *The Ethnography of Manners* (1995), Nancy Bentley has provided the richest account to date of the autoethnographic dimension of Wharton's writing, situating her social novels, *The Age of Innocence* in particular, within a broader turn-of-the-century rise of what Benedict called "culture consciousness."[19] While this emergent relativistic sensibility, argues Bentley, destabilized Victorian notions of moral authority, it also generated a need for specialists capable of unlocking the mysteries of culture—that recently introduced idea that seemed to explain so much about human behavior. Thus, in the early decades of the twentieth century there appears a "new form of expert observation, realized in writing, that gives the observer mastery over a cultural territory."[20] The self-identified practitioners of this emergent mode of intellectual authority were the newly professionalized ethnographers and sociologists. But the rise of culture consciousness, as Bentley compellingly shows, also made itself felt in the realm of fiction, particularly in writers like James and Wharton, who began to "do" polite society in the manner that their contemporary, Malinowski, was doing the Trobriand Islands.[21] Seen this way, these writers' trademark deployment of ethnographic jargon becomes more than a stylistic flourish. Their flaunted primitivism was, as Bentley argues, part of a deliberate strategy aimed at exposing the conventional, socially constructed underpinnings of the real, on the one hand, while asserting a new kind of cognitive mastery over culture, on the other.

---

19. Ruth Benedict quoted in Nancy Bentley, *The Ethnography of Manners: Hawthorne, James, Wharton* (Cambridge: Cambridge University Press, 1995), 102.
20. Bentley, *Ethnography of Manners*, 2.
21. Bentley, *Ethnography of Manners*, 2.

Bentley's study offers an incisive and instructive reading of the welter of discourses that made up Wharton's cultural-historical moment and informed her writing. Much of what I will say below is indebted to her work. And yet, for all its many strengths, *The Ethnography of Manners* suffers, in my view, from the Foucauldian tendency to emphasize the primacy of discourse to such an extent that the subjectivity of its subject all but dissolves. Wharton's belief that she had witnessed the passing of the world of her youth;[22] her acute sense (oft-expressed during the postwar years) of obsolescence and outmodedness; her considered reflections on what it means to write a realist novel at a time when its future seemed in doubt—these and other similarly subjective matters are sidelined, if not ignored, in Bentley's otherwise powerful study. In the reading that follows, I want to take Wharton's own views of her life and times seriously, while also trying to extract more general lessons from them. While I make no claims of epistemological privilege for this kind of reading, I do think that it is more in keeping with the culturalist insistence on the importance of factoring in the "inside" or "first-person" point of view in any interpretative, literary or historical, account. On the line of thought that runs from Herder, through Hegel, to Franz Boas and Wilhelm Dilthey, an account of a human phenomenon, as opposed to the inert facts of nature, will remain one-sided until one complements the detached perspective of the external analyst with the informant's own perspective. This does not mean that the "native's own point of view"—her reported impressions, feelings, thoughts—takes precedence over the perspective of the disengaged observer. But it does suggest that doing justice to the ambiguity, complexity, and richness of human entanglements requires seeing them from (at least) two competing perspectives.

Let me give a concrete example that will help explain how my approach to Wharton's ethnographic novel differs from Bentley's. In the conclusion of the chapter devoted to *The Age of Innocence*, Bentley encourages us to read Wharton's depiction of the passing of Old New York society as a move in a broader WASP strategy for shoring up white privilege and power: "In spite of a pervasive sense of WASP decline [which Wharton's novel echoed and presumably helped to propagate (N.E.)]—*indeed, in part through that very sense*—the northeastern elite expanded its social influence and helped to acculturate the American polity to a new society of consumption and corporate capitalism."[23] In other words, what might seem like an elegiac account of

---

22. Wharton, *A Backward Glance*, 7.
23. Bentley, *Ethnography of Manners*, 113. Emphasis added.

the ending of a way of life, Bentley is implying here and elsewhere in her reading, is in fact the story of how a hegemonic class rebranded itself as an endangered species so as to safeguard and perpetuate its social dominance.

Now, while I do not deny the force of this reading, I am fairly confident that Wharton would have dismissed it as perverse. The suggestion that the "new society of consumption and corporate capitalism"—the society that she (Wharton) personifies elsewhere in the likes of Undine Spragg and Elmer Moffatt—was continuous with her own would have struck her as absurd. Where Bentley sees accommodation and continuity, she saw a decisive, indeed disastrous, break. Time and again in her postwar writing (fiction and nonfiction alike), Wharton depicts the Great War as a radical historical caesura, and refers to her sense of having survived the dismantling of the world in which she had spent the majority of her years. In the introduction to the 1936 edition of *The House of Mirth*, for instance, she compares the war years to that "cataclysmic period from the execution of Louis XVI to the battle of Waterloo," when "out of the savage crimes and senseless destruction of those brief years a new world was born, differing as radically from the old world which it destroyed as that strange amalgam of new forces that grew out of the fall of the Roman empire differed from the civilization it overthrew."[24] Elsewhere she points to the events of 1914–1918 as bringing about the "sudden and total extinction" of the "small society into which [she] was born."[25] The same sense of rupture and loss also finds its way into her novels, and in particular into *The Age of Innocence*, which ends with Newland Archer's bemused recognition that he is stranded in a present that has no more use for his kind. Dallas, his son, is admittedly a more sympathetic figure than Undine or Moffatt, but the new world for which he stands is arguably as alien and inhospitable to his "prehistoric" father as theirs.[26]

Of course, it is easy to dismiss Wharton's invocation of cultural extinction as a bit of melodramatic hyperbole or as a typical elite reflex in the face of a perceived loss of hegemonic power, which it certainly also is. But what happens if we try to take Wharton at her word? Is there a way to view her claim to have witnessed the extinction of a world—her world—as a genuine

---

24. Edith Wharton, "Introduction to the 1936 Edition," in *Edith Wharton's The House of Mirth: A Casebook*, ed. Carol J. Singley (Oxford: Oxford University Press, 2003), 31–37, 32.

25. Wharton, *A Backward Glance*, 7.

26. Wharton, *Age of Innocence*, 213.

(even if hyperbolic) expression of an intimately felt predicament? My point in asking such questions, it should be clear, is not to argue for Wharton's perspective or against Bentley's. The question at stake here is not whether Wharton's "world" *really* met with "sudden and total extinction" sometime between 1914 and 1918, or if, as Bentley claims, it merely adapted to the new environment. (On what grounds would one decide this matter, anyway?) The question to be asked rather is whether, when she claims to have outlived her world, Wharton might not be expressing a kind of truth—one that is not only faithful to her experience, but which is also appropriate to the culturalist self-image that she inhabits and propounds.

The Age of Innocence, as I will read it, is a meditation on the transience of a cultural world, on the triumph of time over the desire for fixity, on the hopelessness of that desire. John Updike is, therefore, only half right when he claims that the novel "beneath its fine surface holds an abyss—the abyss of time, and the tragedy of human transience."[27] For though time's abyss certainly yawns beyond the play of Wharton's limpid metaphors and darting witticisms, the transience it portends is only secondarily that of the individual human life. Personal death is not so much a theme in this novel as is the passing away of social institutions and the way of life that they embody. *The Age of Innocence* is a novel about the unbearable lightness of identity—always collective, received, contextual—not about the flesh-and-blood body on which it is stamped. It is, therefore, not the transience of human life that ticks away under its shining surface, but rather the ephemerality of the webs of meanings that give a life its moral coordinates and meaning. The novel, I will claim, is not only Wharton's most intimate work, representing her personal feelings of untimeliness and dislocation; it is also a text keenly aware of the problems facing the realist genre once it entered the culturalist intellectual climate of the early twentieth century.

Between Wharton and Archer

By choosing to end Newland Archer's story when he is fifty-seven, her own age at the time of writing *The Age of Innocence*, Edith Wharton was clearly inviting comparison. The ground for it, however, is less obvious. It cannot be, for instance, a comparison between the respective contents of Wharton's

---

27. John Updike, "Archer's Way," in *Edith Wharton's* The Age of Innocence, ed. Harold Bloom (Philadelphia, PA: Chelsea House, 2005), 133–139.

and Archer's characters, or between their chosen professional pursuits and accomplishments. For, though formed of the same cultural substance, and launched from comparable levels of social status, what Archer and Wharton each did with the similar cards they were dealt was quite different. Archer—by training a lawyer, by proclivity a dilettante, by achievement undistinguished—does not seem to have evolved into anything like Wharton: a disciplined, committed, and highly successful author.[28] Whereas he remains throughout a fundamentally passive man, all receptivity and pliancy, she was a dynamic woman, unconventional in her way, and uncommonly productive by any standard.

Similarly, the choices Wharton and Archer each made in the intimate spheres of love and family also do not seem to overlap. Some lines of similarity might perhaps be drawn between the passionless marriages, but Wharton's unhappy life with Teddy Wharton was unhappy for reasons that have little to do with what stands between Newland and May Archer (sure and steady May was clearly not composed with the mentally unstable Teddy in mind). Also, Wharton, unlike the resigned Archer, did not give up on passion. Though coming to it late in life in the person of Morton Fullerton, she had dared, however briefly, to realize that part of her self. What she did not experience, however (as opposed to Archer, a warm and devoted father), was parenthood.

Finally, there is the matter of Archer's softness, an outcome of his sheltered life, as well as of a certain narrowness of vision. It is such a fundamental property of his nature that even his fugitive insights into the sacrificial dimensions of Ellen Olenska's banishment and the brutal practices of inclusion and exclusion that underlie his social reality do not seem to harden him or turn him into a cynic. His psychological constitution simply does not have the necessary reserves to sustain a lasting opposition to his social environment. And though he vaguely flirts with the idea of life outside his narrow and privileged slice of New York, his opinions never stray far, or for very long, from the limits imposed by society's sense of propriety. Correlatively, Archer loses "the habit of travel" in his later years, preferring to stay within the narrow confines of the world he knows.[29]

---

28. Blake Nevius comments that "Wharton's career was in one sense a triumph over the very obstacles that defeat her characters—social position, too much money, lack of sympathy, and an everyday environment that is indifferent, if not hostile to art." See, Blake Nevius, *Edith Wharton: A Study of Her Fiction* (Berkeley: University of California Press, 1953), 21.

29. Wharton, *Age of Innocence*, 210.

Wharton, conversely, was an avid traveler and chose to reside away from America altogether during the last decades of her life. Not only possessed of a more independent and cosmopolitan spirit than her protagonist, she was also tougher of mind. Her proto-constructivist conception of selfhood as well as her quasi-Freudian insight into the price exacted by the process of civilization were both harsher and more nuanced than anything the genial Archer might have thoroughly grasped or consistently held. Her sense of affiliation to the social circles in which she moved was likewise more ambiguous than his. Though an Old New York–bred elitist to the marrow, Wharton had no illusions about her milieu and was never as beholden to its strictures as are the New Yorkers she depicts. Instead she used her intimate knowledge of this clannish society's customs and prejudices to become one of its most devastating critics (much more so than James, who was too enamored of the nuanced spectacle of leisured class existence, or F. Scott Fitzgerald who, as Irving Howe points out, came to the subject of wealth as a bedazzled outsider and could therefore only vividly dramatize but not dissect it).[30] In sum, though belonging to the same social class, Wharton and Archer share neither a common outlook, nor a similar psychological constitution, nor still a comparable set of life choices. In fact, in these respects, it is probably Ellen Olenska, not Archer, who resembles her author most closely.[31] Nevertheless, whereas Ellen recedes into the shadows at the end of the novel, the fifty-seven-year-old protagonist remains at center stage. What, then, is the comparison Wharton suggests between herself and her main character?

The answer, I believe, is that it is a comparison not of character but of a particular (and distinctly modern) situation. Wharton, I mean, did not identify with Archer the man but rather with the predicament in which he finds himself at the end of the novel: that of outliving the world that

---

30. Irving Howe, *The Decline of the New* (London: Victor Gollancz, 1963), 131.

31. R.W.B. Lewis argues otherwise: "Edith Wharton divided her own past between Newland Archer and Ellen Olenska" (431). Archer's life, claims Lewis, represented for Wharton what "she might have become had she failed to break free," while Ellen stood for her "nonconformist self" (431). As I see it, however, this reading is committed to the improbable idea that Wharton's conspicuous choice to end Archer's story when he is at her exact age was somehow meant to highlight their differences rather than to point toward to a certain similarity between them. In viewing that similarity as a matter of situation rather than of character, my reading is again opposed to Lewis's. See R.W.B. Lewis, *Edith Wharton: A Biography* (New York: Harper & Row, 1975), 431.

had shaped him. Archer's words in the final scene, "say I'm old-fashioned: that's enough" (the coded message he sends up to Ellen, as an explanation for why he does not come up to see her after all those years of separation) need to be taken in their most literal sense.[32] What he realizes at that moment is that the cultural stuff out of which he was fashioned, and which continues to inform his desires, beliefs, norms, and tastes, belongs wholly to the past. He recognizes, in other words, that he has been left behind by cultural-historical change, that he has become, to the core of his identity, an anachronism.

This strange condition aligns the mature Archer with a long procession of literary characters, leading back to the mid–eighteenth century, whose defining feature consists of surviving the extinction of their cultural milieus. These "remnant-figures," as Ina Ferris calls the type,[33] make their first appearance in the proto-Romantic poems of James Macpherson and Thomas Gray (discussed in chapter 1), whence they made their way into Walter Scott's historical fiction, before becoming a staple feature of regionalist writing in Europe and America.[34] Ethan Frome, the eponymous hero of Wharton's 1911 regionalist novella, belongs to this tradition, as does Archer, the protagonist of her "regional" New York novel. Remnants, writes Ferris, embody "a particular kind of displacement that spotlights disconnection and disengagement in the present rather than (or as well as) the loss of tradition or authenticity rooted in the past."[35] That is, rather than activating the recuperative modalities of nostalgia, figures like Archer and Frome highlight the predicament of finding oneself an exile and a stranger in what were once one's native grounds. The peculiar poignancy of remnants lies in the fact of their "[having] outlived not just their time and their function . . . but, in a sense, their very lives."[36] Outmoded and displaced,

---

32. Wharton, *Age of Innocence*, 217.

33. Ina Ferris, "'On the Borders of Oblivion': Scott's Historical Novel and the Modern Time of the Remnant," *Modern Language Quarterly* 70, no. 4 (2009): 473–494.

34. Notable American examples of the type include Washington Irving's Rip Van Winkle (1819), James Fenimore Cooper's Chingachgook (especially his depiction in *The Pioneers* [1823]), Mary Noailles Murfree's Cynthia Ware (1884), Kate Chopin's Madame Pélagie (1894), the spectral chief in Mary Hartwell Catherwood's "Pontiac's Lookout" (1894), and Mary Austin's Basket Maker (1903).

35. Ferris, *Borders of Oblivion*, 484.

36. Ferris, *Borders of Oblivion*, 477.

they are typically depicted as either unwilling or unable to engage with the new order in which they find themselves, preferring instead to withdraw, in the manner of Archer at the conclusion of the novel, to their memories where the past lives on. As such, remnants spotlight the precarious state of the culturally constituted self, while also underscoring by the sheer fact of their status as survivals "the fragility of the continuum of common life under modern conditions of acceleration and dispersion."[37] The tenuousness of culture and the dislocation of the remnant are, in short, two sides of the same culturalist coin.

It is then the sense of cultural-historical dislocation, if not much else, that Wharton shares with her character. But here too the felt pressures of the situation do not fully overlap. For unlike Archer, whose profession is not much more than a respectable way for a New York gentleman to pass his time, Wharton's identity was tightly bound up with her vocation. As a result, while Archer's sense of his obsolescence is primarily a consequence of shifting social norms and conventions, hers also had to do with the transvaluation of aesthetic values—a process that was quickened by the massive cultural impact of the war. Whereas the fifty-seven-year-old Archer has to contend with the fading away of his way of life, Wharton also had to deal with the sense that her literary methods were becoming inadequate to the task set by the times. This was not merely a subjective impression. In the postwar years, critical esteem (though not popular taste) was indeed moving away from the kind of prose that Wharton was writing to that of a younger generation, whose style of writing was in many respects a rejection of hers. Wharton was well aware of this shift in critical reception and it was a cause of mild alarm. Her distaste for the modernist aesthetic was mingled with a worry that the fervor surrounding the Young Turks was making her seem like a "deplorable example of what people used to read in the Dark Ages."[38] And there is, at least to my mind, more than a hint of defensiveness in her curt dismissals of Joyce, Woolf, and T.S. Eliot.[39]

---

37. Ferris, *Borders of Oblivion*, 485.

38. Lewis, *Edith Wharton*, 442.

39. She famously described *Ulysses* as a "turgid welter of pornography (the rudest school-boy kind)"; Eliot's *The Waste Land* was "unformed and unimportant drivel"; and the comparisons, often made at the time, between her work and Woolf's irritated her. See Cynthia Griffin Wolff, *A Feast of Words: The Triumph of Edith Wharton* (New York: Oxford University Press, 1977), 372.

Be that as it may, the fact that Wharton disapproved of the new course taken by fiction does not mean that she was oblivious to the changes in cultural consciousness that had made it apposite. As her comment to her friend, Bernard Berenson, suggests, she was well aware that the First World War had demolished the prewar range of aesthetic possibilities: "Before the war you could write fiction without indicating the period, the present being assumed. The war has put an end to that for a long time. . . . In other words, the historical novel with all its vices will be the only possible form for fiction."[40] Turning back to the 1870s in *The Age of Innocence* was thus motivated by more than a need to come to a reconciliation with her past, a wish to pay homage to the recently deceased James (whose *Portrait of a Lady* hovers in the background of the novel), or a desire—whether conscious or not—to preserve and thus promote certain class claims to power and wealth, as Bentley and others have argued.[41] Wharton's choice to set her novel in the past represented her way of responding to the changed conditions of writing. These changes already began emerging prior to 1914 (in Conrad and Joyce, Robert Musil and Franz Kafka), but they would become impossible to ignore, at least if one wished to remain a serious artist, only in its wake. As Franco Moretti remarks, "if history can make cultural forms necessary, it can make them impossible as well."[42] Wharton, an attentive observer of culture, was evidently awake to the constraints imposed by her historical moment. As the mention of "form" in her comment to Berenson makes clear, she (no less than her modernist contemporaries) saw the connection between genre and the broader cultural forces that frame its reception and delimit its possibilities.

Despite her successful forays into regionalist writing and other genres, Wharton was first and foremost a novelist of manners. Favoring the contrivances and conventions of nineteenth-century metropolitan realism, her novels typically feature intricate plotting, omniscient narration, interspersed introjections of social and psychological commentary, and the disclosure of self through the filter of class mores and social institutions. In *The Writing of Fiction* (1924), she makes the sources for these preferences explicit, returning time and again to Austen and George Eliot, Stendhal and Balzac,

---

40. Lewis, *Edith Wharton*, 423–424.
41. See Lewis, *Edith Wharton*, 424–425; Bentley, *Ethnography of Manners*, 460; Wolff, *A Feast of Words*, 309–310, 333.
42. Moretti, *The Way of the World*, 229.

Dostoevsky and Tolstoy, whom she regarded as the peaks that overlook the land of prose and which, between them, exhaust its formal possibilities. Evidently thinking of herself as a link in that tradition, Wharton rejected the galvanizing spirit of rebellion and formal experimentation that accompanied the rise of modernism. Thus, while her references to Henry James's later novels were politely equivocal—even Homer nods—her curt asides on the merits of the up-and-coming modernist vanguard (with the exception of Proust) were flatly negative. She abhorred the "formlessness" and "anarchy" with which the modernists threatened to corrupt the tradition.[43] "True originality," she held, "consists not in a new manner but in a new vision."[44] And in practice as in theory: the sparkling surface of her prose bespeaks the graceful manipulation of already available devices and themes, not an investment in the Poundian quest to Make it New. Indeed, when viewed in the context of its time, *The Age of Innocence*, published midway between *Ulysses* and *Jacob's Room*, and the same year as *Women in Love*, seems out of place among its contemporaries.

Wharton was no revolutionary, and *The Age of Innocence*, like most of her work, cannot be co-opted into the modernist procession without violence. Nevertheless, as I will argue, this last of her major novels reveals Wharton's preoccupation with the distinctly late-modern problem of belatedness and an awareness—equally late-modern—of the impasse reached by the nineteenth-century realist tradition once it entered the post-Nietzschean, post–World War I cultural climate. Wharton had struggled with the question of how to write a novel once the epistemological, political, and, above all, moral presuppositions that informed the realist tradition had become profoundly unsettled. *The Age of Innocence*, I claim, was her answer. This historical novel of manners stands as Wharton's most ironic and self-conscious work.

The Realist *Cul-de-Sac*

In "The Dehumanization of Art" (1925), José Ortega y Gasset prophesized that the genre of the novel "if it is not yet irretrievably exhausted, has cer-

---

43. Edith Wharton, *The Writing of Fiction* (New York: Touchstone, 1997), 15.
44. Wharton, *Writing*, 17.

tainly entered its last phase."⁴⁵ A few years earlier, Virginia Woolf expressed a similar sentiment (albeit less apocalyptically): "We only know," she writes in *Modern Fiction* (1921), "that certain paths seem to lead to fertile land; other to the dust and the desert," by which she meant that the future lay with the Georgian innovators rather than the Edwardian imitators.⁴⁶ These statements are important markers of a general sense following the Great War, that some kind of cultural dead-end has been reached, that the old forms and ways will no longer do. The modernist explosion of innovation, the emerging array of new aesthetic and philosophical concepts, the periodical issuing of manifestoes and counter-manifestoes, typical of the period, all attest to this sense.

However, *pace* Ortega y Gasset, the problem facing the novel was not exhaustion, due, as he thought, to a paucity of possible subjects. Rather, it was structural and stemmed from a distinctly post-Nietzschean vein of moral skepticism. The gradual secularization of European and American societies—a process helped along by the contributions of Darwin and Nietzsche, Freud and Dewey—induced a growing tendency to view morality not as a matter of obeying the prescriptions issued by a nonhuman power, nor as a question of following rational categorical imperatives, but rather of observing culturally prescribed guidelines and prohibitions. This is not to say that the emerging discourses in science and philosophy had somehow "disproved," say, Dickens's Broad Church moral outlook or George Eliot's ameliorative humanism. Nothing could. But the culturalist frame of thought that had gradually coalesced since the turn of the nineteenth century had reframed the way morality was viewed. No longer the virtuous highroad, "morality" was rapidly coming to be understood as the honorific that a given community gives to the habits of which it approves, as opposed to the "immoral" practices that it condemns. In this relativistic moral universe, the question "Why be good?" was morphing into the rather differently inflected, "Why be conventional?"

The blurred distinction between morality and convention did not bode well for the realist novel. For morality is to the nineteenth-century realist

---

45. José Ortega y Gasset, "The Dehumanization of Art," in *Theory of the Novel: A Historical Approach*, ed. Michael McKeon (Baltimore, MD: Johns Hopkins University Press, 2000), 294–316, 295.

46. Virginia Woolf, "Modern Fiction," in *Selected Essays*, ed. David Bradshaw (Oxford: Oxford University Press, 2008), 6–13, 6.

novel as truth is to philosophy: it is the sought-after essence that irradiates appearances from within, the reality toward which the form strives. "The novel," Lionel Trilling famously wrote, "is a perpetual quest for reality, the field of its research being always the social world."[47] This view was forcefully seconded by Trilling's midcentury counterpart in Britain, F.R. Leavis, who followed Matthew Arnold in claiming that "a kind of reverent openness before life, and a marked moral intensity" were the distinguishing attributes of great novelistic art.[48] More recently, following literary criticism's "ethical turn,"[49] a number of scholars have revisited the question of the relation between the novel's characteristic preoccupation with ethics the genre's formal attributes. The realist novel, reasserts Andrew Miller in his study of Victorian moral psychology, "was inescapably ethical in orientation: ethical in its form, its motivation, its aims, its tonality, its diction [and] its very style."[50] This view is echoed by Jesse Rosenthal: "we cannot understand the formal principles of the novel," he writes in his aptly titled *Good Form: The Ethical Experience of the Victorian Novel*, "without also understanding the moral principles that have come with them."[51] And finally, writing about the ethics of hospitality in Victorian fiction, Rachel Hollander asserts that issues of "welcome and openness to the other . . . extend to both the content and form of the novel itself."[52] What these complementary studies make salient is that Victorian literary art was pervaded by the era's moral sensibilities on all levels, from the overt handling of plot and characterization to the more subtle registers of rhetorical gesturing and reader-text interaction. To understand the classic

---

47. Lionel Trilling, "Manners, Morals, and the Novel," *Kenyon Review* 10, no. 1 (1948): 11–27, 17.

48. F.R. Leavis, *The Great Tradition: George Eliot, Henry James, Joseph Conrad* (Harmondsworth: Penguin, 1962), 18.

49. For surveys of the "ethical turn," see Michael Eskin, "Introduction: The Double 'Turn' to Ethics and Literature?," *Poetics Today* 25, no. 4 (2004): 557–572; Dorothy J. Hale, "Aesthetics and the New Ethics: Theorizing the Novel in the Twenty-First Century," *PMLA* 124, no. 3 (2009): 896–905. See also, Marjorie Garber, Beatrice Hanssen, and Rebecca L. Walkowitz, eds., *The Turn to Ethics* (New York: Routledge, 2000).

50. Andrew H. Miller, *The Burdens of Perfection: On Ethics and Reading in Nineteenth-Century British Literature* (Ithaca, NY: Cornell University Press, 2008), xi.

51. Jesse Rosenthal, *Good Form: The Ethical Experience of the Victorian Novel* (Princeton, NJ: Princeton University Press, 2017), 2.

52. Rachel Hollander, *Narrative Hospitality in Late Victorian Fiction: Novel Ethics* (New York: Routledge, 2013), 23.

realist novel as a formal as well as an historical or cultural artifact, they conclude, requires engaging with its moral intuitions as well.

Chief among these intuitions was, as George Levine writes, "[the] very Victorian notion [that] goodness is truth, truth goodness": that is, that the good—like the true—remains constant across changes in perspective, time or locale.[53] This is not to claim that the Victorians were in agreement as to where this nonrelative and immutable good in fact lay, what it consisted in, or how society might go about realizing it. Indeed, as the era's culture wars attest, they were no less divided on these questions than we are today. Unlike us, however, the Victorians were united in the basic assumption that the good, regardless of whether it was to be conceived in utilitarian, humanistic, or religious terms, must also be universal. This belief, which the novel both reflected and helped to shape, was not detachable from what Trilling calls its "perpetual quest for [moral] reality," but integral to it. Expressing this intrinsic connection, British essayist Walter Bagehot wrote in 1860 that "an artist who leaves it doubtful whether he recognizes the distinctions between good and evil is blind to artistic as well as moral laws."[54] The assumed existence of a stable and discoverable moral truth that Austen shared with Trollope and Dickens with Eliot is what enabled these writers and their readers to separate the good characters from the bad, tell a successful process of Bildung from a failed one, and locate virtue in the clutter of empty convention. Moral realism (as contemporary philosophers understand it) and literary realism were, in this sense, closely allied.[55] For all its incipient culturalism and historicism, the Victorian novel was as

---

53. George Levine, *Realism, Ethics and Secularism: Essays on Victorian Literature and Science* (Cambridge: Cambridge University Press, 2008), vi.

54. Walter Bagehot, "The Novels of George Eliot, *National Review* (1860)," in *The Victorian Art of Fiction: Nineteenth-Century Essays on the Novel*, ed. Rohan Maitzen (Toronto: Broadview Press, 2009), 171–188, 184.

55. The fact that the nineteenth-century novel, a preeminently culturalist (and thus relativistic) form, was also deeply invested in a universalist conception of the good might offend the logician, but it would come as no surprise to a student of history. For the historical lives of discourses and genres frequently present us with such "contradictions," which result from the incremental, uneven, and piecemeal nature of historical transformations. What appears like a contradiction to us, who stand at the other side of the historical process in question, may well have seemed fully congruent to the historical actors themselves, working as they were from within the conceptual coordinates of their own time and place.

invested as nineteenth-century philosophy and social science in the idea that the good—however conceived—swings free of the contingencies of time and place.

Seen this way, nineteenth-century realism epitomized a monumental and self-contradictory effort by Victorian culture to manage the atomizing tendencies of modernity and perceived sense of " 'meaning loss' " that attended to the ongoing process of imperial expansion, by consolidating an essentially Herderian and Burkean sense of national identity,[56] while, at the same time, holding on to the possibility of morality, understood as an orientation toward a universal good. We've already seen the competing pulls of these two agendas in Walter Scott's expressed ambition to deliver to his readers general truths of the "human heart" ("the object of my tale is more a description of men than manners"), even while, in his subsequent performance, he gives equal weight to the opposing proposition: namely, that "manners" quite literally make "men," which therefore makes the "object" of his tale not the "human heart" but rather the still-unnamed idea of culture.[57] And this tension—between particularity and universality, appearance and reality, convention and truth—became ingrained, as a productive ambiguity, in the nineteenth-century novel, which specialized in extracting allegedly general truths from closely described local circumstances.

The post-Victorian view of morality as a culturally determined, contingent, and mutable set of cultural conventions could not have left the realist novel unchanged. "Once manners are recast as performative ritual rather than as measurable propriety," as Bentley argues, "the novel has transformed an analysis of moral meaning into an anatomy of social power."[58] This formulation points toward the structural problem that arises out of the late-modern shift in cultural sensibility. As the cloud of dubiousness thickened around the robust Enlightenment notion of moral meaning, it became increasingly difficult for the writer to locate an Archimedean moral

---

56. On the phenomenon of " 'meaning loss' attended on the colonial mode of production" (27), see Jed Esty, *A Shrinking Island: Modernism and National Culture in England* (Princeton, NJ: Princeton University Press, 2003), 23–53. On the nineteenth-century British novel as a culturalist response to anxieties about the perceived loss of identity, see James Buzard, *Disorienting Fiction: The Autoethnographic Work of Nineteenth-Century British Novels* (Princeton, NJ: Princeton University Press, 2005), particularly 37–60.

57. Walter Scott, *Waverley; or 'Tis Sixty Years Since*, ed. Claire Lamont (Oxford: Oxford University Press, 2005), 4.

58. Bentley, *Ethnography of Manners*, 112.

point (tacitly shared by author and reader), with which to lever the novelistic world and organize the trajectory of its characters' development. The roots of this problem reach back at least to the mid–Victorian era, but it grew more defined and urgent as the century wore on. The moral resources available to Dickens and Eliot were no longer available in the same way to Hardy and Conrad. To twentieth-century writers and intellectuals, who had already been thinking in culturalist terms when the war toppled the nineteenth century's tottering certitudes, the category of morality itself as it had been hitherto understood started to seem highly suspect.

Wharton was steeped in these discourses and conscious of their implications. At the same time, however, because her aesthetic loyalties lay squarely with the realist tradition, she was also keenly aware of the central role played by a stabilizing moral outlook in organizing the novelistic universe. As she claims in *The Writing of Fiction*: "The art of rendering life in fiction can never, in the last analysis, be anything or need to be anything, but the disengaging of crucial moments from the welter of experience. . . . But there must be something that *makes* them crucial, some recognizable relation to a familiar social or moral standard."[59] That is, in the absence of a steady (and shared) set of guiding moral norms the novel's world loses direction and purpose. The swell of possible perspectives on social experience and conceivable justifications for personal conduct overwhelms the novelist's ability to channel social and psychological reality into meaningful patterns. The result is a collapse of form.

The problem Wharton faced was twofold. On one level, the social milieu that she specialized in analyzing was rapidly becoming extinct. "Gentlemaning as a profession," W.D. Howells has Silas Lapham say, "has got to play out in a generation or two," and this, Wharton felt, posed a serious challenge to the realist writer.[60] "When there is anything whatever below the surface of the novelist's art," she argues, "that something can be only the social foundation on which his fable is built; and when that foundation totters and is swallowed up . . . the poor story-teller's structural problem is a hard one."[61] Fashionable New York, which was both Wharton's native grounds and grist to her mill, was by the 1920s a thing of the past; its craggy

---

59. Wharton, *Writing*, 14.

60. William Dean Howells, *The Rise of Silas Lapham* (New York: The Library of America, 1982), 891.

61. Wharton, "Introduction," 32.

surface of social convention, so handy for the novelist of manners to use as traction, had either been smoothed away or radically altered. Meanwhile, and on another level, the possibility of surveying what Wharton elsewhere calls society's "hot-house of traditions and conventions" from a position external to it—a position whence its *universal* (which is to say *moral*) meanings can come into view—had also drifted out of reach.[62]

The force of this double bind makes itself particularly felt if one's genre operates by extracting moral meaning out of the analysis of parochial customs. For as the two levels—morality and convention—collapse into one, the novel of manners is not only emptied out of one of its key didactic motivations, it loses the selecting function performed by a unifying moral theme: that of disengaging "crucial moments from the welter of experience." To gauge the dramatic impact that the loss of moral meaning had on the structural underpinnings of the novel of manners one need but open one of Henry James's late works. These tortured explorations of voided mores and emptied-out customs repeatedly rehearse the problem of evaluation of self and other in a world that has seen "the collapse of any credible claim to a natural or fixed social order."[63] The result on the page is so dense with moral equivocation, observations so fraught with qualification, sentences so weighed with subordination, that the prose falls time and again into near impenetrability. Wharton, who confessed a lack of sympathy for James's later work, did not wish to follow him down that road.[64] Operating under the same pressures, she chose a different path.

What then was Wharton's solution to the impasse facing the genre? How does *The Age of Innocence* retain the traditional realist format and style without lapsing into moral naiveté? The answer, in a phrase, consists of the explicit culturalization and historicization of the novel's moral theme. By way of illustration, I will now turn to the way Wharton sets up one of the novel's key scenes.

Toward the climax of the main action of the novel, Archer, seizing the opportunity for an intimate *tête-à-tête* with Ellen, volunteers to pick her up from the Pennsylvania terminus in Jersey City. Ellen is arriving by train

---

62. Wharton, "Introduction," 33.

63. Robert B. Pippin, *Henry James and the Modern Moral Life* (Cambridge: Cambridge University Press, 2000), 172.

64. For Wharton's thoughts about Henry James's experimental late novels, see her letter to W.C. Brownell, quoted in Nevius, *Edith Wharton*, 30.

from Washington DC following a summons issued by the family's formidable matriarch, Mrs. Manson Mingott, who had suffered a minor stroke. This being the mid-1870s, there is no question of the young countess making the ferry crossing to Manhattan and then the carriage ride uptown by herself. The rigid code of propriety, religiously adhered to by Old New York's elite, demands that she be met at the station and accompanied by another member of the tribe. Anything less, for people who, in the narrator's words, "dreaded scandal more than disease," would be unthinkable.[65] Thus, society's sense of decorum grants the lovers, as Archer anticipates with excitement, "all of two hours—and it may be more" of privacy.[66] Two hours is the time it would take to get from Jersey City to the residence of the failing grandmother, located in what the narrator (ironically echoing the fashionable opinion, that civilization reaches only as far as Thirty-fourth street) calls the "inaccessible wilderness near the Central Park."[67]

As Archer paces the platform in wait for Ellen, Wharton plants the following in his mind: "[He] remembered that there were people who thought there would one day be a tunnel under the Hudson through which the trains of the Pennsylvania railway would run straight into New York. They were of the brotherhood of visionaries who likewise predicted the building of ships that would cross the Atlantic in five days, the invention of a flying machine, lighting by electricity, telephonic communication without wires, and other Arabian Nights marvels."[68] This passage represents, as Brian Edwards puts it, "Wharton's wink of complicity with [the readers] who inhabit this literally preposterous world."[69] Such appeals to her readers' superior historical knowledge are sprinkled throughout the narrative and are one of the ways Wharton ironizes the world of yesterday.[70] Of course, as a creature of that

---

65. Wharton, *Age of Innocence*, 201.

66. Wharton, *Age of Innocence*, 171.

67. Wharton, *Age of Innocence*, 9.

68. Wharton, *Age of Innocence*, 171.

69. Brian T. Edwards, "The Well-Built Wall of Culture," in Wharton, *Age of Innocence*, 482–506, 483.

70. The opening lines of the novel intimate "talk of the erection, in remote metropolitan distances 'above the Forties' of a new Opera House," which alludes to the Metropolitan Opera House, which opened in 1883 on the corner on Broadway, 39th and 40th Streets (3). Later in the novel we overhear the characters discuss the "fantastic possibility that they might one day actually converse with each other from street to street, or even—

world, the young Archer is oblivious to the irony. Back on the platform, his thoughts quickly fall back into the groove of his desire. "I don't care which of their visions comes true," he thinks, "as long as the tunnel isn't built yet."[71] A tunnel, after all, would mean a shorter trip between Jersey City and midtown, which would not serve the purposes of this New Yorker well. For him, the complications of travel by ferry and carriage translate into something precious: time with Ellen. And it is not only the lovers who profit from Old New York's underdeveloped means of transport, the interests of plot also benefit, as the carriage ride uptown provides some of the novel's most affecting moments and oft-quoted passages.

However, the specifics of that scene do not concern me here. I provided this brief description of the way it is set up in order to point toward Wharton's strategy throughout the novel. It consists of mining the moral and physical infrastructures of Old New York to generate plot, while simultaneously underscoring their specificity and transience. These events, Wharton repeatedly emphasizes as the plot unfolds, could only have taken place in that kind of world and to the particular kinds of people that it produced. Her New York novel thus fulfills the "test of not being possible to have happened elsewhere,"[72] which Austin holds up as the hallmark of genuine regionalism, while also suffusing the institutions and identities that it depicts with the distinctive air of obsolescence characteristic of regionalist representation.

Wharton took great pains, while researching the material for the novel, to complement her formidable memory with factual miscellanea from the period, so as to ensure as vivid a recreation of that cultural-historical moment as possible.[73] At the same time, the energy she expends in resuscitating that vanished world is matched only by the cool determination with which she seems intent on smothering it. Katherine Mansfield, in her generally admiring review in *The Athenaeum*, complained of the somewhat chilling stateliness of Wharton's prose: "Does Mrs. Wharton expect us to grow warm in a

---

incredible dream!—from one town to another" (85). Similarly, during the lovers' last meeting alone, which takes place, tellingly, in one of the Cesnola Collection rooms in the Metropolitan Museum, Archer says prophetically, "some day, I suppose, it will be a great museum" (185).

71. Wharton, *Age of Innocence*, 171.

72. Austin, *Regionalism*, 100.

73. For a description of Wharton's historical research, see Julia Ehrhardt, "'To Read these Pages is to Live Again': The Historical Accuracy of *The Age of Innocence*" in Wharton, *Age of Innocence*, 401–412.

gallery where the temperature is so sparklingly cool?"[74] This coolness is a result of the ironic distance preserved throughout by the narration. Like a bemused Ecclesiastes, her narrator traces the careers of the characters who populate the novel's elaborately recreated cultural world, while repeatedly pressing home its fragility and transience. What seems solid and unchanging from the characters' perspective is revealed as ephemeral and brittle from the narrator's. This bifurcated view is central to Wharton's method. Through the double gesture of concretizing a world and desubstantializing it, she manages both to preserve the moral framework demanded by the formal requirements of the realist tradition and to communicate an evasive disavowal of the selfsame framework. *The Age of Innocence*, in other words, has an Archimedean moral point that holds its world together, drives the plot, and determines the lives of the characters: it is the code of Old New York. But this complex set of prescriptions and prohibitions is explicitly made to seem as binding and, indeed, as morally relevant only for the denizens of that world. For the reader, who hovers alongside the ironic narrator on the other side of the Great War, Old New York's morality—like its broughams, archery clubs, and heavy Eastlake furniture—appears as simply yet another of that world's picturesque cultural quirks.

"After a while nothing matters" or Wharton's Temporalization of Value

Recognizing the parochial and cultural basis of morality and its subjection to time and change is the point of Archer's education and endpoint of his development. The final chapter takes us some twenty-five years into the future, to a world in which "long-distance telephoning had become as much a matter of course as electric lighting and five-day Atlantic voyages."[75] Ellen's ejection from society and banishment back to Europe is long in the past, and Archer is now a widower, having lost May two years earlier. Though a respected citizen, well regarded by his peers, Archer's life did not turn out as he had dreamed. He has become in his eyes "a mere grey speck of a man compared with the ruthless magnificent fellow he had dreamed of being."[76]

---

74. Katherine Mansfield, "Family Portraits," *The Athenaeum* (10 December 1920): 810–811, reproduced in Wharton, *Age of Innocence*, 399.
75. Wharton, *Age of Innocence*, 209.
76. Wharton, *Age of Innocence*, 212.

After a short term in the State Assembly, for which he ran at Governor Roosevelt's urging, he fails to be re-elected and drops back to the "obscure if useful municipal work" more suited to his nature.[77] He could never have become, he now realizes, a man of action, being always more of a spectator than an active shaper of events. But though a contemplative and passive man, his introspection is honest and clear-eyed. As we glimpse his assessment of the course his life has taken, we find a mixed bag of experience: not only the "deep rut" into which he has sunk, but also joy in his children and contentment in his lacking but decent life with May.[78] What we do not find there, however, is a coherent story of moral development.

This is because it is not Archer who undergoes significant change in the course of the plot but rather the world around him. I disagree, therefore, with Cynthia Griffin Wolff's claim that at "the center of this novel is Newland's problem of being and becoming, given the unalterable traditions of this portion of history, this 'place.'"[79] It is, I argue, quite the reverse: the novel's main concern is the being, becoming, and transience of a specific cultural world. At the work's center is precisely the mutability of tradition and its inevitable capitulation in the face of time and change. Throughout, the self is depicted as a function of the whole, not as its dialectic counterpoint. In contrast with the aim of the Bildungsroman, then, the novel does not reconcile the claims of individuality and those of society. The weight of institutions, in Wharton's view, is simply too ponderous and that of the self too slight to pull off the Hegelian balancing act performed by the genre. Archer, at the conclusion of his story, is not the well-rounded Goethean individual that we meet at the end of *Wilhelm Meister* (1821, 1829), nor does he land the perfect match as in *Pride and Prejudice* (1813). He is too spiritually exhausted, "too starved" by a life-long subservience to duty, to be the *Bildungsheld* that Wolff describes.[80] Archer's loss of freedom (or the possibility of freedom) is not recompensed, in the conclusion of the novel, by happiness, nor does it lead him to destruction *à la* Stendhal's Julien Sorel. For his trajectory, in the final analysis, is neither a successful nor a failed version of the initiation plot.

---

77. Wharton, *Age of Innocence*, 207.
78. Wharton, *Age of Innocence*, 210.
79. Wolff, *A Feast of Words*, 314.
80. Wolff, *A Feast of Words*, 215.

Archer, at the end of his story, ceases to be a participant in the plot of his life, becoming instead its retrospective observer. Once a member of an historical form of life, he now stands witness to its death. As Moretti argues, one of the "great symbolic tasks" of the Bildungsroman tradition was to "[contain] the unpredictability of social change," to stabilize it, by incorporating it into the development of the ego.[81] What we find in *The Age of Innocence*, however, is an ego that is simply left behind as history speeds onward. Stripped of their power by time and cultural change, the dreaded social taboos that had so fatefully shaped the lives of Archer, Ellen, and May have, for their children's generation, become merely quaint, as harmless as "an Isabey miniature."[82] Given the gigantic shadow that society's "totem terrors" had cast over Archer's life, there is cruel historical irony in the ease with which his son Dallas simply takes "for granted" his family's approval of his future bride, Fanny Beaufort.[83] For Fanny's background, had she had the misfortune of being born several decades earlier, would have seemed far more intolerably scandalous in Old New York's eyes than Ellen's, with potentially dire results for the lovers. This detail places Archer's sacrifice to the moral perspective of that lost world in a strange and profoundly ironic light. And it sharply illustrates the novel's point: that history can make a mockery of even the most deep-seated values.

"There was good in the old ways," Archer thinks one moment; "there was good in the new order too," he counters in the next.[84] But where does that leave him? On my reading, at the end of the novel, he has become what Richard Rorty has called an ironist: "The sort of person who faces up to the contingency of his or her most central beliefs and desires, someone sufficiently historicist and nominalist to have abandoned the idea that those central beliefs and desires refer back to something beyond the reach of time and chance."[85] The reason Archer sees the positive both in "the old ways" and in "the new order" is not that both partake in a transcultural, ahistorical Good, which he can now sagely assess with the perspective of

---

81. Moretti, *Way of the World*, 230.
82. Wharton, *Age of Innocence*, 211.
83. Wharton, *Age of Innocence*, 211.
84. Wharton, *Age of Innocence*, 208–209.
85. Richard Rorty, *Contingency, Irony, and Solidarity* (Cambridge: Cambridge University Press, 1989), xv.

age and attained wisdom. Rather, it is because he has become sufficiently historicist to regard normative judgments as human creations, which is to say, as cultural artifacts.

Archer's foil, in this regard, is May, whose "incapacity to recognize change" leaves her oblivious of the fact that all around her "the world of her youth had fallen into pieces and rebuilt itself."[86] Cognizant of this blindness, her family silently conspires to shelter her from the realities of the twentieth century, knowing that she is not constituted to deal with them. And so she dies, still ensconced in the "principles and prejudices" that her parents inculcated in her, secure in the groundless confidence that her husband will transmit the "sacred trust" of that ghost world to their youngest son.[87] This will not happen. Archer knows that history has opened a gulf between his generation and that of his children. He understands, in other words, that he is a child of his time and that that time has passed.

Because he does not suffer from May's handicap Archer is able to register the unraveling of "the little world he had grown up in, and whose standards had bent and bound him"—an experience that forces upon him the awareness that morality is immanent to the cultural constellation that produced it.[88] And it is precisely because he had survived the breakup of the social matrix that had propped up his identity as a moral agent that he is able to appreciate the relativity and transience of normative valuations. According to Peter Berger, society can function smoothly only as long as its structures remain largely transparent to its "normal" subjects. To maintain the taken-for-granted status of their norms and prohibitions, social organizations must internalize the latter in the individual to the extent that they become "part and parcel of the universal 'order of things.'"[89] Given the massive societal pressure that is applied to this process of naturalization, it is typically only when the order of things falls apart, or is superseded by another, that it suddenly loses its transparency and becomes visible as a fragile and mutable human creation. This dialectic is familiar from Hegel: a field of social reality that had hitherto seemed straightforwardly identified as the World comes to appear—once *aufgehoben*—as a particular (and hence

---

86. Wharton, *Age of Innocence*, 208.

87. Wharton, *Age of Innocence*, 208.

88. Wharton, *Age of Innocence*, 208.

89. Peter Berger, *The Sacred Canopy: Elements of a Sociological Theory of Religion* (Garden City, NY: Doubleday, 1967), 24.

surpassable) cultural-historical constellation. Archer, who had experienced this kind of perspectival shift, no longer regards meaning and value as inherent in the things themselves. His resigned posture and ironic attitude in the final chapter, which enable him to recognize the good "in the old ways" and "in the new order too," consists of his acceptance that the value of an object, practice, or relationship emerges epiphenomenally from a contingent cultural and historical nexus of practices and institutions.

The historicism and holism that informs *The Age of Innocence* makes it a more nuanced treatment of the dialectic of culture than the unforgiving *The House of Mirth*. Like Lily Bart, Archer too is a figure "subdued to the conventions of the drawing-room," which, robbing Lily of her life, rob him of his desire.[90] Where the novels importantly differ is in Wharton's treatment of those social conventions themselves. Both *The House of Mirth* and *The Age of Innocence* present us with characters who are the "victim[s] of the civilization which had produced [them]," but whereas Lily is crushed by her society, Archer survives the dismantling of his.[91] This difference is crucial for understanding the novels' diverging generic and emotional modalities. In *The House of Mirth*, as in the naturalistic works of Theodore Dreiser and Frank Norris, society figures as an implacable and inhuman force, which determines the lives of its members while remaining itself sublimely impervious to their little struggles and defeats. "Society did not turn away from her," Lily muses toward the end of the novel, "it simply drifted by, preoccupied and inattentive, letting her feel . . . how completely she had been the creature of its favour."[92] What lends Lily's fall its tragic resonance is precisely the depersonalized indifference that such passages attribute to the social body (she is "its" creature), and that hearken back to the form's ancient Greek source. Which is also why, when Lily's fortunes take a turn for the worst, Wharton has her recall her past reading of Euripides.

Though the emphasis on the determining force of class and upbringing remains a constant feature of Wharton novels, the dominant tonality of *The Age of Innocence* is irony rather than tragedy. New York society in the 1870s, though portrayed as no less vicious and unforgiving than its 1900 version, is modeled on a mortal rather than quasi-divine scale. If in *The House of*

---

90. Edith Wharton, *The House of Mirth*, Norton Critical Edition, ed. Elizabeth Ammons (New York: W. W. Norton, 1990), 12.
91. Edith Wharton, *The House of Mirth* (Hertfordshire: Wordsworth Editions, 2002), 7.
92. Wharton, *House of Mirth*, 229.

Mirth society looms like a dark and unperturbed firmament, against which we trace the trajectory Lily's tragic fall, in *The Age of Innocence* we witness its all-too-human demise. Archer, who had bowed before his milieu's values and prohibitions, also lives to see them become denatured and obsolete. The practices and prejudices that had been "part of the structure of his universe" become in the course the novel mere intimations of a "prehistoric ritual," thus illustrating, at once, both culture's power to terminally shapes lives and its own subjection to the forces of time and change.[93]

This theme is brought home in the scene of Archer and Ellen's meeting in the newly established Metropolitan Museum. As they sit together before the exhibits in the Cesnola rooms, Ellen absentmindedly sums up the upshot of the novel's culturalist historicism: "'It seems cruel,' she said, 'that after a while nothing matters . . . any more than these little things, that used to be necessary and important to forgotten people, and now have to be guessed at under a magnifying glass and labeled: "Use unknown."'"[94] The key words here are "after a while." The young Archer's mistake is to think, along Platonist lines, that the discovered arbitrariness of social convention relegates it to the level of mere appearance: something untrue and therefore also unreal. His desire for Ellen and for the kind of freedom that she represents in his mind leads him to yearn for an alternative not only to New York but also to cultural life as such: "I want—I want somehow to get away with you into a world where words like that—categories like that—won't exist. Where we shall be simply two human beings who love each other, who are the whole of life to each other; and nothing else on earth will matter."[95] Ellen knows better. Unlike her companion, she does not entertain notions of ideal worlds beyond the culturally demarcated realm of concrete possibilities. Nor, having already begun to feel their full brunt, does she doubt the power of social conventions. She thus urges Archer "[to look] not at visions, but at realities."[96] In this way, Wharton, as Bentley claims, signals to her reader the "double structure of culture, at once conventional and actual."[97] But the selfsame recognition of the cultural basis of norms and institutions also eventually forces Archer (and the reader) to acknowledge

---

93. Wharton, *The Age of Innocence*, 65, 110.
94. Wharton, *The Age of Innocence*, 186
95. Wharton, *The Age of Innocence*, 174.
96. Wharton, *The Age of Innocence*, 174.
97. Bentley, *Ethnography of Manners*, 107.

their ephemerality. Learning to accept, as Archer ultimately does, that the things that matter *to us* will someday cease to matter, without, however, losing one's sense of their present value, is, for Wharton, the distinguishing mark of intellectual and moral maturity.

Wharton and Archer Revisited

Archer's decision not to go up to Ellen's Paris apartment (to recall Trilling's formulation) represents the conclusion of the novel's quest for reality. His love for Ellen, he finally recognizes, could only survive in the cultural climate in which it had originally bloomed. To expose its memory to the changed conditions would be to kill it. Thus, Wharton's historicist and severely anti-romantic view allows nothing to escape from time and change. Like all else, love in the novel is a contingent phenomenon, inextricably bound to social and historical factors over which the lovers have little control. Whatever remains of it, for Archer, is locked up within him, where Old New York still lives: "It's more real to me here than if I went up."[98] The recognition that his love for Ellen is no longer realizable does not, however, retroactively rob it of its actuality. In its time, it was as real as the social sanctions that had thwarted its consummation. The question of reality is settled once culture and history replace metaphysics. To face up to this idea and its implications, as Archer does at the end of the novel, is to come to terms fully with the finitude and ephemerality of one's cultural world and, by extension, with one's own situatedness and transience.

So described, Archer's state of mind is, I believe, a reflection of Wharton's own in the postwar years. Like Archer, she had come to believe that she had fallen out of sync with the times, that her generation's way of taking up the world and representing it had been displaced by a new understanding of being and a new aesthetic.[99] And, like her protagonist, Wharton was neither able nor willing to give up on the values and tastes that

---

98. Wharton, *Age of Innocence*, 217.

99. This realization no doubt grew stronger as the years wore on. Lewis argues that Wharton's work in the 1920s, specifically *A Mother's Recompense*, "expresses [her] desire to establish some sort of contact with the American authors of the new generation and their new ways of doing things—as well as the difficulties, perhaps the near impossibility, of the effort," Lewis, *Edith Wharton*, 465.

defined who she was and where she had come from (both in personal and in artistic terms). *The Age of Innocence* comes out of the former realization and the latter inability. It is a realist novel that stages its own obsolescence, a belated novel of manners that dramatizes the disappearance of the culture that had made its own genre possible. With it, Wharton came to terms not only with her identity, as a child of an extinct social order, but also with the inevitable evolution of literary form.[100] Placing the novel's action in the past and historicizing its moral theme were the only way left to her to write a novel, as she understood a novel should be written.

The Age of Innocence marks the point in which Wharton's irony, so richly on display in her biting satires of the upper classes, comes full circle to implicate herself. Alexander Nehamas, referring to Thomas Mann, describes this self-implicating species of irony, which results from the inability to espouse *any* moral ground as final and stable, as "the kind that goes all the way down."[101] Translated from the existential register to terms of craft, this kind of irony, this internalization of nominalism and historicism, makes moral realism impossible. For the exploration of moral realism—in literature as in philosophy—is fueled by the belief that an ahistorical, context-independent, perspective-free foundation is to be had. With the withering away of this belief, so withers the motive for the search, calling for new motives for fiction to be sought. This impasse, made an ineluctable challenge by World War I, would inspire much formal and thematic innovation from postwar novelists on both sides of the Atlantic. For Wharton, however, it represented a limit. *The Age of Innocence*, her most self-conscious work, was also, as Edmund Wilson wrote, "her valedictory."[102] It is an ironist's elegy: an elegy to a way of writing about life as much as it is to that life itself.

---

100. Robin Peel locates this tendency already in Wharton's pre-war novels: "On the one hand her interrogation of early modernism is informed by an antipathy to change, but on the other it is informed by a developed aesthetic recognition that all art, including literature, has evolved and must evolve, if it is to be vital and serious." See, Robin Peel, *Apart from Modernism: Edith Wharton* (Cranbury, NJ: Associated University Press, 2005), 12.

101. Alexander Nehamas, *The Art of Living: Socratic Reflections from Plato to Foucault* (Berkeley: University of California Press, 1998), 20.

102. Edmund Wilson, "Justice to Edith Wharton," in *The Wound and the Bow: Seven Studies in Literature* (New York: Oxford University Press, 1965), 159–173.

Chapter 3

"Und siehe da: Es gab also fremde Länder!"
Joseph Roth's Parochializing of Empire

Sie konnten Österreich nicht überleben.

—Joseph Roth, *Radetzkymarsch*

Bringing Joseph Roth and Edith Wharton into juxtaposition calls for some preparatory groundwork. Certainly not much in their biographies suggests they should be read together. For, while Wharton read and admired German writers,[1] and Roth took the time, if not to actually read American literature, then to summarily dismiss it,[2] there is no evidence that the two

---

1. Wharton, who had been taught the language at an early age, would go on to read German fiction and philosophy throughout her life. She was an admirer of Goethe, Schopenhauer, Nietzsche, and Gottfried Keller (she even wrote the introduction to the English translation of his *Romeo and Julia auf dem Dorfe* [1856]), had met Rilke personally, and was acquainted with the works of Hofmannsthal, Schnitzler, and Clara Viebig. Explaining her obliviousness to Thomas Mann's work, Richard Lawson claims that Wharton "ceased to be culturally acquisitive after she began to write serialized fiction for the women's magazines of the twenties" (289–290). Roth only began his career as a novelist in 1923. See Richard H. Lawson, "Thematic Similarities in Edith Wharton and Thomas Mann," *Twentieth Century Literature* 23, no. 3 (1977): 289–298.

2. It is unclear whether Roth did in fact seriously read contemporary American prose. Nevertheless, in a 1928 feuilleton published in the *Frankfurter Zeitung*, "Der Amerikan-

were aware of one another's work. Nor despite the fact that both had lived as exiles in or about Paris during the interwar period is there any indication that they ever crossed paths socially.[3] This mutual ignorance, however, is not surprising. More than thirty years her junior, Roth did not belong to Wharton's generation or move in her rather rarified social circles. For an *Ostjude* from the Galician backwaters of the former Austro-Hungarian Empire, who, despite enjoying considerable renown as a journalist, never tasted real wealth or social prominence, her forbidding milieu was no more than a distant rumor.

Ernest Hemingway and F. Scott Fitzgerald, not Wharton or Henry James, were Roth's American contemporaries—a generational and temperamental affinity reflected in the themes and protagonists of his early novels. Gabriel Dan of *Hotel Savoy* (1924), Andreas Pum of *Rebellion* [*Die Rebellion*] (1924), and Franz Tunda of *Flight without End* [*Die Flucht ohne Ende*] (1927) are the spiritual kin of Jake Barnes and Nick Carraway: young, disaffected veterans who, upon returning from the killing fields of World War I, try and fail to find their bearings in a hypocritical and cynical postwar society.[4] Dwelling insistently on the social and psychological aftereffects of the war, these early works are permeated by the air of bitter disillusionment and jaded knowingness so typical of the international cadre of writers who came of age during the war years (Erich Maria Remarque, Robert Graves, John Dos Passos, E.E. Cummings, and others). "We are the sons," writes Roth, as though speaking for that lost generation,

---

ismus im Literaturbetrieb," Roth dismisses "the 1920s American novel of social criticism as artistically inferior." See Sidney Rosenfeld, *Understanding Joseph Roth* (Columbia: South Carolina University Press, 2001), 102–103.

3. Though it is perhaps idle to speculate how such a meeting might have gone, my guess would be badly. Wharton's single meeting with F. Scott Fitzgerald, who was not only of Roth's age but whose biography and lifestyle (particularly drink-wise) bear interesting parallels to Roth's, would support this conjecture. As it turned out, despite the mutual admiration for each other's work, Wharton and the up-and-coming Fitzgerald did not warm to one another in person. The uncomfortable afternoon the two spent together, after the publication of *The Great Gatsby* in 1925, was made worse by the flustered Fitzgerald's ill-conceived attempt to scandalize his impervious hostess by cracking lewd jokes. Summing up the visit in her diary later that evening Wharton wrote: "To tea, Teddy Chanler and Scott Fitzgerald, the novelist (awful)." See R.W.B. Lewis, *Edith Wharton: A Biography* (New York: Harper & Row, 1975), 468.

4. For discussion comparing Roth's early novels and the "lost generation" works by Hemingway and Fitzgerald, see Rosenfeld, *Understanding Roth*.

We have experienced the relative nature of labels, and of things themselves. In the space of a single instant, which was all that came between us and death, we broke with an entire tradition, with language, science, literature, art—with the whole belief in culture [*Kulturbewusstsein*]. In that instant we knew more about *truth* than all the truth seekers in the world. We are the resurrected dead. We come laden with all the wisdom of the hereafter, back down to the ignorant earthlings. We have the skepticism of metaphysical wisdom.[5]

As a journalist, Roth brought this relativistic sensibility to his depictions of the splintered social landscape of the 1920s; as a fledgling novelist, he tried to bang this recalcitrant material into shape using the methods in vogue at the time (hence his affair with the aesthetics of the *Neue Sachlichkeit* movement). Those hastily produced, structurally unsound, yet sporadically brilliant early novels are perhaps best read as a series of experimental attempts by a self-assured and highly individual voice to negotiate the requirements of narrative form and the unwieldy contents of a disjointed social present.

The difference between Roth's novels of the 1920s and the kind of writing that Wharton practiced and endorsed could not, it would initially seem, be greater. Her major works—*The House of Mirth* (1905), *The Reef* (1912), *The Custom of the Country* (1913), and *The Age of Innocence* (1920)—are novels of manners that combine the genre's trademark social settings, tight plotting, and reliance on dialogue with a dark, pseudo-Freudian emphasis on the renunciations demanded by civilized life. Unlike Roth's apprenticeship novels with their open-ended plots and staccato rhythms, in Wharton no string is left untied and no narrative element is allowed to disturb the architectural harmony of the whole. "Any hesitation, any failure to gather up all the threads," she instructs the would-be novelist in *The Writing of Fiction* (1924), "shows that the author has not let his subject mature in his mind."[6] True to her prescription, Wharton's prose is a tightly controlled affair designed to expose, with a Flaubertian combination of exactitude and distaste, the myriad stupidities and brutalities of genteel society.

---

5. Joseph Roth, *The White Cities: Reports from France 1925–39*, trans. Michael Hofmann (London: Granta, 2004), 74.
6. Edith Wharton, *The Writing of Fiction* (New York: Simon & Schuster, 1997), 78.

As discussed in the previous chapter, the formal and normative conception of the novel that Wharton brought to her own writing and which she used to evaluate the work of others were drawn almost in whole from the nineteenth-century realist tradition. She abhorred the experimentalism of the European modernists, and would no doubt have severely criticized Roth's early works on the same grounds that led her to dismiss Woolf's and Joyce's. They would have struck her as yet another lamentable example of the perverse modern tendency to regard "formlessness . . . as the first condition of form."[7]

When the high modernists heeded Joseph Conrad's siren call and descended into the "lonely region of stress and strife" of the inward self they were, among other things, articulating a literary response to the impoverishment of moral meaning in a secularized, postwar cultural climate.[8] Wharton, as we've seen, felt this crisis keenly. But the modernist solution, with its hypostatization of consciousness and attendant metaphorics of depth, was anathema to her. So much so, in fact, that she once wryly considered writing an article titled "Deep Sea Soundings" against "this tiresome stream-of-consciousness theory," which she charged with the indiscriminate piling on of raw experience without sifting it for the choice nuggets of significance and pertinence.[9]

Wharton's dismissal of the modernist aesthetic was not based solely on considerations of style or form. It reflected a consciously held theoretical view of the nature and makeup of the self. Wharton was what we would call today a social-constructionist, who doubted that there was much of anything to be found "underneath" the contingencies of culture and language. Anticipating Foucault, she asks: "What does 'human nature' thus denuded consist in and how much of it is left when it is separated from the web of custom, manners, culture it has elaborately spun about itself? Only that hollow unreality, 'Man,' an evocation of the eighteenth-century demagogues who were the first inventors of 'standardization.'"[10] To abstract

---

7. Wharton, *Writing*, 15.

8. Joseph Conrad, "Preface" to *The Nigger of the 'Narcissus'* (1897), in *The Nigger of the 'Narcissus' and The End of the Tether* (New York: Dell, 1960), 25.

9. See Wegener's endnote in "The Great American Novel," in *Edith Wharton: The Uncollected Critical Writings*, ed. Frederick Wegener (Princeton, NJ: Princeton University Press, 1996), 174.

10. Wharton, "American Novel," 155–156.

a person from the particularities of her time and place is to lose sight of her altogether. Culture, for Wharton, went all the way down.[11]

And it is here, in this lean, contextual, essentially "flat" conception of the self that a convergence between the works of Wharton and Roth (early as well as late) begins to emerge. Georg Lukács's warning against an "exaggerated concern with formal criteria, with question of style and literary technique [at the expense of examining] the ontological view governing the image of man in the work," is at point here.[12] For though Wharton and the early Roth came at their contemporary subjects with different stylistic sensibilities, the image of the self that emerges from their novels has, in fact, much in common. Consider, for instance, the opening of Roth's *Flight without End*: "Franz Tunda, first lieutenant in the Austrian Army, became a Russian prisoner of war in August 1916. He was taken to a camp some versts north-east of Irkutsk. He succeeded, with the help of a Siberian Pole, to escape. On the remote, lonely and dismal farm of the Pole, on the edge of the Taiga, the officer remained till the spring of 1919."[13] Brisk, concise, and dynamic. Lieutenant Tunda emerges from this excerpt first and foremost as an embodied agent, the drama of whose (already dramatic) life is played out, not in the private theater of the mind, but on the social-historical stage. "Consciousness and self-consciousness," as Roth's faithful translator Michael Hofmann notes, "are both at an absolute premium in [Roth's]

---

11. Wharton was not consistent on this point. As she grew older, her estrangement from postwar culture becoming deeper, and her animosity toward the new fiction bitterer, she began slipping herself into the mode of the "eighteenth-century demagogues" whom she decries here. Sooner or later, she then preached, story-tellers would sober up and rediscover "the enduring characters of human nature under the shifting surface of slang and sexuality." See Edith Wharton, "Tendencies in Modern Fiction," in *Edith Wharton: The Uncollected Critical Writings*, ed. Frederick Wegener (Princeton, NJ: Princeton University Press, 1996), 170–174, 173.

12. Georg Lukács, *The Meaning of Contemporary Realism*, trans. John and Necke Mander (London: Merlin Press, 1962), 17. In its original context, Lukács uses this distinction to warn against a reversed case in which placing exaggerated significance on a similar technique (*monologue intérieur*) used by both Mann and Joyce obscures the opposed *Weltanschaungen* at work in their novels.

13. Joseph Roth, *Flucht ohne Ende*, in *Romane and Erzählungen 1916–1929*, ed. Fritz Hackert (Köln: Kiepenheuer & Fitzsch, 1989), 389–496, 389. All translations, unless otherwise indicated, are my own.

work."[14] And indeed the first thing we learn of Tunda's identity, prior to any datum of perception, affect, or thought is his nationality and rank. (For an instructive comparison, read these lines against the opening of *Mrs. Dalloway*.) In fact, having already mentioned the protagonist's name in the first line, Roth drops it altogether in the fourth. Tunda becomes simply "the officer," a presentation that implies a smooth continuity between the character's private identity and his social role.

This emphasis, in the construction of character, on institutional and public function as opposed to representation of thought processes, inner states, and sense impressions is not exclusive to Roth's expositions or special to *Flight without End*. It consistently defines his approach to character, and goes directly to "the ontological view governing the image of man" in his work. Though not party to Wharton's wholesale rejection of modernist experimentalism, Roth seemed to have shared her view that personhood is inextricable from the cultural web of social practice and belief in which it is entangled (spiders, he once wrote, were his favorite animals).[15] As Roth's friend and the first compiler of his collected works, Hermann Kesten, once observed, "he develops novels from characters, and characters from the external, visible aspects of a human being."[16] Whatever is interesting and story-worthy about the self, Roth consistently held, was to be sought, not in the recesses of the perceiving mind, but in the external and shared domain of action, station, and rank.

This view set Roth's work from its inception at the antipodes from the tradition of German *Innerlichkeit* that found literary expression in such landmarks of psychological fiction as Goethe's *The Sorrows of Young Werther* (1774) and Rainer Maria Rilke's *The Notebooks of Malte Laurids Brigge* (1910), and it may have predisposed him toward the culturalist realism of his later works. Sharing Nietzsche's disdain for the Teutonic "cult of 'inwardness,'"[17]

---

14. Michael Hofmann, "Translator's Introduction," in *The Radetzky March*, trans. Michael Hoffman (London: Granta, 2002), ix.

15. Roth, *White Cities*, 69.

16. "Er entwickelt Romane aus Charakteren und die Charaktere entwickelt er aus dem Äußeren, Sichtbaren eines Menschen." Hermann Kesten, "Der Schriftsteller Joseph Roth," in *Joseph Roth—Sonderband, Text + Kritik*, ed. Heinz Ludwig Arnold (Munich, 1974/1982), 7–9, 8.

17. Friedrich Nietzsche, *The Use and Abuse of History*, trans. Adrian Collins (Indianapolis, IN: Bobbs-Merrill, 1957), 26.

Roth viewed the tendency to mystify the so-called German Soul as a particularly pernicious political myth.[18] The self, as it emerges from his works, is not a deep phenomenon. It has no subtle, unfathomable core that antedates culture or escapes language. As Roth saw it (to quote Hofmann again), "though the world and our lives are complicated, we are simple."[19] The self that his fictions project is a tissue of societal roles and identifications, not an entity that stands above or beyond these accouterments. In his novels, as in Wharton's, to have an identity—be it that of a Habsburg state official or an Old–New York gentleman—is not merely to perform a certain function or role; it is to *be* what one performs.[20]

While Roth's externalist view of character is a constant feature of his work, the thematics of cultural extinction appear only in the second phase of his novelistic career (from 1930 until his death in 1939). This decisive shift in thematic concerns and formal approach—from camera-eye depictions of the chaotic postwar present to a growing preoccupation with the irretrievable past—has been the subject of many and competing interpretations. Several of Roth's early critics, following Kesten's lead, have read the change in Roth's themes and style as an expression of a change in his politics, from left radicalism to right-wing conservatism.[21] Citing his disillusionment with socialism (following his trip to Russia in 1926) as well as his increasing pessimism in the face of the rise of European fascism as contributing

---

18. Joseph Roth, "The Myth of the German soul," in *White Cities*, 233–237, 234.

19. Hoffmann, "Introduction," x.

20. Though neither Roth nor Wharton engaged in any sustained elaboration of his or her contextualist view of identity, their similar positions on identity closely resembles the social-constructivist views espoused at the time by George Herbert Mead and later by Thomas Luckmann and Peter Berger. As the latter writes, "society assigns to the individual not only a set of roles but a designated identity. In other words, the individual is not only expected to perform as husband, father, or uncle, but to *be* a husband, a father, or an uncle." See Peter Berger, *The Sacred Canopy: Elements of a Sociological Theory of Religion* (New York: Doubleday, 1967), 14.

21. So writes Kesten: "In den fünfzehn Jahren, da er Bücher veröffentlichte, ward Roth aus einem skeptischen, zuweilen pessimistischen Moralisten ein legitimistischer Katholik, aus einem Linksradikalen ein Rechtskonservativer, aus einem Mitarbeiter sozialdemokratischer Blätter ein Inspirator sozialdoktrinärer Zeitschriften, aus einem 'Frontsoldaten' ein 'österreichischer Leutnant,' aus einem Neuerer ein Erbe, aus einem witzigen Spötter ein frommer Prediger." See Hermann Kesten, "Joseph Roth," *Wort in der Zeit* 9 (1959): 6.

factors,[22] these critics view *Job: The Story of a Simple Man* (1930) as "the turning point in [Roth's] transformation from a 'socialist' author of the *Neue Sachlichkeit* to a conservative, partly reactionary and delicate stylist, as well as a legend- and myth-maker [*Legenden- und Mythenschöpfer*]."[23] Roth's change of style, it is then argued, flows more or less directly from his change of political heart, as he transformed from the socialist firebrand who signed his early dispatches for the left-wing publication *Vorwärts* "the Red Roth" to a reactionary royalist. Martha Wörching's reading of Roth's later work as an escapist "flight from reality" [*Reise aus der Wirklichkeit*] is perhaps the best-known iteration of this line of interpretation.[24]

Later critics, including Thorsten Juergens, Jon Hughes, and Kati Tonkin, have tended to reject this rather narrowly politicized approach, and to question the periodization of Roth's career into distinct phases. Instead of an abrupt break, these critics see a continuity between the experimental texts of the 1920s and the more straightforwardly realistic novels of the 1930s. Juergens identifies in Roth's oeuvre a persistent commitment to "humanistic-socialistic social criticism" more fundamental than his half-hearted political affiliations.[25] For Hughes, meanwhile, Roth's novels, both before and after *Job*, enact an "ongoing resistance against [modernity's] process of fragmentation."[26] The elegiac works that Roth produced in the 1930s, he claims, should be viewed as part of a career-long search for "existential 'wholeness.'"[27] Arguing in a

---

22. For a reading of the thematic and stylistic changes in Roth as a result of his disillusionment with socialism, see Ingeborg Sültenmeyer, *Das Frühwerk Joseph Roths: Studien und Texts* (Vienna and Freuburg: Herder, 1976). For a discussion emphasizing the writer's *Kulturpessimismus*, see Fritz Hackert, *Kulturpessimismus und Erzählform: Studien zu Joseph Roths Leben und Werke* (Berne: Lang, 1967).

23. Bernd Hüppauf, "Joseph Roth: *Hiob*; Der Mythos der Skeptikers," in *Joseph Roth: Werk und Wirkung*, ed. Bernd M. Kraske (Bonn: Bouvier, 1988), 25–51, 25.

24. Martha Wörching, "Die Rückwärts gewandte Utopie," in *Text + Kritik: Joseph Roth*, ed. Heinz Ludwig Arnold (Munich, 1974/1982), 90–100, 90. Wolf Marchand goes so far as to locate proto-fascist tendencies in Roth's later texts, see Wolf R. Marchand, *Joseph Roth und Völkischnationalistische wertbegriffe: untersuchaingenzur politisch Entwicklung Roths und ihrer auswirkung auf sein Werk mit einem Anhang* (Bonn: Bouvier/Grundmann, 1974).

25. Thorsten Juergens, *Gesellschaftskritische Aspekte in Joseph Roths Romanen* (Leiden: Leiden University, 1977), 5.

26. Jon Hughes, *Facing Modernity: Fragmentation, Culture and Identity in Joseph Roth's Writing in the 1920s* (London: Maney Publishing, 2006), 10.

27. Hughes, *Facing Modernity*, 10.

similar vein, Tonkin claims that the experimental novels of the 1920s and the epic works of the 1930s can be seen as parts of a single, unified project to "[understand] historical processes, specifically the problems created by the historical fact of the collapse of the Habsburg Empire in Central Europe."[28]

While I agree with the latter critics that Roth's disillusionment with communism does not have the explanatory power that some earlier commentators have claimed for it, as well as with the contention that his later works cannot be reduced to reactionary nostalgia,[29] I nonetheless persist in finding the traditional division of his career largely accurate. There are, to be sure, continuities between the early and late novels; Roth's externalist conception of selfhood that I've outlined above is one such. But the mid-career switch in thematic concerns and methodological approach is, in my view, too pronounced to be smoothed over in the interest of critical revisionism. In the following, then, I propose to read the shift announced by *Job* and fully realized in *The Radetzky March* (1932) as a function, not of a change of politics or of the author's deepening despair, but of Roth's increasing mastery of the quasi-ethnographic culturalist outlook that he begins to hone in his reportages from 1925 onward. Roth's marked preoccupation in the latter part of his career with collective and time-bound loci of identity (Catholic Southern France, the Jewish *shtetl*, the Austro-Hungarian state apparatus), I argue, reflects his achieved fluency in the culturalist vocabulary whose development I traced in chapter 1. This literary-conceptual toolkit allowed him to give more nuanced expression to the themes of vulnerability, precarity, and relativity that had already preoccupied him in his early novels, while also satisfying a born storyteller's need for narrative cohesion and closure.

"Translating the Stranger": The Ethnoliterary Roth

The year 1925 was pivotal in Roth's life. Five years into his stay in Berlin, the city in which he made a name for himself but which he intensely

---

28. Kati Tonkin, *Joseph Roth's March into History: From the Early Novels to Radetzkymarsch and Die Kapuzinergruft* (Rochester, NY: Camden House, 2008), 4.
29. Roth was critical of what he called the "infantile longing for the recent past." And while a writer can, of course, succumb to tendencies he or she disparages elsewhere, the latter quote at least suggests that Roth was aware of the dangers of nostalgia. Roth, *White Cities*, 75.

disliked, Roth was hired by the *Frankfurter Zeitung* to serve as its French correspondent. France was the thirty-year-old writer's first experience of the non-German world and, as his ecstatic letters back to his editor and friend Benno Reifenberg amply show, it was a revelation. In France Roth felt he had discovered his true spiritual home: a haven of European humanism as yet untouched by "the ever more apparent Americanization and Bolshevization of our continent."[30] Everything that seemed to him hidebound and stifling about Germany seemed to fall away "on the other side of the fence."[31] Paris was a blessed contrast to the sprawling ungainliness of "stone Berlin" [*das steinerne Berlin*],[32] while the South of France, with its remnants of "the great and mighty cultural traditions of antique and medieval Europe," was a sanctuary of beauty and tolerance—a place "in which one can dream again."[33] In light of this euphoric response, and given Germany's increasing inhospitality to Jews, it is unsurprising that the move to France, like Wharton's more than a decade earlier, would prove to be final. While continuing to write for German audiences, Roth would never again reside in a German-speaking land.

Life in self-chosen exile coupled with the demands of his new position as foreign correspondent would prove to have a gradual yet decisive impact on Roth's writing. Entrusted by his employer with the task of relating non-German worlds to German-speaking readers—an audience from which, to compound matters, he was by then thoroughly alienated[34]—Roth was now

---

30. Joseph Roth, letter to Benno Reifenberg from Marseille (August 30, 1925), in *Joseph Roth: A Life in Letters*, trans. Michael Hofmann (London: Granta, 2012), 54.

31. Roth, *White Cities*, 73.

32. "Das steinerne Berlin" is the title of one of Roth's reports from the German capital, see Michael Bienert, *Joseph Roth in Berlin: Ein Lesebuch für Spaziergänger* (Berlin: Kiepenheuer & Witsch, 1997), 163–165.

33. Roth, *White Cities*, 75.

34. Something of Roth's growing estrangement from Germany can be gauged from the following in his letter to Bernard von Brentano from November 1925: "In diesem Land [meaning Germany] habe ich keinen Verlag, keine Leser, keine Anerkennung. Aber auch keinen Schmerz, weil mich nichts traurig macht, keine Enttäuschung, weil ich nichts erhoffe, keine Wehmut, weil ich gleichgültig bin und kalt." As David Bronson remarks, these defiant early statements of spiritual divorce with the German-speaking world should be read as indicators of the full-blown crisis of alienation that befell Roth after his return from Russia a year later. David Bronson, *Joseph Roth: Eine Biographie* (Köln: Kiepnheuer & Witsch, 1981), 299.

obliged to confront the formal and moral dilemmas involved in the act of cultural mediation, or, as he called it, "translating the stranger."[35] How was one to make sense of the ways of foreign peoples without effacing their otherness? How might group-based differences be represented without resorting to the rank racialist essentialism promulgated by the German nationalists? What is the place of the observer's subjectivity, his emotions and perceptions, in the account that he produces? Such questions, foisted upon Roth by his new position, called for a different set of tools and representational techniques from the ones he employed in his earlier work, precipitating the gradual shift into the culturalist vocabulary that would define the second chapter of his writing career. As Andreas Kilcher argues, the sequence of trips that Roth undertook in the late 1920s—to Galicia (in 1924), Southern France (1925), Russia (1926), and later to Albania, Yugoslavia, Poland, and Italy—marked "the moment of birth not just of the travel journalist, but of the writer, too—in a word, of *ethnoliterature*."[36]

The text that marks Roth's initial foray into the ethnoliterary concerns that define the second phase of his writing career, culminating in *The Radetzky March*, is *The White Cities*, the travelogue of his trip from Lyon to Marseilles in 1925 (published posthumously in 1956). That Roth had issues of craft in mind as he embarked on this project can be gathered from the letter he sent to Reifenberg from Marseilles in August, 1925, in which he expounds on his plans for the book:

> I should like to write a wholly "subjective" book, in other words, something completely objective. The "confession" of a young, resigned, skeptical human being, at an age where he is completely indifferent whether he sees something new to him or not, traveling somewhere. . . . Think of the books of the Romantics. Take away their tools and props, both linguistic and perspectival. Replace them with the tools and props of modern irony and objectivity. Then you will have the book I want to write, and feel almost compelled to write. It's a guide

---

35. Joseph Roth, *The Wandering Jews*, trans. Michael Hofmann (New York: W. W. Norton, 2001), 88.

36. Andreas Kilcher, "The Cold Order and the Eros of Storytelling," in *Writing Jewish Culture: Paradoxes in Ethnography*, ed. Gabriella Safran and Andreas Kilcher (Bloomington: Indiana University Press, 2016), 68–93, 77.

[*Reisebuch*] to the soul of its writer, as much as of the country he's passing through.[37]

As the shoptalk reference to "tools and props" implies, Roth's new role as cultural translator was prompting him to reflect on issues of technique and style. Though he was a proponent of fast writing (who regarded the tendency to obsess over each word and phrase as a species of "laziness"),[38] he evidently did not view writing as the expressive outpouring of spontaneously recollected emotion, but as the conscious employment of literary devices to premeditated effect. Examining his evolving conception of authorship in the years leading up to *The Radetzky March* can therefore shed light on the elements, "both linguistic and perspectival," that he would go on to use in crafting his elegiac masterwork.

Like Bronislaw Malinowski, whose *Argonauts of the Western Pacific* (1922) was published three years earlier, Roth devotes considerable effort in the introductory section of *The White Cities* to distinguishing his mode of cultural observation from the kind one finds in conventional travel guides and tourist reports. But while for Malinowski the problem with the various white administrators, missionaries, and traders who are the ethnographer's first guides into the foreign culture is that they are too "full of the biased and pre-judged opinions inevitable in the average practical man [to take an] objective, scientific view of things,"[39] for Roth it is precisely the striving after disinterested, strictly factual truth that leads the conventional tourist astray. The "'good observer'" [who meets] everything with open but inflexible eyes," he states, "is the sorriest of reporters."[40]

To focus exclusively on the datable features of empirical reality at the expense of "[attending] to what's going on in [oneself]," Roth maintains, is both theoretically misguided and morally problematic. In the first place, it presupposes a mistaken view of the way language works. The signifiers we use do not straightforwardly latch unto stable signifieds. Rather, both the words we employ and what we think we represent when we use them are constantly in flux. Or, as Roth puts it, "before we can set down a single word, it's changed its meaning. Our familiar concepts no longer match the realities.

---

37. Joseph Roth, "Letter to Benno Reifenberg, from Marseilles (August 30, 1925)," quoted in Hofmann, *Life in Letters*, 53–54.
38. Roth, *Life in Letters*, 54.
39. Bronislaw Malinowski, *Argonauts of the Western Pacific* (London: Routledge, 1961), 5.
40. Roth, *White Cities*, 71.

The realities have grown out of the tight clothes we've put them in." The inability to recognize that "the world is continually changing," claims Roth, engenders a false confidence in the inevitability of one's cultural categories, and an equally misguided belief in the stability of what one observes. Both these false beliefs come together in the figure of the "good observer," who inevitably misrepresents what he or she sees. "People talk about the present," Roth writes critically, "with a sense of historic certainty," as though the way things are now will persist forever, as though the world is static rather than plastic, and as though one's imported cultural categories simply hook up to the way things objectively are. The best we can do, Roth concludes, is to come to terms with the inevitably parochial nature of our judgments and observations. "I can't 'report' [on a foreign culture or place]," he writes, "at the most I can say how the experience felt, *to me*."[41]

Lest the uncompromising phrasing of this last statement mislead us, it is important to emphasize that his growing skepticism regarding the canons of objectivity notwithstanding, Roth had too much respect for the brute power of reality to sanction the kind of solipsistic aestheticism occasionally promulgated by Walter Pater or Oscar Wilde. For all his emphasis on and recommendation of the inevitably subjective dimension of experience, the authorial stance that he struggled to articulate in the late 1920s is closer to what Friedrich Schiller famously described as the attitude of the "sentimental poet," who, conscious of his estrangement from the world, nevertheless attempts to give a true account of it by "[*reflecting*] on the impressions which objects make on him."[42] And so, when Roth states that he cannot report on what he sees without bringing his individual response into the frame, he should not be taken as saying with Anatole France that "we speak of ourselves every time that we have not the strength to be silent."[43] His point, rather, is that only through an act of creative intuition can something like a true account of an unfamiliar way of life be captured and communicated.

To truly grasp an alien culture, Roth implicitly argues in the opening of *The White Cities*, it is not enough to record its visible manifestations; one must divine what Lionel Trilling famously called its "hum and buzz of

---

41. Roth, *White Cities*, 71.

42. Friedrich Schiller, *On the Naïve and Sentimental in Literature*, trans. Helen Watanabe-O'Kelly (Manchester: Carcanet New Press, 1981), 42.

43. Anatole France, "The Adventure of the Soul," in *The Literary Life*, trans. Ludwig Lewisohn, in *A Modern Book of Criticism*, ed. Ludwig Lewisohn (New York: The Modern Library, 1919), 1.

implication,"[44] the evanescent half-tones and inflections of value "that for good or bad draw the people of a culture together and that separate them from the people of another culture."[45] This elusive substance cannot be discovered by empirical observation or through the amassing of detail, for it resides on the level of the whole, not in any of its observable parts. Thus, the characteristic weakness of conventional tourist guides and journalistic reports, in Roth's view, is their positivistic bias, their inability to look beyond the realm of observable facts. It is only by sympathetically and imaginatively immersing oneself in the foreign element, while attending closely to one's own experience, that one can provide a true account of it.

Roth's qualification of the role of empirical observation and his emphasis on the significance of subjective immersion and self-reflexiveness signal his gradual shift away from the documentary style of his earlier novels and toward the culturalist mode of thought and description, which was gaining in both prominence and sophistication during the early decades of the twentieth century. As Christopher Herbert has argued, the idea that "culture" is not located in any of its empirically observable parts, but rather on the invisible level of their interaction, is the mark of the modern theory of culture.[46] Its incipience can be traced back to E.B. Tylor's seminal 1871 definition of culture as a "complex whole," as well as to Herbert Spencer's claim in *The Principles of Sociology* (1876–1896) that the true object of social science was to be sought, not in entities themselves, but in "the relations of structures and reciprocities of functions" between them.[47] What these nineteenth-century scientific versions of the culturalist idea added to the holistic and historicist conception of culture introduced by Herder and Burke was their stress on the systematic interconnectivity of the components of the whole. Culture, on the view that these Victorian thinkers bequeathed to Roth's contemporaries (most notably Franz Boas, Malinowski, Ruth Benedict, and E.E. Evans-Pritchard), consisted not of things but of the *relations between things*—a stipulation that made it, by definition, inaccessible to

---

44. Lionel Trilling, "Manners, Morals, and the Novel," *Kenyon Review* 10, no. 1 (1948): 11–27, 12.

45. Trilling, *Manners*, 12.

46. See Christopher Herbert, *Culture and Anomie* (Chicago: University of Chicago Press, 1991), particularly 1–28.

47. Spencer quoted in Herbert, *Culture and Anomie*, 12.

strictly empirical investigation. "*Relationships,*" as Herbert underscores, "*are not observable phenomena.*"[48]

To get a handle on the inner workings of an alien culture, on "the real spirit of [its] natives," writes Malinowski, involves engaging directly in the everyday routines of lived experiences of its members, on the one hand, while simultaneously reserving a quotient of critical distance, so as to be able to reflect upon these group behaviors and reveal their systematic interconnectivity, on the other.[49] The constant oscillation between embeddedness and reflection, which defines the ethnographic practice of participant-observation, corresponds to the ambivalent nature of the object it seeks to describe. Culture, for Malinowski (as for Roth), is that peculiar entity that pops into focus only when the two polarized filters of subjective experience and objective observation are superimposed.

Roth would put the theoretical toolkit that he had begun to assemble in *The White Cities* to work the following year. In 1926, Roth traveled to Russia on behalf of the *Frankfurter Zeitung* to report on the state of the young Soviet Union under the recently ascended Stalin. During his five-month tour, which took him as far east as Baku on the Caspian Sea, Roth sent back some seventeen articles on conditions in communist Russia,[50] while also working on a long essay on the state of the region's beleaguered Jewish minority, eventually published as *The Wandering Jews*. And it is in this alternately sympathetic, ironic, despairing, and celebratory account of Eastern-European Jewry, a world that, by 1926, was already in advanced stages of depopulation and decay, that marks Roth's first foray into ethnoliterature.[51]

While *The White Cities* consists mainly of atmospheric vignettes of spaces and locales (the ancient Roman monuments in Nîmes; the cathedral in Lyons) with only scarce mention of local types and individuals, *The Wandering Jews*

---

48. Herbert, *Culture and Anomie*, 10.

49. Malinowski, *Argonauts*, 14.

50. Kilcher, *Cold Order*, 75.

51. As David Roskies argues, the Eastern-European *shtetl* began to go into decline in the mid nineteenth century "when its two foundations—the feudal economy and the power of the nobility—were overturned." By the time of Roth's trip to the East, this form of life would have been a faint shadow of itself, more myth than reality. See David G. Roskies, *Against the Apocalypse: Responses to Catastrophe in Modern Jewish Culture* (Cambridge, MA: Harvard University Press, 1984), 109–110.

is a work in which human landscapes take precedence over physical ones. The book takes the form of a sequence of pseudo-ethnographic encounters with figures and rituals representative of this vanishing form of life—a visit to a wonder rabbi, a traditional wedding, a description of Yom Kippur in the *shtetl*—in which Roth, taking on the role of participant-observer, alternates between a record of his first-person impressions and knowing, explanatory asides that are intended not only to clarify but also to vindicate and often extol the ways of the Eastern Jews. His explicit aim throughout is not only to "explain" the Eastern Jew to his German audiences; it is also to defend the unjustly maligned and misunderstood culture—to which he stood in an ambiguous relationship of belonging and estrangement—by treating it "with love, and not with that 'scientific detachment' better known as indifference."[52]

Acutely aware of the unequal power relation underlying the ethnographic encounter between what he calls "the European man of learning" and the "helpless objects of [his] inquisitiveness,"[53] Roth is at pains to insist that it is the West rather than the Eastern Jew that stands to profit from the meeting of cultures. Not unlike Maria Edgeworth, who sought to instruct her "*ignorant* English reader" in the ways of Ireland,[54] Roth's description of "how the Eastern Jew and his kind live" is meant as a rebuttal, not only to the slurs of the anti-Semites, but even more so to (what was for him) the maddening condescension of Western-European Jews toward their Eastern brethren. In the heat of this angry polemic, Roth often slips into invidious comparisons between the "authentic and uncontaminated" culture of the East and the "deadly, antiseptic" wasteland of the West.[55] Echoing Edward Sapir's distinction between "genuine" and "spurious" cultures, he draws an exceedingly tendentious contrast between the allegedly pristine, organic culture of the East and the fragmented societies of the West, whose oppressive "narrowness of . . . perspective" finds its objective correlative in a nightmarish landscape "jagged with smoke stacks and . . . power plants."[56] Yet it is important to

---

52. Roth, *Wandering Jews*, 2.

53. Roth, 32.

54. Maria Edgeworth, *Castle Rackrent and Ennui*, ed. Marilyn Butler (London: Penguin, 1992), 63.

55. Roth, *Wandering Jews*, 22, 11.

56. Roth, 5. For Sapir's classic statement, see Edward Sapir, "Culture, Genuine and Spurious," in *Culture, Language, and Personality: Selected Essays*, ed. David G. Mandelbaum (Berkeley: University of California Press, 1964), 78–119.

stress that despite such lapses into the suspect rhetoric of cultural purity, Roth is wholly free of the racialist and essentialist notions that regularly attached to this kind of talk in the 1920s. Jewishness, as he describes it, is neither a racial, nor a national, nor even a (purely) religious category, but a cultural one. Undercutting not only the racialist but also the Jewish orthodox interpretations of Jewish identity, Roth states matter-of-factly that the Eastern Jew is "the product of several generations of mixed marriages."[57] Heredity is not what makes the Jew a Jew. Nor can Jewish identity, in Roth's view, be conceived as a nationality in the traditional European sense, as it is not founded on a territorial claim. (Roth viewed Zionism as an understandable but misconceived endeavor.) In short, Jewishness, as Roth describes it in *The Wandering Jews*, is to be sought after neither on the level of blood and soil nor on that of religion, but in the historically emergent habits, texts, beliefs, and social rituals that distinguish the Eastern Jews from their environment. For Roth, culture's ungroundedness, the fact that it is perpetuated by nothing besides its own self-sustaining rituals, is also what makes it so vulnerable. Indeed, what lends *The Wandering Jews* its poignancy and urgency is its author's repeated reference to the rapid disintegration of this form of life. The Jewish world that he describes is not only fragile; it is already a half-departed thing.

Roth's aim in writing his essay on the Eastern Jews is, thus, both to vindicate and elegize a lost cultural world. This dual agenda sets *The Wandering Jews* squarely within the tradition of salvage anthropology, a genre whose goal, as we've seen in the previous chapter, is to preserve in the amber of language a culture "disintegrating in time and space."[58] Thus, for all his repudiation of ethnography's cold "scientific detachment" and positivist pretensions, Roth, by taking on the role of the representer and preserver of a peripheral way of life at the moment of its vanishing, ends up reproducing the form's ideological and epistemological assumptions. As I argued in chapter 1, while the traditional cultural-extinction narrative (which anthropology inherited from Edgeworth and Scott) helped shape our modern conception of culture as a contingent and ultimately transient collective entity, it also served to keep this unsettling implication at a safe distance. For contained in the genre's consistent association of extinction

---

57. Roth, *Wandering Jews*, 15.
58. James Clifford, "On Ethnographic Allegory," in *Writing Culture: The Poetics and Politics of Ethnography* (Berkeley: University of California Press, 1986), 98–121, 112.

with peripherality is the comforting idea that cultural death is the lot of the geographically marginal other. To depict distant others slipping into historical oblivion is to tacitly reassure the reader at the metropolitan center that her "civilization" is somehow immune to that fate.

And so, despite Roth's relentless and bitter condemnation of "those Western Europeans who . . . peer down with a cheap and sour benevolence from the rickety towers of the Western civilization upon the near East and its inhabitants,"[59] despite his sensitivity to the skewed hierarchy built into the ethnographic encounter and his attempt to reverse it, the longstanding narrative framework that Roth employs in *The Wandering Jews*, in fact, serves to buttress the selfsame complacency that he decries. For that emotional stance rests upon and solidifies the assurance that the moral, political, and epistemological foundations of one's own civilization are rooted in some stable ground, such that renders them immune, if not to change than to extinction.

Nonetheless, it is during his months in Russia that the seeds of what would become *The Radetzky March*, the work in which Roth would relativize and ephemeralize the center, were sown. This period, as Kilcher writes, sees a "Copernican reversal" in Roth's thought and writing: what Roth realized during his time in Russia was that "it cannot be a matter of sizing Eastern Europe—particularly the Eastern Europe of Jews—from a Western perspective and in so doing colonizing it symbolically; rather it is about using Eastern Europe to *put Western Europe into perspective*."[60] It is this realignment of viewpoint, this placing of the hegemonic self "into perspective," Kilcher argues, that is at the core of Roth's ethnoliterary turn, shaping his subsequent journalistic as well as literary writing. Kilcher is, I think, right about this. But, while he holds up *Flight without End* and *Job* as examples of Roth's ethnoliterary turn, I will present *The Radetzky March* as the culmination of this transition. For, while those earlier novels do indeed signal Roth's increasing absorption in the culturalist mode of representation that he broaches in his reportages, it is only in his 1932 masterpiece that he finally applies this culturalist vocabulary to a social world located at the hegemonic center. In *The Radetzky March*, as in *The Age of Innocence*, concepts and metaphors, which had first appeared in early-nineteenth-century colonial contexts, are employed to narrate the identity and fate of a class located at the hegemonic center of an imperial order. If Wharton dresses

---

59. Roth, *White Cities*, 1.

60. Kilcher, *Cold Order*, 77. Emphasis added.

the genteel men and women of Old New York in bows and feathers and casts them in the role of a vanishing tribe, Roth imagines the Habsburg Empire as a *shtetl* writ large.[61]

Empire as Cultural World: *The Radetzky March*

In his favorable 1933 review of Hermann Wendel's *French People*, a forgotten book made up of thirty-two brief biographies of great French historical personages, Roth writes: "Over all the characters hangs a pall of melancholy. Death, with which each one of these minibiographies ends, casts its shadow over the life of this book. And so—because life is occluded by the shadow of death—the book comes to have a metaphysical gravity that contrasts with historical levity. Yes, that seems to be its charm: that it is a description of death. Its value, though, is more practical: it teaches the reader about France, through representative individuals."[62] As is often the case when one writer reviews the work of another, Roth's praise seems more applicable to his own book, *The Radetzky March*, which was published in Berlin the previous year, than to Wendel's. For it is Roth's novel, much more so than *French People*, that is a "description of death": not individual and private but collective and shared. It is *The Radetzky March*, not Wendel's gallery of portraits, that strives to make a now-vanished world "known and understood" by tracing the interlocking fates of a group of "representative individuals." And it is Roth's book, rather than his counterpart's, that depicts its characters as living "[in] the shadow of Death that within a few months would take them all in its clutches!"[63]

This looming shadow is, of course, the war, which had a profound impact on writers who, like Roth, experienced what Marjorie Perloff describes as the "sudden and radical dissolution of the geographical entities into which

---

61. The idea that Roth regarded the empire on the model of the *shtetl* was first raised by Claudio Magris. Roth's partly conscious identification, "zwischen Austriazität uns Ostjudentum, zwischen *Imperium* und *Shtetl*," Magris claims in *Weit von Wo*, is partly what distinguished his work from the nostalgias of other Jewish "*laudatores der felix Austria*," such as Stefan Zweig and Franz Werfel. See Claudio Magris, *Weit von Wo: Verlorene Welt des Ostjudentums* (Vienna: Europa Verlag, 1974), 16.

62. Roth, *White Cities*, 215–216.

63. Joseph Roth, *The Radetzky March*, trans. Michael Hofmann (London: Granta, 2002), 303.

[they] were born."⁶⁴ In her recent study of the cadre of writers she calls the Austro-modernists (Robert Musil, Karl Kraus, Elias Canetti, Roth, and others), Perloff argues that the trauma of the war created in them "a deeply skeptical and resolutely individualistic modernism."⁶⁵ But this description, while applicable to Kraus and Canetti, and perhaps also to Musil, is, I believe, wholly misleading when it comes to Roth. For while Perloff is right to claim that these postwar writers came away from the war with a heightened awareness of the contingency of identity and the precarity of social institutions—the sudden and total liquidation of the empire was an event without parallel since the 1789 termination of the *ancien régime*—this awareness did not lead Roth in the direction of a "resolutely individualistic modernism." In contrast with his contemporaries, it led him to abandon his early modernist preoccupation with fragmentation and alienation in favor of an evermore consistently pursued realist engagement with the communal, social, and historical dimensions of human existence.

The Radetzky March, Roth's preeminent realist novel, is the first work whose composition was accompanied by an extended period of research. During the two years it took him to write the book, Roth studied the ceremonies of the Habsburg court, consulted pictures of the Austrian army and uniform, and investigated the formalities of the empire's state bureaucracy.⁶⁶ The results of this preparatory stage are everywhere in evidence. Like Wharton's reconstruction of Old New York, *The Radetzky March* is invested in giving its readers a sense of what Bill Brown has described as "the way cultural codes become objectified in specific material forms, the way that people shape, code, and recode the material object world, the way they make things meaningful and valuable."⁶⁷ The novel is a trove of period pieces and iconic paraphernalia: Jäger uniforms and Corpus Christi processions; shining sabres and white ceremonial gloves; whinnying horses, cherry dumplings, and bewhiskered men of all ranks and titles (Wharton's attentiveness to headdress finds its analogue here).⁶⁸ However, in contrast

---

64. Marjorie Perloff, *The Edge of Irony: Modernism in the Shadow of the Habsburg Empire* (Chicago: University of Chicago Press, 2016), 4.

65. Perloff, *Edge of Irony*, 4.

66. Bronson, *Joseph Roth*, 394.

67. Bill Brown, *Other Things* (Chicago: University of Chicago Press, 2015), 50.

68. "[Roth's] Epik," as Marcel Reich-Ranicki succinctly puts it, "ist . . . Detailkunst." See his "Der Romancier Joseph Roth," in *Joseph Roth: Interpretation, Rezeption, Kritik,*

with Wharton's novel, where Europe *qua* an alternative cultural paradigm intrudes in the form of Ellen into insular New York society, in *The Radetzky March* there is no clash of civilizations. Throughout the novel the cultural borders of the Habsburg Empire are never overstepped. From the first page to the last, the reader remains within a sharply demarcated realm of meaning. Indeed, few novels offer a more striking example of what Fredric Jameson called "'strategies of containment' whereby [novels] are able to project the illusion that their readings [of their own cultures] are somehow complete and self-sufficient."[69] In *Job*, Roth places the Singers' *shtetl*-bound existence in a broader multicultural perspective: at one point Mac, their departed son's American business partner, makes a surprise visit to the family's Western Russian home; later in the novel we follow the Singers' emigration from Russia to New York. By contrast, in *The Radetzky March* no alternative cultural perspective is allowed to intrude upon the depicted world. From the novel's beginning with the Battle of Solferino to its end with the empire's dying days, Austro-Hungary remains an insular self-contained cosmos that structures its characters' identities and defines the range of their moral experiences.[70] This figuration of culture as a "world" (with everything that this conceit implies) is established early on and maintained regularly throughout the novel to become one of its central organizing metaphors. And while this choice may have been premeditated, it seems more likely that, as the writing progressed, Roth became increasingly taken with the culture-*qua*-world metaphor and began to think ever more seriously in its terms, which may account for the gradual shift in the tone in which it is presented.

The metaphor's initial appearance is in the novel's first episode set in the 1859 Battle of Solferino and San Martino. When during a lull in the fighting, Lieutenant Joseph Trotta, the soon-to-be Hero of Solferino, spots the young Emperor Franz Joseph marking himself as a high-value

---

ed. Michael Kessler and Fritz Hackert (Tübingen: Stauffenburg, 1990), 261–268, 267.

69. From *The Political Unconscious*, quoted in James Buzard, *Disorienting Fiction: The Autoethnographic Work of Nineteenth-century British Novels* (Princeton, NJ: Princeton University Press, 2005), 107.

70. However, though rendered as an insular *Kulturwelt*, the Dual Monarchy is not described as a homogenous monolith that shows one and the same face to all its subjects. As Malcolm Spenser notes, Roth took much care to stress the colonial nature of the empire and the multinational diversity of the Crown Lands over which it ruled. See Malcolm Spenser, *In the Shadow of Empire: Austrian Experiences of Modernity in the Writings of Musil, Roth, and Bachmann* (Rochester, NY: Camden House, 2008), 155–156.

target for enemy snipers, he is gripped by a dread that quickly escalates to Armageddon-like proportions: "Trotta's heart was in his mouth. Fear of the unimaginable, the boundless catastrophe that would destroy himself, the regiment, the army, the state, the whole world sent a burning chill through his body."[71] The spiraling order of magnitudes ("the army, the state, the whole world") injects a modicum of hysteria into Trotta's interpretation of the events, and opens an ironic gap between his parochial perspective and the soberer, because broader, perspective of the narrator. But when the metaphor recurs a bit later in the book, in the description of Count Chojnicki, the irony is already toned down: "The world in which it would have been worth living was doomed. The world that would follow did not merit any decent inhabitants."[72] This markedly more solemn tone persists in the subsequent reflections of District Commissioner Trotta, who, after meeting the jaded count, comes to similar conclusions, and in much the same words: "He could see the world coming to an end, and it was his world."[73] Similarly, the frail but perceptive Emperor Franz Joseph has "still less belief in the continued existence of his world than the jokers all over his great empire who poked fun at him."[74] And again: Carl Joseph, as he faces the ill-fated demonstration of the brush factory workers (easily the novel's darkest episode) has "a sudden premonition [*eine dunkle Ahnung*] of the end of the world."[75] The last chapter of the novel, set after the deaths of Carl Joseph and the Emperor, ends with the words "[District Commissioner Trotta's] world was ended [*untergegangen*]."[76] The culturalist idea, that the limit of one's culture is also the limit of one's world, could scarcely have found a more doggedly pursued fictional representation.[77]

While Roth liked to think of his expansive fatherland as "a large house with many doors and many rooms," his insistent depiction of the empire as a discrete and insular "world" makes exploring this fictional landscape

---

71. Roth, *The Radetzky March*, 4.
72. Roth, *The Radetzky March*, 206.
73. Roth, *The Radetzky March*, 179.
74. Roth, *The Radetzky March*, 236.
75. Roth, *The Radetzky March*, 228.
76. Roth, *The Radetzky March*, 353.
77. Edward Sapir, "The Status of Linguistics as a Science," in *Culture, Language and Personality: Selected Essays*, ed. David G. Mandelbaum (Berkeley: University of California Press, 1949), 160–166, 162.

a decidedly claustrophobic experience.[78] The novel's strategy of combining extended thick descriptions of objects and rituals with narratorial introjections that constantly remind us of this world's imminent demise produces a sense of strolling through a magnificently crafted architectonic structure, which, like Poe's House of Usher, threatens to collapse around us at any moment. And as if to exacerbate this sense, Roth seems intent on leaving his readers (who follow and identify with the doomed characters) with no emotional way out. Emigration is not an option for the Trottas. As the novel repeatedly underscores, the military and bureaucratic institutions of the empire make up the only realm in which they possess an intelligible identity and sense of purpose. This soon-to-be destroyed nexus of customs and institutions makes up the horizon of their world.

This point is embodied in a particularly forceful way in the character of Carl Joseph Trotta, the youngest of the condemned von Trotta line and the subject of the novel's plot of initiation. *The Radetzky March*, as Perloff argues, is better thought of as an anti-Bildungsroman, as it is not what Carl Joseph learns but "what [he] unlearns that matters."[79] More specifically, Carl Joseph's growth as a character—such as it is—involves his coming to recognize that the empire is but one world among many, that its seemingly unalterable social institutions, moral norms, and rules of conduct are neither necessary nor given from all eternity, but are simply the way things are done *here*. This rattling realization creeps up on the young lieutenant as he ponders the upcoming journey of his friend Count Chojnicki to the South:

> The South was a foreign land somewhere! And lo: there were other countries [*Und siehe da: es gab also fremde Länder!*], countries which were not subject to Emperor Franz Joseph, which had armies of their own, with many thousands of their own lieutenants in greater or lesser barracks. In these other countries, the name of the hero of Solferino was without significance. They had their own monarchs. And these monarchs had their own

---

78. The words are Graf Morstin's in *Die Büste des Kaisers* (1935) but are commonly regarded as an expression of Roth's antinationalism in his late legitimist phase. The complete quotation is: "Deshalb hasse ich Nationen und Nationalstaaten. Meine alte Heimat, die Monarchie allein war ein großes Haus mit vielen Türen und vielen Zimmern, für viele Arten von Menschen." *Joseph Roth: Romane, Erzählungen, Aufsätze* (Köln: Kiepenhauer & Witsch, 1964), 361.

79. Perloff, *Edge of Irony*, 45–46.

people to rescue them from mortal danger. It was bewildering in the extreme to follow these thoughts; for a lieutenant in the Monarchy it was just as bewildering as it might be for us to consider that the earth is only one of millions upon millions of heavenly bodies, that there are innumerable other suns in our galaxy, and that each of these suns has it own planets, and that we therefore are relegated to being a very obscure thing indeed, not to say: an insignificant speck of dust! [*ein Häufchen Dreck!*][80]

As a fairly well-educated young man, Carl Joseph knows full well, of course, that the earth does not end at the borders of the empire. Evidently, however, none of the relativistic implications of this fact have yet to occur to him. The formative years spent at the Mährisch-Weisskirchen cadet school had instilled in him a remarkably resilient form of parochialism, which has prevented him from fathoming the significance of the existence of alien lifeworlds. Never before this moment did it occur to him that there is nothing inevitable or natural about the customs he had been taught to follow and the ideals he had been instructed to pursue. The crucial point with respect to the novel's culture-*qua*-world metaphor, however, is that even after Lieutenant Trotta's epiphanic moment, his imagination continues to bear the official stamp of the empire. While finally able to grasp theoretically the facticity of such *fremde Länder*, he is unable to envision any concrete content with which to populate them. He thus lamely projects the only narrow slice of life that he knows unto the blank screen of his ignorance, where he can barely make out distant lieutenants, marching out from their remote barracks to rescue their own faraway emperors.

Roth, evidently, could not resist poking fun at his pitiable protagonist. But there is, I think, a more serious point being made here. As I've argued at the beginning of this study, Roth was skeptical about the individual's capacity for self-reinvention. Like Wharton, he thought that we are far less autonomous and self-directing than we perhaps like to imagine. As I see it, therefore, it is not Carl Joseph's feebleness as a character that explains his failure to reinvent himself. On the view that Roth shares with Wharton, selfhood is entangled with its cultural niche to an extent that makes the range of self-transformation exceedingly narrow. With that said, however, Carl Joseph's discovery that his cultural world is "only one of millions upon

---

80. Roth, *The Radetzky March*, 220.

millions of heavenly bodies," like Newland Archer's analogous recognition of the cultural basis of his identity, marks the moment in which his process of unlearning reaches its conclusion. His dizzying glimpse into what Milan Kundera calls "the essential relativity of things human" shatters the stifling yet secure sense of inevitability that had underwritten his fatalistic devotion to the empire, and eventually enables him to quit the military career and begin to form, however briefly, some kind of life apart from the expectations he inherited with his name and title (before his sense of duty sends him back into the army and eventually to the front).[81] This is, to be sure, a rather modest conception of individuation, but it is the most that the culturally constituted self—the kind of self that Roth's and Wharton's novels imply—can hope to attain.

Roth's admittedly hyperbolic representation of the self's dependence on its cultural environment recalls Arjun Appadurai well-known critique of ethnography's "metonymic freezing" effect, whereby the discipline's proverbial "natives" are repeatedly "confined" within the spatial and moral coordinates of their culture.[82] For like the natives of the anthropological imagination, Roth's characters not only appear to us exclusively within the iconic space of the empire; they are also somehow "*incarcerated*" by its moral geography. But there is, of course, a crucial difference between Roth's characters and the Azande people of E.E. Evans-Pritchard's ethnography (Appadurai's example), or, for that matter, the ill-fated Highlanders of Scott's *Waverley*. While the latter cultures are defined as "[belonging] to those parts of the world that were, and are, distant from the metropolitan West,"[83] Roth's officers and officials make up its ruling elite.

That Roth is fully conscious of this reversal can be gathered from the scene in which he describes the emperor's beloved military officers from the perspective of the Slavic inhabitants of one of the empire's far-flung garrison towns: "To the shopkeepers and craftsman of the little town, these strange gentlemen went about like the baffling followers of some remote and cruel godhead, which simultaneously cast them as its colourfully disguised and

---

81. Milan Kundera, *Art of the Novel*, trans. Linda Asher (New York: Harper & Row, 1988), 7.
82. Arjun Appadurai, "Putting Hierarchy in Its Place," *Cultural Anthropology* 3, no. 1 (1988): 36–49, 37–38.
83. Appadurai, "Hierarchy," 37.

magnificently decked sacrificial animals."[84] This description (which recalls Roth's depiction of the "exotic" *Hasidic* communities in the East),[85] effectively casts the ostensibly more "Western" officers as the objects of anthropological curiosity, while turning the local population—a mixture of stalwart Ruthenian peasants and entrepreneurial Jews—into what Appadurai calls "the movers, the seers, the knowers."[86] On this picture, it is the agents of the emperor, not the prototypical "natives," who are trapped by their bewildering customs and beliefs. And, tellingly, while "the shopkeepers and craftsman of the little town" will survive the coming storm, the officers, along with the world for which they stand, will perish in it.

What does this reversal suggest about the idea of culture? What happens when the culturalist discourse is used to describe the colonizer rather than the colonized, when categories and metaphors typically associated with exoticized strangers are applied to the hegemonic Western self? According to Appadurai, classical anthropology's tendency to trap "natives" in their cultural and spatial niches was closely bound up with the "urge to *essentialize*, which characterized the Orientalist forebears of anthropology, [and which leads] back to Plato."[87] On this postcolonial line of argument (echoed in Edward Said's, Johannes Fabian's, Mary Louise Pratt's, and Lila Abu-Lughod's critiques of classic anthropology), the ethnographic gaze is first and foremost a means to fix living, evolving communities into a timeless present, so as to render them amenable to knowledge and domination. Drawing on anthropology's long and sordid record as a handmaiden for imperialism, these critics thus reduce the ethnographic perspective to an other-making tool: a way, as Pratt writes, of abstracting an indigenous people "out of the landscape that is under contention and away from the history that is being made—a history into which they will later be reinserted as an exploited labor pool."[88]

While I acknowledge the force of these meta-anthropological critiques, I agree with James Buzard that to "[identify] an 'ethnographic perspective' [exclusively] with the brutal 'othering' powers and aims of colonization"

---

84. Roth, *The Radetzky March*, 121.

85. "To the Western European," writes Roth in *The Wandering Jews*, "[the *hasids*] are as exotic and remote as, say, the inhabitants of the Himalayan region, who are now so much in fashion." See Roth, *Wandering Jews*, 32.

86. Appadurai, *Hierarchy*, 37.

87. Appadurai, *Hierarchy*, 41.

88. Mary Louise Pratt, "Scratches on the Face of the Country; Or, What Mr. Barrow Saw in the Land of the Bushmen," *Critical Inquiry* 12, no. 1 (1985): 119–143, 126.

is to overlook the massive effort conducted under the aegis of culturalist discourse to construct a vision of social life "as *both* merely contingent *and* worthy of rededicated participation."[89] To culturalize a human community need not involve essentializing and dehistoricizing its practices and habits. Indeed, on the story that I've been telling in these pages, culturalist discourse has been charged from its earliest beginnings with an awareness of the historical and transient nature of social and cultural practices and institutions. This is not to deny that, like every other discursive tool, it can and has been put to a variety of other uses. But the fact that the idea of culture has been historically implicated in projects of imperial domination and scientific reification does not reduce it to nothing but an instrument of power and control. Indeed, in the hands of Roth and Wharton, the vocabulary of culture works precisely to reveal the fragile and relative (yet still morally binding) nature of social values and conventions. Culture, as these writers imagine it, constructs and anchors the identities of its members while being itself anchored in nothing more stable or permanent than the collective will of this constituency. Its norms and conventions are, at once, relative and real, contingent and effective.

I've said above that *The Radetzky March* (like Wharton's *The Age of Innocence*) constantly toggles between two perspectives on the represented world. On the first, manifested by the novel's numerous high-resolution descriptions of iconic cultural objects and practices, the narrated reality appears like a loosely articulated assortment of social customs and relations. On the second viewpoint, realized through the totalizing perspective of the third-person narrator, the culture of the Habsburg Empire becomes a complex whole, an integrated and systematically coordinated "world." The novel's constant shuttling between these two perspectives, I now want to claim, are the key to its ethnoliterary realism.

As Seyla Benhabib notes, "all analyses of cultures, whether empirical or normative, must begin by distinguishing the standpoint of the social observer from that of the social agent."[90] Seen from the first, external perspective of the observer, culture appears as a "clearly delineable [whole]"; when seen from the internal perspective of the participant, it "forms a horizon that recedes each time one approaches it."[91] Culture, on this classical anthropological

---

89. Buzard, *Disorienting Fiction*, 14.
90. Seyla Benhabib, *The Claims of Culture: Equality and Diversity in the Global Era* (Princeton, NJ: Princeton University Press, 2002), 5.
91. Benhabib, *Claims of Culture*, 5.

view, is that elusive collective entity that only becomes salient when viewed simultaneously from two competing perspectives. Or, as Buzard writes, "a culture amounts to 'that which it takes a Participant Observer to find.' "[92] The Participant side of the equation delivers what Malinowski memorably called the "*imponderabilia of actual life*,"[93] the phenomenological, concrete, material aspect of reality as experienced by the natives/characters. When seen from their view, culture forms an ever-receding horizon of objects, practices, and institutions. But, when framed by the distanced and detached view of the Observer, it comes into view as a comprehensible whole. Observation without participation is empty; participation without observation is blind. It is only by combining the two perspectives that culture in its fullness and interconnectedness can emerge.

Roth does not only follow this culturalist procedure in *The Radetzky March*, there are good reasons to suppose that he was consciously reflecting on it. In 1930, while he commenced work on the novel, Roth published "Enough with the 'New Objectivity!'" the essay that explicitly announces his break with the documentary style in favor of what he describes as a more *künstlerisch* (but which I would call more culturalist) style of writing:

> Only an artistic [*künstlerisch*] report of a train crash (any train crash) will appear to the reader as a "true" account of the misfortune that he himself experienced. The "artistic report" attains the level on which details are unnecessary to render it valid. The eyewitness's account was "authentic." But in the reader it failed to attain even the level of credibility because the eyewitness was a (chance) participant in the event and thus can *only* recognize the true immediacy of his impressions in the "poetic" immediacy of the artistically shaped report, and not in the unshaped simplicity of the "documentary" report. What appears to attest to "life" itself is far removed both from the "inner" or "higher truth," but also from the power of reality. Only the "work of art" is as "genuine as life itself."[94]

The point struggling to emerge from Roth's forest of scare-quotes is more cogently expressed by Clifford Geertz when he observes that "[the] ability

---

92. Buzard, *Disorienting Fiction*, 9.
93. Malinowski, *Argonauts*, 20.
94. Quoted in Rosenfeld, *Understanding Roth*, 35.

of anthropologists to get us to take what they say seriously has less to do with . . . a factual look . . . than it has with their capacity to convince us that what they say is a result of their having actually penetrated (or, if you prefer, been penetrated by) another form of life."⁹⁵ The upshot of Geertz's and Roth's converging views is that the persuasive force of an anthropological or journalistic account is, first and foremost, a stylistic matter. The mere accumulation of details cannot compel the reader's assent. To be convincing, a report must signal—by whichever means—the shaping presence of an authorial consciousness able to separate the essential from the incidental and in this way to penetrate into the "inner" significance of its subject, be it the life of an individual or of a group.⁹⁶

These metafictional reflections, I want to claim, also make an appearance in *The Radetzky March*. Consider the following minor episode early on in the book, when Carl Joseph, here still a cadet, slips into his father's drawing room where the portrait of his celebrated grandfather hangs. Fascinated by the enigmatic gaze of the Hero of Solferino, the boy climbs on a chair to take a closer look. From up close, "[the portrait] disintegrated into numerous deep shadows and bright patches, into brushstrokes and dabs of colour, into a myriad web of painted canvas, into the hard play of dried oil paints."⁹⁷ Having examined the portrait in close up, the boy now steps off the chair to view it again, this time from a more distant perspective, whence "the green shadow of the trees played over his grandfather's brown jacket, the brushstrokes and dabs reassembled themselves into the familiar, inscrutable physiognomy, and the eyes recovered their customary remote expression of pondering the dark ceiling."⁹⁸ On the psychological level of interpretation, the portrait can be viewed as an embodiment of Carl Joseph's prosecutorial super-ego, of the unattainable standard that he will continually strive, and fail, to achieve. On the level of its sociohistorical meaning, the portrait may well stand for the accumulated ideological burden that a generation of grandfathers foisted on their grandsons, who would soon perish in the trenches. But there is, I want to suggest, a self-reflexive dimension to the scene as well. For Carl Joseph's shifting between the close-up view of the portrait, from which it disintegrates into a random sequence of "brushstrokes and dabs," and the

---

95. Clifford Geertz, *Works and Lives: The Anthropologist as Author* (Stanford, CA: Stanford University Press, 1988), 4–5.
96. Michel Foucault, "What is an Author" quoted in Geertz, *Works and Lives*, 6.
97. Roth, *The Radetzky March*, 36.
98. Roth, *The Radetzky March*, 36.

more distant view, from which the physiognomic interconnectedness of the object as a whole becomes perceptible, correlates with the novel's strategy of repeatedly toggling between the participatory perspective of the characters and the comprehensive but detached viewpoint of the narrator. From the first, the empire appears to us as an open horizon replete with tactile and sensuous surfaces but deprived of final meaning. From the second, it becomes an organic totality, but at the expense of tangibility and immediacy. In combination, these two perspectives project a vision of "culture" as that paradoxical object whose reality is founded on its ambivalence.

The "Abysmal, Worthless, Stupid, Steely Law" of Culture

The juxtaposition of the two perspectives that brings the Habsburgian culture into view as an ontological entity also determines its representation as a moral one. The novel's most complex and unsettling exploration on the perspectival nature of moral evaluation is contained in the section devoted to the tragic death of Max Demant. In this episode we observe the nearsighted doctor, who had foolishly challenged a fellow officer to a dual after the latter had insinuated that Demant's wife had been unfaithful to him, as he struggles to make sense of this strange and final turn in his life. At one point during the harrowing night before his appointed rendezvous with his opponent, the doctor helplessly curses the "abysmal, worthless, stupid, steely law [that is sending] him bound in chains to a stupid death."[99] Seen against the backdrop of the upcoming duel, the code that has forced Demant, on pain of disgrace, to defend his unfaithful wife's besmirched honor suddenly appears to him as terrifying and arbitrary, and his imminent death as meaningless and absurd. He feels, correctly, that he had faultlessly stumbled into a situation that compels him, against his will, to a certain death.

However, though Demant's point of view remains valid and wholly believable, his death cannot be said to be meaningless when viewed from the recuperative, backward-looking perspective of the narrator. From that extradiegetic point of view, the duel and its consequences, however tragic and exasperating, are shown to be continuous with the cultural logic that regulates the depicted social world as a whole. That is, though the doctor's looming death seems meaningless to him, it is rendered legible and thus

---

99. Roth, *The Radetzky March*, 114.

meaningful when placed in the context of the logic governing the culture to which he belongs. The force of the scene lies precisely in Roth's masterful manipulation of these two perspectives: allowing the reader to share in the doctor's helpless terror, in one moment, he shifts to a cool, emotionally muted depiction of the protocols of dueling in the next. Invited to keen over the fate of the sympathetic doctor and to share in his distress, the reader is also made to recognize and understand the rationale that underlies the sordid custom. What seems meaningless from Demant's standpoint as he faces his death becomes meaningful from the narrator's, leaving the reader with an uncomfortable awareness of the perspectival and relative nature of such determinations.

It is important, at this juncture, not to confuse the question of the meaningfulness of Demant's death with that of its moral justification. Roth's manner of depicting the duel and the circumstances that lead up to it leaves little doubt as to his negative appraisal of this practice. However, at the same time, he also contrives to make such moral evaluations seem almost beside the point. Roth's handling of the scene is not didactically geared toward *justifying* the dueling practice, but toward making it *comprehensible* as a cultural reality. As in Wharton's account of the tribal violence of genteel New York, Roth, a fellow ironist, is trying to make the ethos that dooms Demant legible, but without vindicating (let alone espousing) it. Demant's death, like Ellen's banishment, which is depicted as an inescapable consequence of transgressing the code of Old New York, is rationalized to the extent that it is shown to fit within the order of values that prevail in the represented world. What makes this episode so remarkable is the facility with which Roth modulates between cool-headed elucidation of this unwritten cultural code and warm-blooded sympathy for its human consequences. And the same is true of the scene of Ellen's banishment in Wharton's novel. The point in both cases is that the arbitrariness of social custom does not render it any less real or effective. This is illustrated when Demant, half mad with desperation and fear, contemplates escape: "It seemed perfectly possible to him that he might still elude all the threats to himself. Vanish! He thought. Accept dishonor, relegation to the ranks, serve three years as a private, or run away abroad! Not be shot!"[100] "Vanish!"—this, surely, is what any reader of the nerve-racking episode wants to cry out. But Demant stays put to play his part in his own execution. Why?

---

100. Roth, *The Radetzky March*, 114.

Demant's choice to go through with the duel is not due to a failure of nerve or weakness of character. His decision, like his friend Carl Joseph's choice to return to the army at the conclusion of the novel, illustrates a more general point. In Roth's socially constructed universe (as in Wharton's), the law is at once culturally contingent and operative. Demant is right to recognize the arbitrary nature of the code that compels him to duel—arbitrary in the sense that the only answer to the question "Why duel at all?" is "Because this is *our way* to resolve certain issues." However, though arbitrary and (from our and the narrator's perspectives) unjustifiable, it is still interwoven with an entire world-making web of meaning. For Demant, Carl Joseph, and the rest of the characters, that already-disintegrating web represents the only meaning-making framework they know, the only world they have.

Seen this way, Demant's momentary fantasy "[to] run away abroad!" is the analogue of Newland Archer's dream of escaping New York with Ellen ("I want—I want somehow to get away with you into a world . . . [where] we shall be simply two human beings who love each other").[101] The reason that both Roth and Wharton describe these thoughts as fantasies is not their impracticality—Demant, like Archer, could conceivably get on a ship and flee. What makes them fantasies, on the level of the novels' emphatic, indeed hyperbolic, investment in the notion of the culturally constituted self, is that at their root is a wish for absolute autonomy, the desire to be *sui generis*, uncreated. Seen this way, Demant's decision not to attempt escape becomes no less exasperating but much more comprehensible. For Demant to take the dishonorable route and back down from the duel would signify more than accepting disgrace; it would mean the death of his identity.

What Roth and Wharton repeatedly underscore is that one's identity is a cultural variant that is dependent on a continual interaction with one's social environment. This does not mean that one cannot leave one's environment, but it does mean that one cannot do so and remain the same person. To transgress a cultural world's taboo is to overstep its nomic borders, to fall over the edge, to become an outsider. Had Demant evaded the duel, he would have ceased being the person he is, and would have become temporarily (or fatally) worldless. Which is why, when Demant looks at Carl Joseph (while entertaining the thought of escape) the latter seems to him "like a being from another world."[102]

---

101. Edith Wharton, *The Age of Innocence*," Norton Critical Edition, ed. Candace Waid (New York: W. W. Norton, 2003), 174.

102. Roth, *The Radetzky March*, 114.

What Demant's choice to remain signals is that he prefers a socially meaningful death to the loss of identity. Had he escaped, he would have inflicted upon himself what Richard Rorty describes as the "ultimate humiliation" that a person can endure. By this Rorty means the point at which the individual discovers that "the story I have been telling myself about myself—my picture of myself as honest, or loyal, or devout—no longer makes sense. I no longer have a self to make sense of. There is no world in which I can picture myself as living, because there is no vocabulary in which I can tell a coherent story about myself."[103] In the face of the possibility of such symbolic death, Demant opts for real, yet meaningful death, thus illustrating, yet again, how thoroughly a social animal the Rothian self is.

What makes the death he chooses meaningful, however, is not Demant's own capacity to tell a story, but his community's ability to do so. The norms and values that prevail in the culture of which he and Carl Joseph are members make death in a duel or in defense of the emperor legible, comprehensible, and defensible. That is, the real threat to meaning and value, in Roth's view, is not individual but cultural death. For the possibility of leading a meaningful life and dying a meaningful death depend, in his novel, on the presence of a value-sustaining framework within which—and only within which—meaning can be articulated.

Alien Children

Like Wharton at the conclusion of *The Age of Innocence*, Roth is intent on highlighting the strange power of cultural change to render the obvious dubious, to transform the taken-for-granted assumptions of one generation into a disposable burden for the next. Though he would have agreed with Edmund Burke about the shaping power of tradition, he evidently did not share his view of culture as a site of continuity and stability—"a partnership not only between those who are living, but between those who are living, those who are dead, and those who are to be born."[104] Culture, as Roth views it, is a punctual, time-bound affair, not "a contract of eternal

---

103. Richard Rorty, *Contingency, Irony, and Solidarity* (Cambridge: Cambridge University Press, 1989), 179.

104. Edmund Burke, *Reflections on the Revolution in France* (London: Penguin, 2004), 194–195.

society."[105] Rather than binding successive generations into a unity of identity, it is what cleaves them apart. And indeed, *The Radetzky March* is rife with fathers who look on in a mixture of bafflement and grief at the strange alien beings that came of their loins.

Here for example is Master of the Horse Jelacich, one of the novel's minor figures. In the following, the loyal infantry officer of the empire and devoted father reflects on his two sons, enthusiasts in the fight for national independence: "He loved his sons! [And so he] shut his eyes when he saw them reading their dubious newspapers, and he shut his ears to their seditious talk. He was wise, and he understood that he stood powerlessly between his ancestors and his descendants, themselves destined to be ancestors, one day, of an entirely different breed [*eines ganz neuen Geschlechts*]. . . . At forty, the Master of the Horse felt like an old man, and his sons were like bewildering great-grandchildren to him."[106] Jelalich's sense of bewilderment is occasioned by the realization that the causal biological link between himself and his descendants has not issued in a cultural continuity between the generations. The "breed" to which he belongs extends backward and forward in time only so far as its cultural habitat does. One day, Jelalich recognizes, the islets of sameness that still tenuously bind him to his children will be subsumed by the rising current of historical change, and any meaningful, moral connection between himself and his descendants will evaporate.

These reflections are echoed by Dr. Skovronnek, when he shares his thoughts about his two sons with District Commissioner Trotta: "I look at them sometimes when they're asleep. Their faces look strange to me, almost unrecognizable, and I see that they are strangers, from a time that's yet to come and that I won't live to see. . . . There's cruelty in those sleeping faces."[107] The "cruelty" that Skovronnek intuits in his sleeping children is not a deliberate desire to harm; it is a function of the rift that time and change have opened between them and their father. It is the cruelty that comes of misapprehension, or even more so of indifference. What both Skovronnek and Jelalich intuit in their children's faces is the violence that the future always perpetrates upon the past. What causes both men to shudder is the realization that everything that has gone into making them into the particular people they are may well appear ludicrous, irrelevant, or reprehensible to their descendants, that nothing can defend them from

---

105. Burke, *Reflections*, 194–195.
106. Roth, *The Radetzky March*, 326–327.
107. Roth, *The Radetzky March*, 268.

what E.P. Thompson called "the enormous condescension of posterity."[108] This is the condescension that the narrator vocalizes when he looks back at the world of the fathers from the perspective of the sons, which is to say, of the intended reader: "Nowadays, the notions of professional honour and family honour and personal honour, by which Herr von Trotta lived, seem nothing more than the final residue of implausible and childish tales."[109] The code by which Herr von Trotta has lived, and which forced Max Demant into an early grave, becomes here infantile and absurd. The seemingly unalterable rules of conduct that had led an entire civilization to its doom, Roth is saying, was ultimately nothing more—or less—than a contingent concatenation of rituals and beliefs, a collectively maintained but exceedingly frail fiction.

It is this double emphasis on the pervasiveness and ephemerality of culture, I have been arguing, that is at the root of Roth's elegiaco-realist poetics. In his novel, Austro-Hungary's military-bureaucratic complex appears, at once, as an unsurpassable horizon and as a discrete and breakable whole. Another way to put this point is to say that culture functions in *The Radetzky March* both as a quasi-divine power and as vulnerable entity drawn on a human scale. These conflicting metaphors of society have been with us for at least two hundred years, and have been echoed and re-echoed by countless writers. Trilling writes, "our modern idea of culture may be thought of as a new sort of selfhood bestowed upon the whole of society . . . as having a certain organic unity and personality which it expresses in everything it does"[110]—to which Irving Howe counters: "society now hovers over mankind like a crushing weight, sometimes with a willful malevolence. It's notable that the conflicting visions of society bear a curious similarity to conflicting visions of God."[111] Constructive and repressive, brittle yet all-powerful, mortal yet God-like—these competing conceptualizations of culture, both operative in Roth's novel, come together in the figure of Emperor Franz Joseph, to whom I briefly turn now.

---

108. E.P. Thompson, *The Making of the English Working Class* (New York: Vintage, 1963), 12.

109. Roth, *The Radetzky March*, 292.

110. Lionel Trilling, "Freud: Within and Beyond Culture," in *Beyond Culture: Essays on Literature and Learning* (London: Secker & Warburg, 1955), 104.

111. Irving Howe, *A Critic's Notebook*, ed. Nicholas Howe (New York: Harcourt Brace Jovanovich, 1994), 186.

The All-Too-Human Emperor Franz Joseph

In his depiction of the emperor, Roth again modulates between two seemingly opposed but ultimately complementary perspectives. From the first, the emperor, whose solemn portrait appears everywhere, from barracks to brothel, functions as the symbolic center, the transcendental signified, of the empire. When, early in the novel, Count Chojnicki tries to impress upon his guests that the empire is on its last legs, the narrator tells us that "those who listened to the Count laughed and refilled their glasses. They didn't get it. . . . The Emperor was still alive."[112] For the Count's guests, the fact that Franz Joseph is still on his throne is guarantee enough that their world is secure. When later in the novel young Carl Joseph's fall into debt endangers his honor, the hand of the emperor reaches down, like God from some distant heaven, to set things aright for the grandson of the Hero of Solferino.

Roth's representation of the emperor as a quasi-divine figure was no doubt influenced by the way Franz Joseph was perceived by his ethnic subjects, particularly the Jews, for whom he was a beacon of relative tolerance and benevolence in a world growing increasingly hostile to their presence. "The Habsburg Jews," writes Gershon Shaked, "worshiped him: they prayed for his health and even included lyrics in his honor in their prayer books."[113] This veneration for the emperor and the values he was taken to stand for, as Shaked goes on to argue, continued to course through the postwar fiction of his erstwhile Jewish subjects. For all their modernist iconoclasm, S.Y. Agnon, Franz Kafka, and Roth "[longed] for the order that used to be guaranteed by that authority."[114] There is, however, an important difference between the ways the emperor's shadow figures in the works of the latter writers, and the way he is represented in Roth's. For, while in Agnon and Kafka, symbols of absolute authority are typically presented as radically inaccessible, incomprehensible, or *absconditus*, Roth goes to great lengths to empty the emperor of his sublimity and otherworldliness. Franz Joseph appears in *The*

---

112. Roth, *The Radetzky March*, 149.

113. Gershon Shaked, "After the Fall: Nostalgia and the Treatment of Authority in the Works of Kafka and Agnon, Two Habsburgian Writers," *Partial Answers: Journal of Literature and the History of Ideas* 2, no. 1 (2004): 81–82. For more on Jewish attitudes toward the Habsburg Empire and its emperor, see Robert S. Wistrich, *The Jews of Vienna in the Age of Franz Joseph* (Oxford: Oxford University Press, 1989).

114. Shaked, "After the Fall," 83.

Radetzky March as all too human—a sympathetic and not unwise man, but one who is as constrained by his inherited role as the last of his subjects:

> The Emperor was an old man. He was the oldest emperor in the world. All around him, Death was drawing his circles, mowing and mowing. Already the whole field was bare, and only the Emperor, like a forgotten silver stalk, still stood and waited. His hard and bright eyes had been looking confusedly into a confused distance for many years. The curve of his skull was as bare as a desert. His whiskers were as white as a pair of snowy wings. The creases in his face were a tangled shrubbery where the decades lived. His body was lean, his back slightly stooped. At home he walked around with short pattering steps.[115]

The emperor's titanic function as the symbolic center of the empire is here offset by his portrayal as a frail and declining old man.[116] He is at once the focal point of an immense social structure and a failing octogenarian, an emblem of a centuries-old edifice of imperial might and "a skinny old man, standing in front of an open window." These two perspectives on the emperor's person combine to make him a perfect embodiment of Roth's former home "adrift on a sea of time—not heading for anywhere."[117]

---

115. Roth, *The Radetzky March*, 235.

116. For a discussion of the function of the emperor in Roth's novel, see David Dollenmayer, "History and Fiction: The Kaiser in Joseph Roth's 'The Radetzky March,'" *Modern Language Studies* 16, no. 3 (1986): 302–310.

117. Roth, *The Radetzky March*, 239.

Chapter 4

The Culturalization of Zionism

Yaakov Shabtai's *Past Continuous*

> Goldman plodded through the sand and passed the place where the big shack, which had disappeared without a trace, had once stood, skirted the wild mulberry tree and arrived at the place which had once been the garden in front of Shmuel and Bracha and Grandfather Baruch Chaim and Grandmother Hava's shack, which had been demolished like most of the others, but of which the concrete blocks forming the foundation had miraculously remained standing.
>
> —Shabtai, *Past Continuous*

A Different Kind of Elite

Despite all that separates them in terms of nationality, language, and style, Wharton and Roth can be placed with relative ease in a well-defined historical moment—the immediate aftermath of the Great War—which both writers, like so many of their contemporaries in Europe and America, viewed as the unmaking of one world and the beginning of another. Wharton and Roth, whose lives straddled the violent shift from the long nineteenth century to the short century that followed, were exceptionally placed to dramatize this transition (at least as its meaning was perceived by their contemporaries) and explore its implications.

Given this periodization, it might initially seem that Yaakov Shabtai (1934–1981), belongs to a different story altogether. A contemporary of Philip

Roth and Günter Grass, Shabtai was thoroughly a writer of the twentieth century. By the time he began his writing career, the motorcar that had so thrilled Wharton and the telephone that Roth's District Commissioner Trotta eyes with wary distrust had long been unremarkable appurtenances of everyday life. European fascism, whose rise had darkened the final years of both writers, had been defeated, while Zionism—ignored by Wharton and scorned by Roth as "a kind of Jewish Crusade"—emerged triumphant.[1] Indeed, much as Roth had feared, by the time Shabtai's single completed novel, *Past Continuous* [*Zikhron devarim*] (1977) was published, the young Israeli state was knee-deep in its own imperialist venture, having already began to settle the territories it had conquered in the 1967 War.

Further, the nineteenth century, so present to Roth and especially to Wharton, was not much more than a shadowy abstraction for Shabtai's *sabre* [native-born] generation. This felt remoteness was not merely a result of temporal distance. Formally established in 1948, Israel simply did not have a nineteenth century. Even the *yishuv*, the pre-state Jewish settlement in Palestine, was largely a twentieth-century affair. The past, for those like Shabtai, who were born in mandatory Palestine and raised in the early post-Independence years, was literally a foreign country: it happened on a different continent (Europe), in a different language (Yiddish), and to a form of life (diasporic Jewry) that Zionism had done its utmost to disavow.

And yet, for all these differences, Shabtai's masterpiece has more in common with *The Age of Innocence* (1920) and *The Radetzky March* (1932) than with anything produced by his immediate Hebrew predecessors. Indeed, when seen against the backdrop of the century or so of modern Hebrew literature that preceded it, *Past Continuous* stands out as a radical departure, an idiosyncratic achievement that broke new thematic and formal ground, dramatically extending its tradition's sense of possibility. But when read in tandem with the latter texts, the novel is revealed as part of the broad tendency that I have been tracing in previous chapters. For although Shabtai's novel was written at a significant cultural and historical remove from Wharton's and Roth's postwar elegies, its underlying culturalist poetics and preoccupation with collective endings are clearly of a piece with theirs. In all three novels, the relativizing and temporalizing view, which was originally developed to render cultural *outsiders* legible to audiences at the imperial and

---

1. Joseph Roth, *The Wandering Jews*, trans. Michael Hofmann (New York: W. W. Norton, 2001), 19.

national center, is applied to social groups that their original readers would have recognized as their own. All three writers train their readers to view their own lifeworld through the metaphors and assumptions traditionally reserved for the objects of metropolitan curiosity and manipulation. In so doing, they both defamiliarize and culturalize the milieus at the center of their novels: insisting on their independent value as unrepeatable human realities, on the one hand, while parochializing and ephemeralizing their moral beliefs and human types, on the other.

Like Wharton, Shabtai was born to a social-political class, which, though barely three generations old, already possessed a sense of itself as a hegemonic establishment with sturdy institutions and ideological battlements. Like Old New York, whose geography stretched roughly from Washington Square, along Fifth Avenue, to the southern border of Central Park, so-called Little Tel Aviv was no more than a smallish knot of streets in what is today the center of the city. In the early decades of statehood, this area—today one of the city's priciest precincts—was home to an unusual elite. Its social prominence was derived neither from wealth nor from hereditary rank but from its historical role as Israel's founding generation and its control of the state's highly centralized government apparatus. As Irving Howe writes in his perspicuous review of the 1984 English translation of *Past Continuous*: "Nothing about the manners or appearance of these people would suggest this, and they would hotly deny they ever did form an elite, except perhaps an elite formed to eliminate all elites. Israeli readers would have no more trouble in recognizing these figures—the people of the Histadrut, the cadres of labor Zionism—than southern readers a few decades ago would have had in recognizing the aristocracy of the Sartorises and the Compsons."[2] What these people lacked in financial capital they made up for in cultural and political clout. The late Israeli sociologist Baruch Kimmerling famously dubbed this sector and its descendants "AHUSALIM," a Hebrew acronym that stands for "Ashkenazi, Secular, Veteran Residents, Socialists and Nationalists [i.e., Zionists (N.E.)]." It was the AHUSALIM, as Kimmerling writes, "who built [Israeli] society and this country; who won the 1948 War, while driving out a substantial portion of its Arab population; and who absorbed a massive number of immigrants, whom they then put through a cultural and political grinder so as to turn them into a new people using

---

2. Irving Howe, "Absalom in Israel," *The New York Times Review of Books*, October 10, 1985. www.nybooks.com/articles/1985/10/10/absalom-in-israel.

melting-pot mechanisms."[3] With their interests and values represented by MAPAI, David Ben Gurion's Zionist Labor Party, the AHUSALIM remained Israel's unchallenged hegemonic class from independence until well into the third decade of its existence, effectively casting the young state in their image while repressing (sometimes actively, but more often simply by dint of sheer cultural dominance) alternative conceptions of Israeli identity.

By the late 1970s, however, it became increasingly clear to many that a change was coming. Demographic shifts resulting from the large waves of immigration of Sephardic Jewish communities from North Africa and the Arab countries, the political ascendance of the religious right in the wake of the 1967 War, and the mounting frustration with the single-party domination of the public sector all signaled that the long hegemony of MAPAI was drawing to a close, and with it the first chapter in Israel's short history. This prospect was realized with the victory of Menachem Begin's right-wing Likud party in the 1977 elections. Popularly known as the *mahapach* or "turnaround," this political upheaval not only wrested political power away from the Labor Party, but also dealt a severe blow to the self-image of its still-hegemonic constituency. Though the secular Ashkenazi elites would continue to control many of the state's social and cultural institutions for decades to come, their symbolic position as the sole representers and arbiters of Israeli identity no longer went unchallenged. Israel, in the wake of 1977, was poised to become a different country from the one envisioned by its founders—a change that many among the AHUSALIM interpreted, not without reason, as the ending of an epoch. It was against this backdrop that *Past Continuous* was written. Published in 1977, on the eve of the "turnaround," Shabtai's elegy to Little Tel Aviv remains the subtlest exploration of the intimate effects that this watershed historical transition had on Israel's founding elite.

Nothing in Shabtai's earlier writings suggested the scale of the achievement of his first novel, which came out when he was in his forties.[4] Prior to *Past Continuous*, Shabtai had published a book of short stories (*Uncle*

---

3. Baruch Kimmerling, *The End of Ashkenazi Hegemony* [in Hebrew] (Jerusalem: Keter, 2001), 11–12. Unless otherwise indicated, translations are my own.

4. Not long after the publication of *Past Continuous*, Dan Miron remarked that "even those who looked favorably upon [Shabtai's] early works stand before the novel in utter amazement." See Dan Miron, "Hazikaron ke'idea," in *Pinkas Patuach* (Tel Aviv: Sifriyat poalim, 1979), 20.

Peretz Takes Off [1972]), as well as eleven plays, a handful of translations (among them of Gogol, Harold Pinter, and Robert Lewis Stevenson), and a few poems and song lyrics. He was a minor figure, recognized but marginal. The publication of *Past Continuous* would change all that, catapulting its author (who would die of heart failure only four years later) to the rank of Israel's foremost realist writer—a position he has held ever since. It is fair to say that Shabtai's novel has come to occupy in Israeli literary culture a position akin to that which Marcel Proust's *Remembrance of Things Past* (1913–1927), Thomas Mann's *The Magic Mountain* (1924), and William Faulkner's *The Sound and the Fury* (1929) occupy in theirs. Four decades after its first publication, *Past Continuous* remains a literary touchstone and a cultural monument.

Examples that illustrate the novel's prominence in highbrow Israeli culture are many and telling. Dan Miron, the *éminence grise* of the Israeli critical establishment, has consistently championed Shabtai as "the greatest Hebrew storyteller of his generation; its most measured, profound, nuanced and disciplined artist."[5] Young Israeli writers routinely acknowledge Shabtai's influence, as do leading Israeli filmmakers, including Asi Dayan and Amos Gitai (who adopted the novel to the screen in 1996). Articles about Shabtai, about his milieu,[6] and even about the different dishes depicted in his work (including recipes!)[7] are published periodically in Israel's major newspapers— the latest in 2016.[8] The novel has also inspired more communal types of worship. In 1994, on the sixtieth anniversary of Shabtai's birth, a marathon reading of *Past Continuous* (emulating Bloomsday, the annual celebration of James Joyce in Dublin) was held in Beit Bialik in Tel Aviv, a Mecca of

---

5. Yaakov Shabtai, "Postscript," in *Sof Davar* (*Past Perfect*) (Israel: Hakibbutz hameuchad, 1985), 247. *Sof Davar*, Shabtai's second and last novel, was published posthumously by the author's widow, Edna Shabtai, who also edited the manuscript together with Dan Miron.

6. Shabtai, like Mann in *Buddenbrooks*, Arthur Schnitzler in *Der Weg ins Freie*, and Virginia Woolf in *To the Lighthouse*, modeled many of his characters on his family and members of his close social circle.

7. See Chana Soker-Schwager, *Mechashef hashevet memeonot haovdim: Yaakov Shabtai batarbut hayisraelit* (Tel Aviv: Hakibbutz Hameuchad, 2007), 67–75.

8. See, Liat Alkaiam, "Why Did Goldman Commit Suicide: Revisiting Shabtai's *Past Continuous*" [in Hebrew] *Haaretz*, March 30, 2016. www.haaretz.co.il/magazine/the-edge/.premium-1.2898583.

the city's literati.⁹ Among the readers were some of Israel's most prominent writers, philosophers, journalists, actors, and politicians. Finally, in 2007, a survey of publishers and editors conducted by the *Maariv* newspaper named the novel the best work of prose fiction since 1948. As this overview of the novel's reception suggests, *Past Continuous* has come to stand for something more than a literary benchmark for Israel's left-leaning intelligentsia. In a country whose politics have shifted in recent decades consistently toward the religious right, the book has become something of a sacred text, and its author a "secular prophet."[10]

In the aforementioned essay of Howe's, where he lays out the suggestive comparison between Shabtai's figures and Faulkner's "Sartorises and the Compsons," he goes on to argue that artistic triumphs like *Past Continuous* and *The Sound and the Fury* become possible "when a writer gains possession of his own culture, uncovering its deepest sentiments and secrets."[11] This is no doubt true—if anything, too true. After all, what social novel of any distinction has ever been produced by a writer who has failed to see deeply into his or her culture? So, in this chapter, I would like to offer what I hope is a more precise description of Shabtai's achievement. On my proposed variation of Howe's words, what aligns Shabtai with Faulkner as well as with Roth and Wharton is not simply that these writers gained possession of their cultures, but that each gained possession of his or her society *as a culture*. That is, what is common to their novels is that each sees the cultural elite, with which its author identified, not by its own self-universalizing lights, but as a parochial and time-bound nexus of practices, beliefs, and institutions.

On the argument I have been advancing in this book, the twentieth-century emergence of novels depicting the cultural extinction of hegemonic social formations is an index of the deepening hold of the vocabulary of culture on the self-image of modern Western societies. For viewing one's own society in culturalist terms also entails regarding its social practices and institutions as historically emergent human creations that are, for that very reason, grounded in nothing more stable or enduring than their own self-perpetuating mechanisms of socialization. So long as the means of cul-

---

9. A similar event titled "Goldman Day" was held in 2016.
10. Soker-Schwager, *Mechashef hashevet*, 260.
11. Howe, "Absalom in Israel."

tural transmission (myths, canons, collective rituals) succeed in maintaining a sufficient degree of continuity between generations—such that the worldview of the one overlaps to a large degree with that of its successor—we can speak, with Edmund Burke, of culture "as a partnership . . . between those who are living, those who are dead and those who are to be born."[12] But once the process of transgenerational transmission breaks down, the members of the older generation find themselves in a position not unlike Newland Archer's and District Commissioner Trotta's: namely, that of standing witness to the ending of the way of life they recognize as their own, and thus of experiencing the strange hollowing out of identity that is peculiar to that fate.

This unsettling prospect, I have been arguing, can occur only to people whose sense of identity—both personal and collective—is bound up with the culturalist assumptions and metaphors that began to gain ground in the wake of the French Revolution. This is not to deny that "cultures" collapsed or died out (due to internecine conflict, genocide, foreign conquest, or exile) prior to that time. But the men and women who lived through those local extinction events did not process their experiences in the way we do now. Cultural extinction became a human possibility only when people started to think of themselves as products of their time, place, and milieu. We thus have no reason to suppose that our distant forebears, who did not conceive of their identities in these terms, were troubled by this prospect, nor that it will be a matter of concern for our distant descendants, whose ways of thinking and feeling may, for all we know, be wholly alien to our own. To accept this possibility is to come to terms with the parochial and timebound nature of the mental universe that we inhabit—an acceptance that is *itself* a consequence of adopting a thoroughgoing culturalist viewpoint. The promotion and dissemination of this viewpoint seem to me one of the main moral contributions of the novels at the center of this study.

Seen this way, what distinguishes Wharton's, Roth's, and Shabtai's novels from those of their literary predecessors is not only their descriptions of their respective milieus as complex social wholes. The ambition to total representation has been a stable feature of realism since the early nineteenth century. What sets *The Age of Innocence*, *The Radetzky March*, and *Past Continuous* apart from earlier realist works (while aligning them

---

12. Edmund Burke, *Reflections on the French Revolution* (London: J. M. Dent & Sons, 1951), 93.

with much nineteenth-century regionalist writing) is their emphasis on the frailty and ephemerality of the cultural worlds they construct. In each of these novels, the distinctive habits and belief systems of a social elite is presented in a way that subverts its members' self-image, exposing the tenuousness and contingency of everything that seems (to their characters) so firm and unimpeachable. Combining the realist aesthetics of solidity with the regionalist poetics of precarity, these novels effectively harmonize the two major literary traditions that issued from Maria Edgeworth's and Walter Scott's seminal novels.

In what follows, I shall begin by closely describing Shabtai's distinctive and highly innovative mode of narration, which I want to hold up as the most sophisticated formal medium yet devised for emplotting and communicating the culturalist outlook. In the second part of the chapter, I will turn to discuss Shabtai's close attention to his characters' intellectual lives, with special emphasis on his critical examination of the desire to transcend culture and time—the desire that his Goldman shares with Wharton's young Newland Archer. Though often read as a philosophical novel, *Past Continuous*, I will argue, looks askance at the philosophical dream of transcendence. It is a therapeutic text whose aim is not to offer an all-encompassing theory of life but to warn its intellectual reader against trying for such a theory in the first place. Shabtai's novel, I want to show, assumes a world to which neither religion nor philosophy—when understood as an attempt to transcend one's cultural and historical embeddedness—are adequate. Bringing Shabtai's sensitive treatment of the philosophical temperament into focus will not only challenge some of the dominant interpretations of *Past Continuous*; it will also help shed light on the antimetaphysical implications of the culturalist and historicist worldview that it projects and endorses.

"A world with no place to hide": Shabtai's Knowing Narrator

If any novel deserves to be called a "narrative of community," it is *Past Continuous*. This category was coined by Sandra Zagarell to describe regionalist texts where the individual lives of the characters are made ancillary to the depiction of the social body as a whole. Such narratives, writes Zagarell, tend to "ignore linear development or chronological sequence and remain in one geographic place. Rather than being constructed around conflict and progress, as novels usually are, narratives of community are rooted in process. They tend to be episodic, built primarily around the continuous small-scale negotiations and daily procedures through which communities sustain themselves."[13] Though set in a markedly urban rather than rural setting, Shabtai's novel fits this description to a tee, provided of course that we substitute Zagarell's emphasis on the life of a community with an emphasis on its demise.

At the foreground of the novel are three middle-aged men roughly of Shabtai's age: the morose and philosophically minded Goldman, the comically lecherous Caesar, and the artistic, withdrawn Israel. But while these figures serve as our entry point into the social world of the novel, they cannot in good conscience be called its protagonists. Indeed, *Past Continuous* is a novel without a hero. Goldman, Israel, and Caesar's joint function is to serve as triangulation points, helping the reader find her bearings in Little Tel Aviv's forbiddingly complex social network, but they do not stand at the narrative's center. No single character does. Instead, the narrative voice meanders between the biographies of over one hundred characters, tracing their familial, professional, and social connections to one another, recounting old feuds, frustrated longings, and buried secrets, to produce a dense social fabric that comprehends all the characters while centering on none. If there is a protagonist in *Past Continuous*, it is Little Tel Aviv itself.

The novel's lack of a unitary protagonist is mirrored by its lack of a central plot. In line with Zagarell's definition, *Past Continuous* is not a plot-driven work (which is partly why its storyline is so hard to summarize) but a text that seeks to exhaustively catalog, explain, and evaluate a "knowable community" at the moment of its collapse.[14] Shabtai's art, as Howe writes, is "an art of the group. A community is releasing its experience, a generation is sliding toward extinction."[15] And so, unlike Sarah Orne Jewett's *The Country of the Pointed Firs* (1896) or George Eliot's *Adam Bede* (1859) (which Zagarell uses as her examples), works that aim at establishing a restorative

---

13. The works that Zagarell identifies as falling within this category are regionalist sketches written in the latter half of the nineteenth century, mainly by "white women of the middle classes," and in "response to the social, economic, cultural, and demographic changes caused by industrialism, urbanization, and the spread of capitalism." But if my argument in this book is correct then the purview of Zagarell's study is too restrictive. See Sandra A. Zagarell, "Narrative of Community: The Identification of a Genre," *Signs* 13, no. 3 (1988): 498–527, 503.

14. Raymond Williams, *The Country and the City* (New York: Oxford University Press, 1973), 165–181.

15. Howe, "Absalom in Israel."

Burkean continuity between a broken present and "the common culture of the past," *Past Continuous* is concerned with underscoring the one-off quality of the cultural world whose exhaustion and disintegration it maps.[16]

What makes *Past Continuous* the definitive twentieth-century work of cultural extinction, however, is not only its brilliant thematic exploration of the human consequences of such a collective collapse (which I will explore in the second part of this chapter), but also the way it manifests the perspective of the community on the level of narrative form. The novel's signature sinuous sentences, its complex imbrication of temporal frames and its unusual handling of narrative voice all combine to construct a literary terrain that is the closest approximation of E.B. Tylor's ideal of culture as a "complex whole"—a closed interconnected system in which nothing has an autonomous or discreet existence.[17] As in Saussure's structuralist model of language, each individual element in Shabtai's Tel Aviv attains its identity by virtue of its relationship to other elements of its kind in what adds up to a vast interlocking semiotic system of differences "*without positive terms.*"[18] Shabtai, as Robert Alter observes, assumed that "we live . . . in the most complicating connexity."[19] His great achievement was to synthesize a narrative style that incorporates this culturalist principle into its very grammar.

Hebrew (biblical as well as modern) tends to favor relatively short, verb-driven sentences. Its typical rhythm, one might say, is more Ernest Hemingway than Henry James. Long subordinated constructions or elaborate adjectival prose tends to clash with the language's congenital preference for the compact and concise. Therefore, the initial encounter with Shabtai's prose, for Hebrew readers accustomed to the terseness of their native tongue, is often experienced as something of a shock. In its Hebrew original, the text confronts its reader as a single extended paragraph, a seamless expanse of

---

16. Zagarell, "Narrative of Community," 514.

17. Edward B. Tylor, "The Science of Culture," in Primitive Culture: Researches into the Development of Mythology, Philosophy, Religion, Art, and Custom (London: John Murray, 1871), 1.

18. Ferdinand de Saussure, *Course in General Linguistics*, trans. Wade Baskin (New York: McGraw-Hill, 1959), 120.

19. Robert Alter, *Hebrew and Modernism* (Bloomington: Indiana University Press, 1994), 98.

words that runs unbroken for 275 pages,[20] averaging about two sentences per page (with some extending for several pages).[21] These winding paratactic structures are, moreover, extraordinarily supple: shifting easily between present, past, and future; gliding in and out of Tel-Avivian apartments, cemeteries, and restaurants; and moving freely in and out of the characters' lives. Each of these figures (who, as mentioned above, number over a hundred) is introduced to the reader, critically evaluated according to his or her relative merits and demerits, before being allowed to recede back into the dense human backdrop, only to reappear unexpectedly somewhere down the line like an old acquaintance. In many cases, as in the famous opening lines of the novel—"Goldman's father died on the first of April, whereas Goldman himself committed suicide on the first of January"—a character's fate is given to us in advance, before we've had a chance to observe him or her in action.[22] In other cases, it is the past rather than the future that colors our perception of a person or a setting; as, for example, in the numerous instances where old Tel Aviv's vanished cityscapes are made to shimmer, palimpsest-like, through the urban developments that had displaced them. Slow, evenly paced and seemingly interminable, the novel's grammatical units weave a web of significance, in which each node—be it a person, place, or event—appears (to quote Christopher Herbert) as "a corollary of, consubstantial with, implied by, immanent in, all the others."[23] Little Tel Aviv thus bodies forth as a single, unified but not unitary field of significance whose "reality" is vouchsafed by the sheer density and interconnectedness (syntactic as well as semantic) of its parts. More like George Eliot in this respect than like any of his Hebrew predecessors, Shabtai's culturalist realism attains the stamp of authenticity from its conceit of recording what Eliot called "the stealthy convergence of human lots."[24]

---

20. The one exception is an inset advertisement for a body-building device called the "Bullworker," which is presented as a set of standalone sentences, thus briefly breaking the narrative's otherwise continuous flow.

21. These statistics are drawn from Moshe Ron, "*Zikhron Devarim*: ha'mishpat," [In Hebrew] *Siman Kriaa* 16–17 (April 1983): 272–278, 273.

22. Yaakov Shabtai, *Past Continuous*, trans. Dalya Bilu (New York: Overlook Press, 2002), 3.

23. Christopher Herbert, *Culture and Anomie* (Chicago: University of Chicago Press, 1991), 5.

24. George Eliot, *Middlemarch* (Peterborough: Broadview Press, 2004), 102.

For all its complexity, however, *Past Continuous* does not revel in difficulty for difficulty's sake. Despite its unceasing procession of characters, its constant shifts between temporal frames, and repeated juxtaposition of memory and fact, at no point does the novel's reader find herself forced to puzzle out obscurities, circumnavigate rhetorical roadblocks, or decipher abstruse allusions. The narration, which is delivered in a straightforward, fully idiomatic Hebrew, regularly supplies the reader with all the information she needs in order to keep her bearings in the ever-thickening welter of places, anecdotes, and characters. Incidents mentioned in passing at one moment are almost always revisited and clarified before long; characters glimpsed at the early parts of the novel are usually fleshed out at later ones. As the Hebrew title of novel suggests (*zikhron devarim* means memorandum or protocol) Shabtai's narrator is intent on eliminating any ambiguity or ambivalence. Everything is to be revealed, analyzed, justified; nothing is to remain mysterious or puzzling. It is a verbal performance without precedence in twentieth-century literature (Hebrew or otherwise) that needs to be experienced firsthand to be appreciated.

The following, then, is a description of Ephraim, a representative of the old Zionist guard, whose death (along with that of Goldman, his son) is announced in the novel's opening line. To recapture something of the relentlessness of the Hebrew original, I've eliminated the paragraph breaks introduced into the English translation:

> He knew what was right and good, not only for himself but also for others, and could not tolerate error or sin, and for him every error, beginning with the breaking of a cup or the ill-considered purchase of a pair of shoes and ending with stealing or adultery, was a sin, and despite his own inherent generosity and even sentimentality he could not bring himself to forgive anyone, even his own family or friends, because his integrity verged on insanity and his sense of justice was dark and murky, and above all because he had a tyrannical, uncontrollable desire to impose his principles on the whole world, which went heedlessly along its different, lawless ways, leaving Goldman's father battling between disappointment and rage. There were always people who didn't know what was good for them and people who made mistakes, never mind those who actually sinned, often consciously, and in the end everyone violated the proper order of things, everyone, that is, except him, since he was the representative of this order, and accordingly he never knew a single hour of peace of mind,

and his whole life, which was full of hostility and humiliation, passed in denunciation and accusations and argument. Because of his principles he succeeded in quarrelling with almost all his friends and acquaintances, and those he did not quarrel with he ostracized and drove from the house—all except Joseph Levitan, Avinoam and Sonia and Hanoch's father—surrounding himself with a protective wall of loneliness, but by virtue of the same principles he also succeeded in overcoming his loneliness and disappointments and his despair when his daughter Naomi, Goldman's older sister, was killed in a traffic accident—according to one version—or committed suicide—according to another version. He received the news with a terrible outburst of violence and rage, and buried his daughter with a stony face and dry eyes, since in the depths of his heart he had turned his back on her a long time ago, because she was having an affair with a married man, apparently an Englishman at that, and according to his principles she deserved to be punished, and she was punished. It was only at night when he switched off the light and lay down on his bed, which for some years now had been separated from Regina's bed, that he turned his face to the wall and covered his head with the blanket and wept bitterly, but then he recovered and wiped his eyes with the sheet and toward morning fell asleep with his lips tightly clamped together.[25]

The first thing to note here is that the despite the surface similarity between Shabtai's serpentine sentences and the kind of writing one finds in Proust or Woolf, the narrative technique used in *Past Continuous* is in fact at the antipodes of Proust's and Virginia Woolf's lyrical, introspective styles.[26] Shabtai's narrative of community does not deny psychological depth to its characters, but it never adopts their perspective or invites its reader to share in their experience phenomenologically—from "inside" their consciousness as it were. The doctrine of the primacy of the individual—the doctrine that Romanticism bequeathed to the high modernists—is wholly eschewed here, as is the modern preference for showing over telling. Ephraim is laid out and dissected down to "the depths of his heart," but from a carefully maintained analytic distance and in a dispassionate (though not necessarily

---

25. Shabtai, *Past Continuous*, 18–19.
26. See Miron, "Hazikaron ke'idea," 24–25.

indifferent or unsympathetic) voice. The character's distinctive thought style is made available to us through free indirect discourse ("[there] were always people who didn't know what was good for them"), but it is presented as merely one more piece of evidence, on par with his behavior at Naomi's funeral or the sterility of his marriage with Regina, to be adduced in corroboration of the narrator's final judgment of the man. *Past Continuous* is, in this sense, the least polyphonous of novels. Its characters are never "ideologically authoritative and independent," in the manner that Bakhtin admired in Dostoevsky.[27] Authority rests fully and exclusively with the brooding monologic narrator.

Not for nothing does Howe claim that "the voice of *Past Continuous* achieves an authority quite beyond that of the omniscient narrator in the traditional novel."[28] For Shabtai's narrative voice not only transcends the limitations of intradiegetic first-person narration; it also has no qualms about handing down summary judgments on the men and women whom it summons before us. We thus learn of one character that "he was, in fact, an arrogant man," or of another that he was "absolutely shameless, both in his cruelty and in his sycophancy."[29] The liberality with which Shabtai's narrator dispenses such verdicts as well as the tone of composed assurance in which they are delivered set *Past Continuous* at odds with the prevailing literary tendencies of the last hundred and fifty years. As Moshe Ron argues, since the latter part of the nineteenth century, the realist novel has tended, by and large, to gravitate toward reticent narrators that refrain from passing explicit judgments,[30] preferring instead to show their characters in social play. This is what Wharton does when she teaches us to recognize Archer's pliability and conformity by dramatizing his capitulation to his society, or Roth when he unfolds District Commissioner Trotta's deep humanity through his changing relationship with his son Carl Joseph. Shabtai's narrative voice, in contrast, rarely shows; it tells—and this with a degree of finality that seems to brook no dissent. Consider the following description of Erwin, another member of the fading older generation:

---

27. Mikhail Bakhtin, *Problems in Dostoevsky's Poetics*, ed. and trans. Caryl Emerson (Minneapolis: University of Minnesota Press, 1984), 5.

28. Howe, "Absalom in Israel."

29. Shabtai, *Past Continuous*, 63, 240.

30. Ron, "Zikhron Devarim: ha'mishpat," 273–273.

Erwin, who in his youth had been a Zionist and a socialist and who had emigrated to Eretz Yisrael as a pioneer and lived for a number of years as a member of a kibbutz, continued to regard himself as a Zionist and a socialist with political, social, and moral principles, and although during the course of time these principles had been subjected to an almost imperceptible process of erosion until they were distorted beyond recognition, nevertheless Erwin, who had come to an agreement with himself that in the last analysis there was always a gap between the world of values and that of action, and that actually everything was permitted, went on believing that in some roundabout way he still stuck to his principles.[31]

We do not need to wait until we have had a chance to observe Erwin's behavior to know what we are to think of him. Having only just been introduced to this former socialist and *halutz* [pioneer], we already know him better than he knows himself. It is we, not Erwin, who understand that the principles to which he continues to pay lip service have been "distorted beyond recognition"; it is we, not him, who recognize the full extent of his betrayal of his former self. Whereas he goes on believing "in some roundabout way" in his integrity, we know better. To enter Shabtai's Tel Aviv, as Ron succinctly sums up the accumulating effect of this narrative method, is to find oneself in "a world with no place to hide, with no real interiority (except in madness), where everything is revealed and known, or can in principle be revealed and known."[32]

Confronted with this display of narratorial mastery, conventional critical parlance inclines us to reach for the term *omniscience*. The narrator's ability to peer into the hearts and minds of its characters, its unrestrained movement across space and time, and the sheer scope and density of the represented reality all recommend this term to us. As Richard Maxwell remarks in connection with Dickens's vaunted mastery of Victorian London: to grasp a cultural world "all at once . . . as a physical and moral totality [must be] a God-like task."[33] And indeed, a number of influential readings

---

31. Shabtai, *Past Continuous*, 92.

32. Ron, "Zikhron Devarim: ha'mishpat," 277.

33. Richard Maxwell, "Dickens' Omniscience," *ELH* 46, no. 2 (1979): 290–313, 290.

of *Past Continuous* (most notably Miron's, Howe's, and Gershon Shaked's) have invoked the concept of omniscience or one of its cognates to describe Shabtai's ostensibly all-knowing, all-seeing, and all-judging narrator.

It is not clear, however, that omniscience is a useful term for describing Shabtai's mode of narration or, for that matter, third-person extradiegetic narrators generally. As Jonathan Culler, speaking to the more general issue, argues, the idea of omniscience collapses a set of independent phenomena—"the conventional establishment of narrative authority, the imaginative or telepathic translation of inner thoughts, the playful and self-reflexive foregrounding of creative actions, and the production of wisdom through the multiplication of perspectives and the teasing out of intricacies in human affairs"—thus obfuscating rather than clarifying the distinct textual effects of each of these separate narrative functions.[34] If we habitually conceive of extradiegetic narrators on the model of God, Culler goes on to claim, it may be because we habitually assume that narrating agents come in only two variations: "mortal persons [or] a divine person." Given this range of options, those narrators that do not belong to the first category inevitably fall into the second, thus leaving the critic with a resounding but dubious narrator-as-God metaphor.[35]

Past Continuous makes the limitations of this forced choice particularly salient. First, for all its flaunted mastery over the represented world, Shabtai's narrator refrains from engaging in what Culler calls the "production of wisdom."[36] Though the novel is populated by characters who obsess over the so-called Great Questions—death, salvation, the problem of free will, and others—the narrating voice itself never philosophizes or pronounces on the human condition. At no point in the text is the reader offered the kind of exportable maxims that characterize Trollope's and Eliot's narrators (think, again, of those famous one-liners from *Middlemarch*: "the quickest of us walk about well wadded with stupidity" or "for the growing good of the world is partly dependent on unhistoric acts").[37] The narrator's knowingness and moral authority, unimpeded when it comes to the lives of the novel's characters, does not extend beyond the cultural and geographical boundaries of Little Tel Aviv. It is as though this cultural locale represents the only locus of value and meaning in what is otherwise an entropic expanse of

---

34. Jonathan Culler, "Omniscience," *Narrative* 12, no. 1 (2004): 22–34, 32.
35. Culler, "Omniscience," 25.
36. Culler, "Omniscience," 32.
37. George Eliot, *Middlemarch* (Peterborough: Broadview Press, 2004), 180, 640.

non-sense. Within that culturally demarcated space, the narrator's authority is absolute; beyond it, it makes no pretense to wisdom.

Further, when we examine the actual phrasing of the novel's unequivocal judgments of its characters we find that these often seem "too one-dimensional and simplistic to be accepted as omnisciently reliable," as Chana Soker-Schwager observes.[38] At one point in the novel, a character is briefly introduced only to be brushed aside as "a mean man"; at another, a single-sentence analysis of Eliezra culminates in her indictment as "a vain and capricious woman."[39] Such displays of infallibility seem more a parody of omniscience than an expression of it. Whose perspective, then, is invoked in such passages? How are we to understand this peculiarly moralistic narrator? Soker-Schwager suggests that Shabtai's mode of narration is best viewed as a variation on *skaz*, in which the narrator becomes a representative member of the community whose voice enjoys no special privilege over the voices of the other characters. Arguing in a similar vein, Shai Ginsburg has more recently claimed that the markedly one-sided quality of the novel's apparent omniscient assertions is intended to signal its narrator's unreliability, thus encouraging us to question rather than uncritically accept the ideological assumptions that underwrite its interventions.[40] While both these interpretations seem to me an advance on the earlier critical consensus regarding the alleged omniscience of Shabtai's narrator and the source of its authority, I would like to present a somewhat different view—one that is more in line with the culturalist grammar informing the novel as a whole.

On this view, derived from Elizabeth Ermarth's discussion of realist narration in *Realism and Consensus in the English Novel* (1983), Shabtai's narrator is construed neither as a human person nor as a divine one—indeed, not as a person at all. Rather, it is a "a specifier of consensus": a coordinating perspective that cannot be identified with the embodied point of view of any single individual, but from whose vantage point a shared social world comes into view as a unified totality.[41] To put this perspective in the terms of the present study, in Shabtai's novel it is *culture itself that speaks*. (This

---

38. Soker-Schwager, *Mechashef hashevet*, 298.

39. Shabtai, *Past Continuous*, 99, 47.

40. See Shai Ginsburg, *Rhetoric and Nation: The Formation of Hebrew Culture 1880–1990* (Syracuse, NY: Syracuse University Press, 2014), 317–335.

41. Elizabeth Ermarth, *Realism and Consensus in the English Novel* (Princeton, NJ: Princeton University Press, 1981), 65–66.

claim need not involve reifying culture into an "entity" or some kind of Hegelian "subject," whose essence precedes its existence.[42] Culture *just is* the shared habits of speech and action that distinguish one human community from another, not an essence or thing that precedes these performative iterations.) In its function as the specifier of consensus, the narrator is, in a sense, speaking in the voice of each member of the community, but only from that part that each member shares with his or her cultural peers. At the same time, however, because no person is defined exclusively by what she has in common with her peers, the narrator could also be said to speak from a position beyond or outside any single individual. It is this relative distance—a "distance" that is nothing but the sum of internal differences between the characters—that enables the narrator to grasp the social field as though from the "outside," as a discrete totality. But this outsidedness is not a position above or beyond the moral and epistemological horizon of the represented world. Shabtai's narrator remains anchored to that social reality, even while it reflexively brings it into view as a circumscribed site of meaning and value. Seen this way, Shabtai's narrator is neither a human speaker nor an autonomous semi-divine entity, but a symphonic, collective intonation. Unified but not unitary, it is the articulated distillation of a shared ethos.

By way of illustration, let us look at a moment from the conclusion of the novel. The following scene describes Zipporah, a venerated pillar of the community, but who is now old and infirm, as she is wheeled into a wedding ceremony of one the novel's minor characters:

> At that moment there was a stir in the crowd and Zipporah appeared in the doorway to the hall. She was sitting in a wheelchair and Esther pushed her slowly among the guests, who came up to her one after the other and respectfully, admiringly, and also affectionately shook her hand and kissed her cheek and exchanged a few words with her, and Goldman remained standing where he was and he looked at her and saw her approaching him in her wheelchair—a small, erect woman in a dark woolen dress, with one foot shod in a white canvas shoe peeping out from under it, her short, curly gray hair tied in a black ribbon and her little face, as rosy and wrinkled as an old apple, shining with

---

42. Ermarth, *Realism and Consensus*, x.

intelligence and authority which were nothing but the expression of her own integrity and her confident and tireless affirmation of life with all its difficulties and suffering.⁴³

This passage stages a gradual movement from the external camera-eye view of Zipporah's arrival, through Goldman's reported impressions, and finally to the narrator's evaluative summary of her. On the first level, Zipporah's social stature is conveyed indirectly: by the stir caused by her appearance and by the way the guests line up to pay homage to her. This is followed by a closer view of Zipporah's person, as focalized from Goldman's perspective. Now the reader is invited to take in the details of her physical appearance, the toll that diabetes has taken on her, as well as her modesty, indicated by her simple dress. The likening of her face to a "rosy and wrinkled" apple is still anchored to Goldman's private allusions, but with the conclusive "nothing but" we move beyond his perspective to that of the narrator, who then proceeds to lay bare the essence of her moral identity: her "integrity" and "tireless affirmation of life." The voice is no longer Goldman's own, but it includes his perspective as well as the perspectives of the other guests. For it is the voice of the community that speaks in this and similar passages. Its summary of Zipporah reveals her not as she is in herself—a meaningless proposition in Shabtai's culturalist world—but as she is (or was) *for those people*.

Shabtai's narrative voice, as we see, speaks not from some godlike vantage point but from within Little Tel Aviv and the story that it had told itself about itself. It reveals that community's internal contradictions, its parochialism and ideological violence, but also something of the grandeur of its original ambitions and the inevitable disillusionment that followed the establishment of the State of Israel as revolutionary vision hardened into prosaic fact. Indeed, *Past Continuous* is, in many respects, a prolonged quarrel with the culture in which its author was reared: with its self-righteousness and inflated view of itself as the culmination of history's grand design for the Jewish people. Importantly, however, the novel's critique of this milieu—the AHUSALIM—is not launched from an alternative (anti- or post-Zionist) worldview.⁴⁴ Shabtai, as Soker-Schwager argues, remained a loyal son of the Zionist labor movement to the end, identifying with its

---

43. Shabtai, *Past Continuous*, 373.
44. Soker-Schwager, *Mechashef hashevet*, 259.

ideological program and lamenting its felt retreat following 1977. Insofar as his novel reveals and condemns this movement's failures and excesses, it is on the basis of its own values and aspirations—those embodied in figures like Zipporah—not from the position of universal judge and jury. Consider, for instance, the novel's description of Ephraim's absolutism: "He was a Zionist and a Socialist and believed in plain living, hard work, morality, and progress . . . all this as part of a system of clear, fixed, uncompromising principles embracing every area of life and action, which he never doubted for an instant despite all the external changes and difficulties, and from which he saw no reason to deviate in the slightest degree."[45] *Past Continuous* does not attack the substantive articles of Ephraim's Zionist-Socialist creed; what it unremittingly lampoons is the conviction, shared by several of the novel's characters, that these values are part of a "system" of commandment, that they express some kind of "proper order,"[46] which transcends the realm of cultural compromise and negotiation. For it is this belief—the belief, to quote Isaiah Berlin, "that somewhere, in the past or in the future, in divine revelation or in the mind of an individual thinker, in the pronouncements of history or science, or in the simple heart of an uncorrupted good man, there is a final solution"—that drives Ephraim's intolerance and violence, and which destroys the lives of so many of the novel's other characters.[47] Shabtai shared Berlin's mistrust of what he called "[our] deep and incurable metaphysical need": the need to hook our moral identities to an order that is immune to the contingencies of language, culture and chance. It is the belief in the possibility of such anchoring that gives rise to Ephraim's "tyrannical, uncontrollable desire to impose his principles on the whole world," as well as to Archer's desperate proposal to Ellen that she escape with him "into a world where words like that—categories like that—won't exist."[48] What is common to these two characters—otherwise so unlike—is the need to believe in an Other to culture, in some ground or source to which they might attach their values and beliefs, thus ensuring not only their objectivity but also their imperishability. Like Wharton, Shabtai makes

---

45. Shabtai, *Past Continuous*, 17–18.

46. Shabtai, *Past Continuous*, 18.

47. Isaiah Berlin, "Two Concepts of Liberty," in *Liberty*, ed. Henry Hardy (Oxford: Oxford University Press), 212.

48. Shabtai, *Past Continuous*, 18; Edith Wharton, *The Age of Innocence*, Norton Critical Edition, ed. Candace Waid (New York: W. W. Norton, 2003), 174.

dark comedy of this attempt. His novel, as I will now turn to argue, is a therapeutic text: one that, by dramatizing the futility of the desire to reach beyond time and culture, seeks to defuse it.

On Knowing and Dying: Shabtai's Anti-Philosophicalism

As I've pointed out at the beginning of this chapter, no Israeli novel is nearer and dearer to contemporary Israeli intellectuals than *Past Continuous*. Teeming with philosophical discussions and ideas, Shabtai's novel may be viewed as the Hebrew counterpart to Musil's *The Man without Qualities* (1930–1943), Jean-Paul Sartre's *Nausea* (1938), and John Barth's *The End of the Road* (1958). Visit an Israeli home where these or similar titles grace the bookshelves, and you will almost certainly find *Past Continuous* there, too—flanked by a white hardcover of Nietzsche in translation and a tattered compilation of essays by Israeli polymath Yeshayahu Leibovitch.

One of the reasons for the novel's ardent highbrow following is the serious attention it devotes to the intellectual lives of its characters. Prior to Shabtai, post-1948 Israeli literature's attitude toward the figure of the intellectual ranged between wariness and hostility. Despite being hatched in the imagination of central European urban literati, Eretz-Israeli Zionism had little time for the homegrown variety. Social veneration, during those precarious early years, was reserved for more practical types: the intrepid *halutz*, the industrious *kibbutznik*, and the stalwart soldier. The intellectual, meanwhile, was something of an embarrassment to the reigning ethos (so much so that the very term, as Nissim Kalderon comments as late as 1988, "is still faintly embarrassing in Hebrew").[49] This instinctual aversion was echoed by the blatantly engaged literature of the era. While the protagonists of the early Israeli novel, notes Tzipora Kagan, were often shown to wrestle with the pressing "economical and political problems" that beset the young state, "metaphysical questions, including philosophical and theological [ones] were pushed beyond the pale."[50] As a consequence, notwithstanding a few

---

49. Nissim Kalderon, "Eize gvulot ata mesugal lesamen bamidron," in *Hargasha shel makom* (Tel Aviv: Hakibbutz Hameuchad, 1988), 21–42, 32.
50. Tzipora Kagan, "Sifrut shel shki'a ke'sifrut shel hitgalut," *Moznaim* 74, no. 6 (2000): 4–6, 5.

notable exceptions,[51] intellectuals were virtually absent from the landscape of the pre-1977 Israeli novel. As Shabtai himself commented on one occasion: "An entire subdivision of perfectly kosher *sabres* had been thoroughly excluded from the representation of the *sabre* in Hebrew literature. I am referring to the children of the *moshavot*[52] and the old *yishuv*, to the sons of merchants and of the petit-bourgeoisie, to all those pale, refined, cultured types."[53] By way of a corrective, *Past Continuous* offers its reader a gallery of "cultured," cerebral types who worry, solemnly and earnestly, about ultimate things: the value of life in an entropic universe; the meaning of suicide; the problem of free will; the question of suffering; the existence of God; and the craving for metaphysical certainty. They include Goldman, the forty-something lawyer-cum-spiritual seeker; Uncle Lazar, the erstwhile revolutionist purist turned stoic; Manfred, the one-time rationalist academic turned skeptic; Besh, the unreconstructed nihilist; as well as more minor figures, such as Zahara's defeated husband Phillip, and others. In marked contrast to his Israeli precursors, Shabtai devotes significant swaths of his novel to these characters' intellectual biographies, spiritual torments, and occasional philosophical debates. Case in point: "[Manfred] said [to Goldman] that he did not believe in the absolute autonomy of man . . . that he had come to the conclusion that a rational morality was impossible and that the achievements of reason were mainly in the area of destruction, including its own self-destruction, of course, by the admission of its own limitations, and that this was its strength, but in the area of construction reason had not achieved much, because in the last analysis life was a purposeless chaos and therefore in order to build anything you needed something which

---

51. These exceptions include Herbst in S.Y. Agnon's *Shira* (1971), Doctor Ginat and Gabriel Gamzo in Agnon's "Edo and Enam" (1948); A.B. Yehoshua's narrator in "Mul hayearot" (1963), a history student working to complete his thesis on the crusades; and Amos Oz's Michael Gonen, a Hebrew University doctoral student, in *My Michael* (1968). Yet the intellectualism of these figures is an ancillary feature that is used to enhance their function within the symbolic economy of the narrative as a whole. Michael Gonen's Apollonian rationalism, for example, functions as the foil to his wife's Dionysian tempestuousness, within the overall Manichean scheme of Oz's novel, not as a theme in its own right.

52. The Israeli *moshava* was an early form of agricultural settlement. As opposed to the more collectivized *moshavim* and *kibbutzim*, lands in the *moshavot* were privately owned.

53. Shabtai's comment is taken from a 1980 symposium on "The Figure of the Sabre in Hebrew Literature." Quoted in Soker-Schwager, *Mechashef hashevet*, 131.

transcended pure reason."[54] As suggested by the tone and substance of this passage (to which I will return later), the denizens of Shabtai's moribund Little Tel Aviv do not go gently into that good night; they philosophize along the way to their cultural extinction.

Impressed by the proliferation of such passages in the novel, many of Shabtai's early critics have described *Past Continuous* as a philosophical as well as literary achievement. As in all matters Shabtai, it was Miron who set the tone early on, arguing that the novel's sprawling social panorama, its regionalist authenticity and its close depiction of familial entanglements are all "but illustrations of more general and abstract truths." The novel's true meaning, argued Miron, lies not in its ethnographic realism but in its hypostasizing of memory, which "[breaking] free of the limits of the individual consciousness . . . becomes an idea, almost a metaphysical principle . . . a kind of autonomous logos."[55] Gershon Shaked soon followed suit, discovering in *Past Continuous* the workings of a "non-arbitrary dialectical force . . . whose different variations one finds in Hegel, Marx and Spengler."[56] Kagan describes *Past Continuous* as "redemptive literature," claiming that the novel affords its readers "a glimpse into the infinite dimension of our world."[57] Soker-Schwager, critical of the approaches of her predecessors, cautiously describes the book as "a 'philosophical' novel about the impossibility of philosophy."[58] Miron's choice to eulogize the recently deceased Shabtai as not only the best craftsman of his generation but also as its "greatest metaphysician" is exemplary of this critical tendency.[59]

The temptation to read a philosophical meaning into Shabtai's chronicle of cultural extinction, I want to claim in this final section, should be resisted. It should be resisted not only on theoretical grounds—because it demotes literary narrative, as the New Critics argued, to the auxiliary

---

54. Shabtai, *Past Continuous*, 363.

55. Miron, "Hazikaron ke'idea," 22–23.

56. Gershon Shaked, *Hasiporet haivrit: 1880–1980*, vol. 4 (Tel Aviv: Hakibbutz Hameuchad, 1993), 382.

57. Kagan, "Sifrut shel shki'a," 4–5.

58. Soker-Schwager, *Mechashef hashevet*, 274.

59. Miron is in fact quoting the early scholar of Hebrew literature Fishel Lachover, who used this epithet to describe Hebrew modernist Uri Nissan Gnessin. See Dan Miron, "Afterword," in Yaakov Shabtai, *Sof Davar* (Tel Aviv: Siman Kria'a and Hakibbutz Hameuchad), 247.

role of vehicle for an abstract paraphrasable core—but primarily because, by looking for riches where they are scant, such an approach obscures the novel's actual achievement. Shabtai, it should be admitted, possessed neither Mann's prodigious learning and capacity for allusion nor Borges's startling knack for producing mind-twisting vignettes. He does not use his novel as a platform for the interrogation of ideas, in the manner of Musil or Barth, or for unfolding a philosophical view, à la Camus or Sartre. His novel's strength lies not in the philosophical views it purportedly imparts but in what it has to show us *about* philosophy, or, more specifically, about the need to hold philosophical views in the first place. To describe Shabtai as the "greatest metaphysician" of his generation is to suggest that *Past Continuous* has something philosophically important to tell us. But, as I see it, the novel's real contribution consists in helping us see something important about philosophy.

Shabtai, I like to think, would have agreed with this description. In an interview conducted four years after the publication of *Past Continuous*, he described his aesthetic preferences as follows: "I very much prefer the surface [of the work] to be more or less flat. . . . I don't like it when a text carries a kind of hump of ideas and all sorts of symbols."[60] This statement might seem hard to square with the profusion of philosophical discussions and concepts that confront the reader of his novel. If any novel carries such a "hump of ideas," one might object, it is *Past Continuous*. But the contradiction is only apparent. What Shabtai decries in this passage is idea-driven prose, not the depiction of idea-driven human lives. Shabtai was keenly interested in the power of ideas to shape lives—a recurring theme in his work. What he rejected, at least as I read his remark, is the notion that novels (to quote Miron) are in the business of illustrating "general and abstract truths." In my view, the critical challenge we face when confronting *Past Continuous* is how to make interpretive sense of its obvious preoccupation with philosophy without philosophizing the work itself.

What Shabtai does in *Past Continuous*, I will now turn to show, is to foreground a series of characters who are consumed by what John Dewey called "the quest for certainty," in order to analyze and ironize this intellec-

---

60. Ilana Zuckerman, "Shabtai, Yaakov: Hareayon ha'acharon" [Yaakov Shabtai: The Last Interview], *Yedioth Achronot* (April 9, 1981).

tual type.⁶¹ *Past Continuous* does not share the metaphysical obsessions that variously determine the lives of Goldman, Uncle Lazar, and Manfred. It is concerned with revealing the motivational infrastructure that underlies the metaphysical cast of mind. On this reading, far from sponsoring a philosophical worldview, *Past Continuous* is in fact a cautionary tale, warning its reader against the desire to philosophize, against the wish to reach beyond narrative and culture.

To view Shabtai's novel in this way is to regard it as a therapeutic text in the sense used by Richard Rorty when describing the mature work of Wittgenstein, Heidegger, and Dewey. As Rorty tells it, after spending their youth trying to formulate "an ultimate context for thought," these philosophers devoted their later years to the attempt to dissuade would-be system-builders from undertaking similar projects.⁶² With the authority of rehabilitated metaphysicians, they strove to discredit the assumptions and metaphors that had long sustained the philosophical tradition and that had captivated their younger selves. Their later anti-metaphysical texts should be read as "therapeutic rather than constructive, edifying rather than systematic, designed to make the reader question his own motives for philosophizing rather than to supply him with a new philosophical program."⁶³ As they came to view the matter, the very need for a philosophical system discloses an essentially religious wish to anchor one's identity to some fixed framework, such that might absolve the metaphysician from the vulnerability and temporariness of human life.

Shabtai had no stake in the specialized debates on system building, Cartesianism, or truth as representation to which Rorty's intellectual heroes made their contributions. But *Past Continuous* can nevertheless fruitfully be read as part of a therapeutic, anti-metaphysical tradition that includes the kind of cautionary philosophical tales found in Dewey's *Reconstruction in Philosophy* (1926), Wittgenstein's *Philosophical Investigations* (1953), and Rorty's own *Philosophy and the Mirror of Nature* (1979). A fellow traveler, Shabtai shared these card-carrying philosophers' suspicion of the tendency to theorize and universalize the terms of one's existence. Like them, as we'll

---

61. John Dewey. *The Quest for Certainty*, in *John Dewey: The Later Works, 1925–1953* (Carbondale and Edwardsville: Southern Illinois University Press, 1984).

62. Richard Rorty, *Philosophy and the Mirror of Nature* (Princeton, NJ: Princeton University Press, 1979), 5.

63. Rorty, *Mirror of Nature*, 5.

soon see, he too repudiated the demand for justification and validation from above, and viewed the desire to system as the mark of a distinct intellectual disposition or temperament—one that needs to be isolated, described, and overcome.

Past Continuous can lay claim to yet another tradition concerned with questioning the very practice of philosophizing: that of the anti-philosophical satire as practiced by Aristophanes, Voltaire, George Eliot, and Woolf. Neurotic, self-obsessed, pietistic, and ultimately self-destructive, his Goldman is the direct descendant of Eliot's Casaubon and Woolf's Mr. Ramsay—men driven by the futile desire to fasten an incontestable mental grip on the universe, to discover the key that opens all locks, to make final sense of it all. Shabtai's "anti-philosophicalism," to borrow Michael Lackey's term,[64] consists of dramatizing the moral and psychological perils that attend to the intellectual obsession common to these characters—the selfsame obsession that the early Heidegger and the late Wittgenstein both sought to surmount and neutralize.[65]

To describe philosophy, at bottom, as the expression of a particular intellectual temperament is to broaden the term's scope beyond its usual definitions as a branch of knowledge, an academic discipline, or a textual tradition. A philosopher in the fuzzy, nonprofessional sense that I evoke here is an intellectual who has been touched by the Platonist yearning for the eternal and unchanging, and who therefore spends her life seeking access to what Derrida has called "a full presence beyond the reach of play," or what Shabtai, in his portrait of Ephraim, describes as a "system of clear, fixed, uncompromising principles."[66] The self-image that informs this search is propped up by two master tropes: that of man-as-knower and that of truth-as-liberating. In combination, these metaphors give rise to the belief that salvation runs through the mind, that knowing the truth is redemptive.

---

64. Michael Lackey, "Modernist Anti-Philosophicalism and Virginia Woolf's Critique of Philosophy," *Journal of Modern Literature* 29, no. 4 (2006): 76–98.

65. For an account of the late Wittgenstein's turn away from the foundational ambitions of the *Tractatus* as a foil for the late Heidegger's retreat into "the escapist mood in which the *Tractatus* was written," see Richard Rorty, "Wittgenstein, Heidegger, and the Reification of Language," in *Essays on Heidegger and Others: Philosophical Papers* (Cambridge: Cambridge University Press, 1991), 52.

66. Jacques Derrida, *Writing and Difference*, trans. Alan Bass (Chicago: University of Chicago Press, 1978), 279; Shabtai, *Past Continuous*, 17.

It is this belief that Shabtai makes the engine of Goldman's personality: "Goldman, who could not endure the experience of 'being-in-the-world' [*havayat hakiyum*], had decided to turn over a new leaf in his life—which in this particular instance meant the absolute liberation from it and the transition to a new way of life, or to use his own expression: 'a different mode of being' [*tsurat havaya akheret*] possessing absolute freedom and complete certainty."[67] What marks Goldman as a philosopher is not his wish for freedom or certainty. The desire to liberate oneself from constraints or to assure oneself of the reasonableness of one's actions and beliefs need not be metaphysical. Nor, for that matter, is the wish for "a different mode of being," if understood to mean the desire to reimagine and thus remake oneself. What makes Goldman into a metaphysician, rather, is his desire for "*absolute* freedom and *complete* certainty" (emphases mine). These adjectives do more than modify their nouns; they disclose Goldman's otherworldliness: his negation of this world—the world of history and culture—in favor of a world of unchanging intelligible essences. For, as Dewey argues, "the only universality and certainty is in a region above experience, that of the rational and conceptual."[68] It is this hankering after the immutable and timeless that marks Goldman as a philosopher.

That Shabtai was consciously establishing his character's affinity to the metaphysical tradition is evidenced by Goldman's jargon-laden speech. In Hebrew, the abstract nouns "*havaya*" [being] and "*kiyum*" [existence] belong to a much more rarified register than their English cognates. While "being" and "existence" may pop up in a host of quotidian contexts, "*havaya*" and "*kiyum*" are recherché terms that connote the atmosphere of a university philosophy seminar.[69] Shabtai's choice to place these abstract nouns in quotation marks (i.e., in Goldman's own voice) is meant to alert us that Goldman's wide-ranging reading—"in all kinds of scientific fields, as well as literature and current affairs, sociology and psychology, travel diaries, biographies, books about religion and geology and history"—presumably also includes some contemporary philosophy, whence he borrows the half-digested terminology that routinely crops up in his speeches.[70]

---

67. Shabtai, *Past Continuous*, 4.
68. John Dewey, *Reconstruction in Philosophy* (Mineola, NY: Dover, 2004), 46.
69. Dalya Bilu's apt choice to translate these phrases using Heideggerian neologisms indicate her attunement to these nuances in Shabtai's diction.
70. Shabtai, *Past Continuous*, 72.

But the conspicuous use of quotation marks, which punctuate the passage's flow, serves another important function. By presenting the passage's sound bites ("being-in-the-world," "different mode of being") in Goldman's own voice, the text opens an ironic gap between the narrator's view of Goldman and his philosophized view of himself. Keeping this irony-generating disjunction of voices in mind is necessary if we are to avoid the error made by Shabtai's earlier critics: namely, that of modeling the interpretation of the text on Goldman's own interpretation of his world. In my view, by trying to penetrate beyond narrative to the alleged philosophical meaning of the text, these critics effectively replicate (on the interpretative level) the procedure for which Goldman is censured on the diegetic level. If, however, we manage to keep the novel's ironic treatment of Goldman's metaphysical yearnings in view, we will be able to read his philosophical utterances not as windows into the novel's purported "deep" meaning or as bits of extractable wisdom, but as part of its critical portrait of an intellectual type.

Rather than have us take Goldman's philosophizing at face value, Shabtai invites us to regard it, along with the fantasy of "a different mode of being," as abortive attempts to use theory in order to circumvent emotional impasses, which are biographical and sociohistorical—not metaphysical—in nature. Two such impasses loom large in Goldman's life. The first is the ruinous psychological legacy of his father's violent tyranny; the second is the cultural threat posed by the influx of "invading outsiders" who, by gradually changing the ethnic and political landscape of Little Tel Aviv, Goldman feels, "had turned him into a stranger in his own city."[71] Rather than face up to these personal and cultural pressures, Goldman's response is to withdraw further and further into a solipsistic realm of abstract quantities and ideal relations. By the end of the novel, the middle-aged Goldman has ensconced himself in his childhood room, where he spends his time translating Johannes Kepler's 1634 text, *Somnium* [*The Dream*]—a project cut short by his suicide.

But even before his final seclusion, Goldman's interactions with friends and relatives reveal his inability to sustain an interest in conversations that do not speak to his lofty philosophical concerns. Any chat, no matter how banal, becomes an occasion for him to soliloquize on the human condition. Here, for instance, is Goldman on the question of the motorcycle: "Eliezra suddenly interrupted with the words, "I cannot understand, Goldman, why you need a motorcycle in the first place," and Goldman, embarrassed, said

---

71. Shabtai, *Past Continuous*, 269.

that the motorcycle was a very convenient form of transportation in town, much more convenient than the automobile and much cheaper too, and then he smiled and added, as if he weren't completely serious, that he was fascinated by the speed of the motorcycle and that he had a kind of urge, which perhaps exists in every man, to challenge death."[72] What makes this passage a prize piece of Goldmania is the subtle switch of registers between his admission of his private fascination with the speed and danger of the motorcycle and his conjecture that the urge to challenge death "perhaps exists in every man." It is this compulsion—the chronic need to recast the local and particular as universal and necessary—that is the real "urge" illustrated by the passage. And, as Eliezra's impatience with his response indicates, it is one of the least attractive qualities of this generally unsympathetic character. Goldman annoys not merely because of his strained air of knowingness but also because the white noise of his monologic neurosis overwhelms the imperatives of conversation, rendering him deaf to any voice but his own.

The ultimate victim of Goldman's philosophicalism is himself, but it also affects those around him. As in the cases of Casaubon and Mr. Ramsay, his overriding desire for cognitive mastery issues in an inability to properly recognize or empathetically attend to the suffering of others. A telling moment in this regard is when Caesar attempts to unburden himself to his friend regarding his dying son's deteriorating medical condition. As in the previous example, the rhetorical shifts in Goldman's response reward close analysis:

> [Goldman] had tried to encourage him by saying that there was no reason to panic and even the best doctors sometimes made mistakes and he was sure that everything would be all right in the end, and in the middle of all this *his tone suddenly changed slightly* and he said that life was nothing but a journey towards death, as the ancients had known, and that this was the one certain thing in life, and not only that but also death was actually the very essence of life, growing inside it hour by hour until it enclosed and embodied it completely—like the larva forming itself inevitably into the chrysalis from which the butterfly will eventually emerge—and thus man had to train himself to accept death, which never comes too early, and even when it seemed to come too early, there was no point in rebelling against it.[73]

---

72. Shabtai, 49. Translation modified.
73. Shabtai, 351–352. Translation modified; emphasis added.

One can imagine the solemn look that steals over Goldman's eyes as his tone changes. Evidently oblivious to the sensitive demands of the situation, he falls into his habitual pattern of transforming a concrete context into a pretext for speculative flight. Though he is still ostensibly speaking to his distraught friend, Caesar and his predicament have retreated from the darkening stage of Goldman's mind, as he steps forward to act out the role of vatic conduit for the timeless wisdom of "the ancients." It is a singularly obtuse performance. Trite consolatory mutterings, a comforting hand, even silence would have all been preferable to the tired chestnuts that Shabtai lets drop from his character's mouth.

In his interpretation of this scene Shaked argues that Goldman's assertion that "death [is] actually the very essence of life" should be taken as a summative statement of the novel's philosophy. "This 'theory' of Goldman's," he writes, "is a biological version of the dialectical view that regards the eventual decline of ideologies, nations, and peoples as already inherent in their inception and process of development."[74] But this critical gesture, as I've argued above, is a repetition of the very tendency that the novel criticizes in Goldman. By reading the latter's musings as revelations of the novel's core philosophical message, Shaked replicates the character's disregard for the particularities of the scene—the dying child, the hapless father, the unresponsive friend. Once these specificities are brought into the interpretative frame, the declarative content of Goldman's speech becomes of secondary significance. What matters, we now see, is not Goldman's philosophical theory but the function that the very turn to theoretical abstraction plays in his overall psychological economy. Far from expressing the core meaning of Shabtai's novel, the significance of the scene is better grasped by the furious Caesar, who later sums it up as "impotent intellectual bullshit."[75]

While Goldman rarely redeems himself, there is one precious moment in which he momentarily drops his habitual declamatory tone and succeeds in seeing himself as we see him. When discussing the death of his father with Israel, Goldman speaks plainly and, for once, perceptively about the psychological short-circuit in which he is trapped: "'You know that I didn't love him, but when I saw him helpless and sinking I felt sorry for him. Anyway, it was awful. And in any case it's hard to accept that someone's dead and gone forever. Because if that's the way things are, what's it all for?' And he fell silent for a moment and then said, 'You see, I'm talking

---

74. Shaked, *Hasiporet haivrit*, 393.

75. Shabtai, *Past Continuous*, 352.

about myself again.'"⁷⁶ The novel's approbation of this insight is signaled by its effect on Israel: "Goldman spoke very simply, and he thus succeeded in transferring his sadness to Israel."⁷⁷ Rather than being met with impatience or irritation—often the case when Goldman speaks—his admission elicits a measure of sympathy in the typically apathetic Israel. But this isolated moment of clarity is the exception. As a rule, Goldman is incapable of outgrowing his philosophicalism. Having caught "a whiff of the absolute,"⁷⁸ he is unable to accept the limitations imposed by a finite life within a finite cultural world. Ultimately, his will-to-truth is revealed as a will-to-death. Acting on his theory that suicide represents "the only true freedom granted to man,"⁷⁹ he arrives at the self-destructive consummation of his "rationalist-nihilist utopia."⁸⁰

Goldman's fate has obvious cautionary implications. It suggests that the desire for philosophical salvation results in an inability to endow the contingent and transient with significance and value, while also incapacitating one from responding appropriately to one's fellow sufferers. The therapy that Shabtai offers in *Past Continuous* consists of dramatizing these perils. Should his novel's therapeutic intervention reach home, it might convince readers who see something of Goldman in themselves to stop trying to view their lives, grandiosely and neurotically, from God's point of view and abandon the search for "absolute freedom and complete certainty."

But Shabtai's proffered therapy is not entirely negative. There is a way, in the world of *Past Continuous*, to remain an intellectual without becoming Goldman. This option is embodied in the impressive figure of Uncle Lazar.

The Twice-Born Uncle Lazar

During his early years, Uncle Lazar (Ephraim's brother) was a fervent communist idealist who left his family and country to join the International Brigade and fight in the Spanish Civil War. Unlike his brother and nephew,

---

76. Shabtai, *Past Continuous*, 73.

77. Shabtai, *Past Continuous*, 73.

78. Howe, "Absalom in Israel."

79. Shabtai, *Past Continuous*, 206.

80. Nancy Ezer, "Memelancholia shel yachid lemelancholia shel ma'amad: me'shkhol vekishalon le'Brenner le'Zikhron Devarim leshabtai," *Dapim lemechkar besifrut* 13 (2001–2002): 23–30, 27.

however, Lazar manages to shed his earlier foundationalist self and, as his name implies, be reborn. The extended description of Lazar's second self is one of the novel's highlights:

> Uncle Lazar was not a taciturn man by nature, and if he hardly ever spoke it was only because he knew the limitations of human knowledge, the invalidity of human reason, and the restrictions of human possibilities, and everything was so contradictory and ambiguous that doubt seemed the only thing which possessed any reality, and the ability to believe was possessed by only a few, and there was no use hoping for much, and he also knew just how far a person had to deceive himself in order to live through a single day, and how fate could play tricks on people, as it had on him, and that all the words in the world were incapable of moving the world a single centimeter from its course, or bringing back one single day that had passed, or filling in the gaps, or consoling a man whose eyes had been opened, and Uncle Lazar's eyes had been opened, and they remained open, although he was not at all despairing or embittered, but simply very realistic and sober, with all the calm detachment of a man who had experienced much and who saw clearly and for whom life held no more surprises.[81]

Lazar, who is Goldman's occasional chess partner and principal philosophical interlocutor, also serves as his intellectual foil, the ideal type against which *Past Continuous* measures the younger man and finds him lacking. A "realistic and sober" stoic, whose "eyes had been opened, and . . . remained open," Lazar is the novel's paradigm of intellectual maturity. He represents the rehabilitated metaphysician whose soul had been tested and refined by the fires of experience, and whose conclusions therefore receive the narrator's stamp of approval.

While the novel treats Goldman's expressed ideas with an insinuating irony, Lazar's speeches are made to resonate with quiet authority. Importantly, however, this differential treatment is not rooted in a substantive difference in the characters' basic views. Like Goldman, who is persecuted by a constant awareness of "how everything [is] wearing out and coming to an end,

---

81. Shabtai, *Past Continuous*, 177.

bodies and people and the ties between them,"[82] Uncle Lazar regards the ineluctable disintegration of human things as "the very essence of life and its sadness, because it [is] very hard to accept that what was once one and whole disintegrate[s] and fall[s] apart."[83] As these formulations suggest, not only do both men subscribe to an entropic picture of the universe, their articulations of this shared view are practically interchangeable. Nor is the disparity in the treatment of Goldman and Lazar attributable to the degree of intellectual force or in the originality with which each man expresses his ideas. Goldman, as we've seen, has a penchant for jargon and cliché, but Lazar's speculations do not fare much better. What is being contrasted when Lazar and Goldman are placed side by side, in short, is neither their worldviews nor the degrees of eloquence with which these are expressed, but rather the *manner* in which each man holds his views.

Uncle Lazar, who after fighting Franco's forces in Spain found his way to the USSR where he was tried as a Trotskyite and sent to an eighteen-year sentence in the barren Siberian wastes, has learned to "endure arbitrariness and uncertainty and even to renew himself with them."[84] His links to his family severed and his utopianism shattered by the long term in exile, he nevertheless finds ways to shore up the fragments of his earlier self and survive. He emerges from his ordeal, not with new ideas exactly, but with a quasi-pragmatist suspicion of ideological and philosophical systems in general. Louis Menand, in his account of Oliver Wendell Holmes's experience in the American Civil War, describes a similar process. The war, writes Menand, "made [Holmes] lose his belief in beliefs. It impressed on his mind, in the most graphic and indelible way, a certain idea about the limits of ideas."[85] The future Supreme Justice did not emerge from the war a nihilist. He did not see in his experience proof of the nullity of beliefs or ideologies. Nor did he imagine himself to have arrived at some privileged standpoint beyond good and evil. Instead, what Holmes came to realize was that systems of belief, along with the laws and customs that they engender, are contingent and parochial human creations. Men's laws,

---

82. Shabtai, *Past Continuous*, 294.

83. Shabtai, *Past Continuous*, 214.

84. Shabtai, *Past Continuous*, 191.

85. Louis Menand, *The Metaphysical Club: A Story of Ideas in America* (New York: Farrar, Straus and Giroux, 2001), 38.

in his memorable pronouncement, "do not flow from some mysterious omnipresence in the sky."[86]

Like Menand's Holmes, the twice-born Lazar does not abandon his earlier moral-political outlook. Notwithstanding his long decades of imprisonment and exile, he continues to affirm the anarchism of his youth as "the only meaningful social theory."[87] Nor, despite his recognition of the "limitations of human knowledge" does he forsake the life of the mind. Lazar was and continues to be an enthusiastic and curious reader: "[Lazar] had never stopped pursuing knowledge or reading books, partly out of interest and curiosity and the love of learning, but mostly in an ever-renewed passion to understand the ever-changing world in which he lived and whose random chaos and arbitrariness had shaped his life."[88] The chastening of his youthful idealism, in other words, does not dampen Lazar's intellectual curiosity or desire for knowledge. But, having surmounted his youthful absolutism, he is free of the awful earnestness that destroys his nephew.

The distance that separates Lazar from Goldman is thus not epistemological but attitudinal. While Goldman's strives to see himself vertically, from an absolute perspective, Lazar is content to view himself horizontally, as embedded in an "ever-changing world." Whereas the former stands for the type of person who yearns for "unity and coherence," for contact with a realm beyond the shifting sands of culture and time,[89] the latter represents the kind of intellectual who has cured himself of this self-consuming passion and has made peace with an existence that proceeds *solely* along the horizontal (which is to say social and dialogic) axis. As he tells Goldman: "Although on the face of things a sober examination of his life and its inexplicable vicissitudes might well have driven him either to complete nihilism or to the conclusion that there was, in fact, something that could be called 'God' or 'Providence' or 'ultimate being' running the world according to mysterious laws of its own, and nevertheless he was an atheist and remained an atheist . . . [and did not] see any need to breach the frontiers of life and realize his freedom in an ultimate sense."[90] Lazar's atheism is not only anti-theological but also

---

86. Francis Biddle, *Justice Holmes, Natural Law, and the Supreme Court* (New York: Macmillan, 1961), 49.
87. Shabtai, *Past Continuous*, 205.
88. Shabtai, *Past Continuous*, 178.
89. Shabtai, *Past Continuous*, 170.
90. Shabtai, *Past Continuous*, 207.

anti-theoretical. His gentle chiding of Goldman is not intended to convert him from a bad theory to a better one. Rather, he is trying to disabuse his nephew of the bad idea that one needs theory at all in order to live. His repudiation of the need to reach beyond life's "vicissitudes" is a repudiation of the notion that life is something for which one should or can provide systematic justification—of the kind that something like "'God' . . . or 'ultimate being'" can provide. After Goldman relays to him his theory of suicide as "the fullest and purest expression of free choice," Lazar observes that "he [Goldman] was expressing the point of view of a man who was already religious or who had a deep need for religion."[91] In contrast to Lazar's anti-theoretical Nietzscheism, Goldman's will-to-theorize is presented here as already religious and, therefore, in Lazar's view, antipathetic to life.[92]

The tendency among Shabtai's early commentators to treat *Past Continuous* as a philosophical novel is related to the social-political climate of the 1970s. By way of introduction, let us briefly revisit Manfred's speech, quoted at the beginning of this chapter:

> [Manfred] said [to Goldman] that he did not believe in the absolute autonomy of man . . . that he had come to the conclusion that a rational morality was impossible and that the achievements of reason were mainly in the area of destruction, including its own self-destruction, of course, by the admission of its own limitations, and that this was its strength, but in the area of construction reason had not achieved much, because in the last analysis life was a purposeless chaos and therefore in order to build anything you needed something which transcended pure reason.[93]

---

91. Shabtai, *Past Continuous*, 206–207.

92. A closeted theologian, Goldman could be viewed as a sardonic (if anachronistic) commentary on Yitzhak Orpaz's well-known ideal of the "secular pilgrim"—a figure whose pointless pilgrimage to nowhere *Past Continuous* traces step by futile step. Orpaz uses this term to describe the modern individual who, despite having lost his belief in God, still strives to make contact with some source of absolute value, such that might infuse his world with final meaning. In his 1982 *Hatszalyan hachiloni* (*The Secular Pilgrim*), Orpaz uses this concept to analyze the works of Camus, Hemingway, S.Y. Agnon, Shabtai, and others. See Yitzhak Orpaz, *Hatszalyan hachiloni* (Tel Aviv: Hakibbutz Hameuchad, 1982).

93. Shabtai, *Past Continuous*, 363.

The crucial thing to note in this and similar moments in the novel is not only the confident way Shabtai has with this jargon, but also the kind of implied reader that it both appeals to and constructs. Locutions such as "the absolute autonomy of man," "rational morality," "in the last analysis," and "pure reason" belong to a particular dialect—call it *intellectualese*—and interpolates a particular readership. "Every fiction," writes Roland Barthes, "is supported by a social jargon, a sociolect, with which it identifies . . . and finds a sacerdotal class (priests, intellectuals, artists) to speak it generally and to circulate it."[94] The publication of Shabtai's text coincided with the emergence of the requisite audience, the "sacerdotal" enclave, whose members not only knew how to speak Manfred's language but savored it. And it is the savoring that matters. For by assuming a certain cultural-intellectual competence, Shabtai's text had helped define, delimit, and thus lend a sense of group identity to an emerging community of Israeli readers. The same remains true today. The novel's philosophical terms of art continue to function as linguistic merit badges, conferring a pleasing sense of membership on the initiated. Thus even prior to the processing of the propositional content of Manfred's speech, its "sociolect" already invokes in Shabtai's intellectual reader a strong, because exclusive, sense of identification with the work, as well as with the imagined community that it constructs.[95]

Past Continuous came out as this urban-intellectual readership, to and about which it speaks, was congealing into its recognizable present-day shape. The 1970s were a period of accelerated transformation of Israeli society, witnessing not only the ousting of MAPAI and the rise of settlement movement, but also more diffused cultural shifts. The hoary prestige of the old Zionist establishment's intellectual wing had by now all but vanished,[96] and on both sides of the recently established Green Line new forms of intellectual life were attaining self-consciousness. In the yeshivas affiliated

---

94. Roland Barthes, *The Pleasure of the Text*, trans. Richard Miller (New York: Hill & Wang, 1975), 27–28.

95. Few novels in the history of modern Hebrew prose have developed such a cult following. The only equivalent case, I believe, is Pinhas Sadeh's *Hakhaim kemashal* (*Life as a Parable*) (1958).

96. This nation-building élite consisted mainly of party ideologues, such as Berl Katznelson and Meir Ya'ari; writers and poets, such S.Y. Agnon, Nathan Alterman, Moshe Shamir, and S. Yizhar; and the founding professorate of the Hebrew University: Martin Buber, Gershom Scholem, Yeshayahu Leibovitch, Hugo Bergmann, and others.

to the settlement movement, rabbis and other religious intellectuals were weaving together a Hebraized version of romantic *volksgeistlich* nationalism, which combined stringent observance with mystical messianism and Hegelian historicism.[97] Meanwhile, on the other side of the Line, left-wing literati in Tel Aviv and Jerusalem were modeling themselves and their students on more contemporary European trends, becoming at first existentialist and then, as the years wore on, Foucauldian in theory, universalist in politics, and exclusivist in attitude. As Shlomo Sand observes, "With the collapse of MAPAI's hegemonic status and the rise of the Likud party, intellectualism becomes a mark of separateness from the 'masses.' High culture turns into a way of distinguishing 'us' from the 'others,' who had hijacked the country."[98] Faced with the loss of direct political power, Israeli intelligentsia assigned to itself the task of defending the universalist ideals of knowledge and reason against its non-liberal "others." An island within the island of MAPAI's ethno-political hegemony, Israel's secular intellectual culture grew increasingly spectatorial and hyper-philosophized in direct proportion to the felt erosion of its base's social-political sway.

Shabtai's response to this (still ongoing) process of cultural realignment was complex. Like Wharton's and Roth's elegiac novels, *Past Continuous* is partly a nostalgic requiem to the disappearing world of the AHUSALIM. Born to this tribe, Shabtai could not help but share in (what we now know) were its moral prejudices and blind spots. Like other similarly positioned writers, he is thus susceptible to the charges of cultural conservatism and chauvinism that have been routinely leveled at social elegists from Walter Scott onward. At the same time, however, *Past Continuous*, I've tried to show, also presents us with an incisive and highly pertinent diagnosis of the modes of thought and action to which the loss of cultural power often gives rise. As Soker-Schwager's detailed study of Shabtai's reception shows, the embrace of *Past Continuous* by Israel's intelligentsia was intimately linked to this milieu's need to validate its threatened identity.[99] And it is in this context that the tendency to philosophize the novel should be understood.

---

97. Gideon Aran, *Kukism: shorshei gush emunim, tarbut hamitnakhalim, teologia zionit, meshikhiyut bezmanenu* (Jerusalem: Carmel, 2013), 138.

98. Shlomo Sand, *Haintelktual, haemet vehakoach* (Tel Aviv: Am Oved, 2000), 166.

99. See chapters 2 and 3 in Soker-Schwager, *Mechashef hashevet*, in particular her comment on the critical tendency (prevalent during the 1970s and exemplified by Miron) toward "universalizing abstraction" (110).

For implicit in the attempt to extract a metaphysical meaning from Shabtai's text is the wish to make the contingent necessary and the particular universal, to naturalize culture by essentializing its human types. It thus became the ironic fate of Shabtai's therapeutic, anti-philosophical novel that it has so often been interpreted in the selfsame manner that it caricatures.

Chapter 5

Culturalism and Historicism in Contemporary Intellectual Life

I opened this book by claiming that the novel of cultural extinction, in general, and the works of Wharton, Roth, and Shabtai, in particular, have a moral lesson to teach. I did not mean by this that we should go to these writers in search of moral truths as these have traditionally been conceived: as insights into our shared "human nature" or as intimations of the Moral Law. Indeed, on my account, each of the novels examined above could be said to thwart such a moralistic reading. For what *Past Continuous* has in common with *The Age of Innocence* and *The Radetzky March* is that each emphatically culturalizes—which is to say, parochializes and temporalizes—the norms, values, and human types that populate its world. In so doing, each of these works deliberately frustrates the readerly desire to use the lives of its characters as substantive moral models.

It is, of course, still possible (and, for certain purposes, also useful) for contemporary readers to draw analogies between the moral predicaments that determine, say, Newland Archer's or Max Demant's fates and some present-day ones. However, such analogies, precisely because they make the characters' moral frames continuous with our own, effectively blur the *specificity* and even *strangeness* of those particular moral predicaments. Old New York's views on marriage and the Habsburgian military honor code, Wharton's and Roth's texts emphatically insist, are no longer relevant moral realities, having been rendered obsolete along with the (putative) disappearance of the communities in which they manifested. The reason for this emphasis is that morality, on the culturalist view that Wharton and Roth share with

Shabtai, is no longer understood as a reflection or expression of something more universal or enduring than culture. In the culturalist world that their novels project, moral norms, like the languages in which they are articulated, come neither from the starry heavens above nor from the moral law within, but are simply one more contingent petal of the blossom which we are.

My suggestion above that the novels at the center of this study "actively thwart" or "deliberately frustrate" the attempt to extract general moral meanings from their narratives will be misunderstood if read to mean that they deploy arguments to that effect. Cleanth Brooks's well-known warning against putting literary texts "into an unreal competition with science or philosophy or theology" remains apposite here.[1] For unlike philosophical tracts or scientific treatises, which tend to defend the truth of their assertions by rational or empirical means, literary works instruct by inviting us to assume a certain perspective (or perspectives) and thus to inhabit a possible world. One might walk away from a novel with a keener awareness of human depravity or with a heightened sensitivity to cruelty or with a fuller recognition of the limits of egotism. But whatever the takeaway, it will not have come about as a result of learning a new fact about the world or of drawing new inferential connections between propositions, but because the text has encouraged or compelled its reader to see herself and her world in a new light. The experience of literature thus belongs to the category that includes, at its extreme limit, religious or political conversions. Such transformations, when they occur, typically have little to do with argument: one rarely finds religion as a result of a debate with a really persuasive theist or after tabulating the relative pros of cons of religious belief versus unbelief. Instead, changes of this kind follow upon the experience of suddenly seeing one's familiar world from an unfamiliar and compelling alternative perspective, such that alters what William James in *Pragmatism* (1907) calls "[one's] more or less dumb sense of what life honestly and deeply means."[2] The contents of the world remain the same; what has changed is one's angle of vision.

The latter claims are not special to the particular novels discussed in this book. Every novel, if it belongs to the tradition that begins with Maria

---

1. Cleanth Brooks, "The Heresy of Paraphrase," in *The Well Wrought Urn* (New York: Harcourt, Brace & World, 1947), 201.

2. William James, *Pragmatism: A New Name for some Old Ways of Thinking* (Cambridge, MA: Harvard University Press, 1975), 9.

Edgeworth and Walter Scott, strives to introduce its readers to a thickly described constellation of mutually animating practices, beliefs, and human types. Every realist novel (even if it professes no aims beyond providing casual entertainment) tries to foster the complex dynamics of identification and recognition between reader and characters that countless writers and critics, from George Eliot to Rita Felski, have identified as the genre's chief mode of moral education.[3] What distinguishes the novel of cultural extinction from its realist counterparts, therefore, is not that it constructs a complexly integrated social world or that it encourages its readers to identify with the characters they find there. It is that, having done these things, it then goes on to depict the disarticulation and collapse of its characters' socially constructed reality. To the extent that we succeed in identifying with the novel's characters, vicariously feeling as they feel and valuing as they value, we become (for the duration of the reading at least) honorary members of their cultures. But to the same extent, we also experience—albeit in a controlled, distanced, attenuated manner—the collapse of the normative systems of practice and belief that had infused their lives with meaning and purpose. The novel of cultural extinction thus carves out a unique vantage point for its reader, from which she can appreciate *both* the unavoidable, all-pervasive, identity-shaping power of culture *and* its fragile and perishable nature.

To be sure, human beings did not have to wait on the realist novel to know that all things must pass. The ancient Greek worldview, as James comments elsewhere, "was full to the brim of the sad mortality of this sunlit world,"[4] as were the wisdom books of the Hebrew Bible, most notably Ecclesiastes (from which Wharton drew the title for *The House of Mirth*). There is, however, a crucial difference between the attitude toward earthly things that has come down to us from ancient Judeo-Christian and philosophical sources and the attitude of the novel. On the view common to Ecclesiastes, Plato, and St. Augustine, the frailty of the flesh, the contingency of social

---

3. For George Eliot's description of art (literary art in particular) "as a mode for amplifying experience and extending our contact with our fellow-men beyond the bounds of our personal lot," see *Essays of George Eliot*, ed. Thomas Pinney (New York: Columbia University Press, 1963), 270–271. For Rita Felski's illuminating exploration of the dynamics of recognition in literary art, see *Uses of Literature* (Malden, MA: Blackwell, 2008), 23–50.

4. William James, *The Varieties of Religious Experience: A Study in Human Nature* (London: Routledge, 2002), 72.

institutions, and the ephemerality of human achievements *ipso facto* robs them of genuine value. The biblical preacher's final judgment on the value of transient things—"Vanity of vanities . . . all is vanity"—is of a piece with Plato's prioritizing of Being over Becoming and with St. Augustine's polemic against everything that is "time-bound and transient": "woe to those who cling to things that pass away, because they will pass away with them!"[5] Genuine value, on the view that these figures helped weave into the fabric of Western thought, can only ever be the property of permanent, immutable things.

Conversely, on the culturalist and historicist view that begins to take shape in the final decades of the eighteenth century, and which would find its most powerful promulgator in the realist novel, value is no longer a function of the object's participation in the divine; it is the name for the specific gravity that an object assumes in the this-worldly medium of human linguistic and social practice that we call a culture. This is the view of value that Freud recommends in his 1915 "On Transience," where he writes that "[a] time may indeed come when the pictures and statues which we admire to-day will crumble to dust, or a race of men may follow us who no longer understand the works of our poets and thinkers, or a geological epoch may even arrive when all animate life upon the earth ceases; but since the value of all this beauty and perfection is determined only by *its significance for our own emotional lives*, it has no need to survive us and is therefore *independent of absolute duration*."[6] Freud's claim that the value of the things that we cherish is determined solely on the basis of their "significance for our own emotional lives" is tantamount to the claim that it is a cultural affair through and through. This culturalist assertion dovetails with Freud's subsequent historicist claim, that the value of our institutions and achievements "has no need to survive us and is therefore independent of absolute duration." With these two claims, Freud sets himself squarely against the longstanding premise that "only the completely fixed and unchanging can be real," which John Dewey identified as the foundational assumption common

---

5. Ecclesiastes 12:8 King James Bible; Augustine *Homilies on the Gospel of John* 1–40, trans. Edmund Hill, ed. Allen D. Fitzgerald (New York: New City Press, 2009), 202.

6. Sigmund Freud, "On Transience," in *The Standard Edition of the Complete Psychological Works* XIV, trans. James Strachey (London: Hogarth Press, 1957), 305–307, 306. Emphases added.

to Greek and Judeo-Christian metaphysics.[7] Not only is cultural value real, Freud might have said, it is the only kind of value there is.

If, as Terry Eagleton writes, "[the] realist novel represents one of the great revolutionary cultural forms of human history [on par with the] importance of steam-power or electricity in the material realm, or of democracy in the political sphere,"[8] this is because of its signal role in making the kind of position that Freud takes above possible. And again, while this great labor of transvaluation is one of the chief glories of the realist novel as a whole, it achieves a particular pitch in the novel of cultural extinction. For this subsection of the realist enterprise throws the historicity, contingency, and mortality of human institutions into sharpest relief, while insisting, at the same time and with equal force, on their real value *for their members*. As we've seen, Wharton's, Roth's, and Shabtai's backward glances at the worlds of their youth do not liquidate the latter as distinct moral realities; quite the opposite: they bring them to life as such. But, at the same time, by emphatically localizing and historicizing these collectively maintained webs of value and meaning, these novels also defuse the temptation to universalize upon their respective moral norms and social types. Indeed, the poignancy of these worlds is derived precisely from their singularity. Those particular kinds of people, with their distinctive manners, commitments, and habits of mind, the novel of cultural extinction tells its reader, will never exist again.

All of which brings us back to the question of the moral upshot of this particular narrative form. If, as I have been arguing, novels of cultural extinction implicitly deny the existence of a common human essence by insisting on the irreducible singularity and unrepeatability of the now-vanished worlds that they describe, what kind of commonality *do* they posit between their readers and their characters? Put differently, if the novels examined in this book strive to accentuate the cultural strangeness of their characters' moral norms and assumptions, what possibility for readerly identification do they hold out? What of ourselves do we recognize in the fates of Newland Archer, District Commissioner Trotta, or Uncle Lazar? The answer, on the view I been advancing, is that these characters and their numerous counterparts from 1800 to the present, give narrative shape to

---

7. John Dewey, *The Quest for Certainty* in *John Dewey: The Later Works, 1925–1953*, ed. Jo Ann Boydston (Carbondale: Southern Illinois University Press, 2008), 18.
8. Terry Eagleton, *The English Novel: An Introduction* (Malden, MA: Blackwell, 2005), 20.

the "peculiar form of human vulnerability" that Jonathan Lear describes in his book (see chapter 1), and to whose historical emergence I had devoted the early parts of mine.⁹ That is, what Newland Archer has in common with District Commissioner Trotta, Scott's Highlanders with Shabtai's Tel Avivians, and all of the above with their assumed modern readers is not a relation to some positive, ahistorical, and supracultural entity (be it God or human nature, or the moral dictates of reason), but a susceptibility to a particular vulnerability that we all, *qua* cultural creatures, perforce share.

"Recognition," Rita Felski observes, "is not repetition": it does not work by affirming what the reader necessarily acknowledges about herself. Rather, in moments of recognition "something that may have been sensed in a vague, diffuse, or semi-conscious way . . . takes on a distinct shape, is amplified, heightened, or made newly visible."¹⁰ What gets amplified or rendered salient for us, as we sojourn through the foredoomed worlds of Old New York, the Habsburg Empire, and Little Tel Aviv, is just how dependent we are on the tenuous webs of meaning in which we are suspended, and how exposed we become when they unravel. But these novels also invite us to recognize that it is *we* who spin those webs, that there are no backstage operators, no puppet masters pulling the strings of history. The belief in progress and metropolitan exceptionalism that protected the nineteenth-century readers of Walter Scott or James Fenimore Cooper or even Thomas Hardy from the full implications of the view contained in these authors' tales of cultural extinction were no longer available in the same way to twentieth-century readers and writers. The view of the universe that Wharton's, Roth's, and Shabtai's novels assume is one in which we are all alone with one another, without any external source of validation or consolation. Thus, insofar as the novels I have examined in this study have a moral lesson to teach, it is a purely negative, therapeutic one: that we wean ourselves off the need to hook up our institutions and beliefs to something powerful and enduring that lies beyond our way of life, and accept the parochial and transient nature of the cultural worlds we inhabit.

Coming to terms with the implications of the thoroughly culturalist and historicist outlook expressed by these novels is difficult to do for sev-

---

9. Jonathan Lear, *Radical Hope: Ethics in the Face of Cultural Devastation* (Cambridge, MA: Harvard University Press, 2006), 6.

10. Felski, *Uses of Literature*, 25.

eral related reasons. In the first place, it denies us of the ability to claim metaphysical privilege for our own cherished beliefs and practices, such that might assure us that they are inherently and objectively superior to their alternatives. Ruth Benedict's observation that "[we] are still preoccupied with the uniqueness, not of the institutions of the world at large, which no one has ever cared about anyway, but of our own institutions and achievements, our own civilization" remains, in my view, as relevant today as it was in 1934.[11] Thus, most decent liberals today, I suspect, still want to believe that there must be some way to *prove* that liberal-democratic institutions are superior to their current ethnic-populist alternatives, not merely by our own liberal-democratic lights but unconditionally. For we still feel that to admit that there is nothing that *makes* our way of life objectively better than its alternatives—nothing, that is, apart from what Freud called "its significance for our own emotional lives"—is to jeopardize our ability to defend it. And by the same token, when we are confronted by practices such as state-sponsored prosecution of homosexuals or female genital mutilation, many of us still feel that it is not enough to claim that these rituals are reprehensible from *our* parochial cultural perspective. When faced with such egregious cruelties, we often find ourselves wanting to agree with David Enoch that "taking morality seriously" demands that we insist on the "perfectly objective, universal [and] absolute" reprehensibility of those practices.[12] Anything less, we worry—wrongly, in my view—will handicap our ability to condemn such horrors or will cripple our capacity to take resolute action against them.[13]

The second reason it is hard to let go of the belief that our cherished values and institutions are grounded in something beyond themselves, something like capital-R Reason or "human nature," is that doing so would deny us of the kind of pseudo-religious consolation that these Enlightenment notions were originally designed to preserve. As Richard Rorty argues, to

---

11. Ruth Benedict, *Patterns of Culture* (New York: The New American Library, 1934), 20.
12. See David Enoch's *Taking Morality Seriously: A Defense of Robust Realism* (Oxford: Oxford University Press, 2011), 1.
13. I readily agree with Enoch as to the reprehensibility of female genital mutilation. The difference between a philosophical realist like Enoch and a Rortyian like myself is that while he believes that it is very important that we have a *theory* that proves that our shared moral perspective is more "rational" than its pro-FGM alternative, I believe that such a theory is neither necessary nor obtainable nor even desirable.

understand the lasting hold of objectivism and universalism on our intellectual culture, we must factor in the spiritual solace these modes of thought have traditionally provided:

> The picture of a common human nature oriented towards correspondence to reality as it is in itself comforts us with the thought that even if our civilization is destroyed, even if all memory of our political or intellectual or artistic community is erased, the race is fated to recapture the virtues and the insights and the achievements which were the glory of that community. . . . [It assures us] that something reasonably like *our* world-view, *our* virtues, *our* art, will bob up again whenever human beings are left alone to cultivate their inner natures.[14]

On Rorty's Deweyan account, what gave rise and continues to drive the age-old hankering after nonlocal and immutable truths is the powerful (yet rarely acknowledged) need to assure ourselves that transience is not the final word: that although we are finite, mortal beings, we nonetheless have access to something that transcends this fate. On this view, if we are reluctant to let go of the possibility that at least some of our values or achievements are as we say "timeless," it is because we find consolation in the belief that people reasonably *like us* will eventually inherit the earth, thus retroactively proving that we have lived in the truth. If Rorty is right about this—as I think he is—then Enoch's insistence that "there must be *some* examples . . . of normative (and indeed moral) truths that are perfectly objective, universal, absolute" (even if we have not discovered what these are yet) is as much an expression of an inability to come to terms with our historicity and finitude as it is a plea for moral seriousness.[15]

To adopt the view that informs the fictions of Wharton, Roth, and Shabtai entails giving up on both kinds of metaphysical reassurance: on the belief in the inherent value of (at least some of) our achievements, values and institutions, as well as on the concomitant belief in the timeless validity and thus perdurability of these achievements, values and institutions. It is to recognize that everything that goes into making us into who we are

---

14. Richard Rorty, "Solidarity or Objectivity," in *Objectivity, Relativism, and Truth* (New York: Cambridge University Press, 1991), 21–34, 31.

15. Enoch, *Morality*, 1.

may be condemned by or deemed wholly irrelevant to our descendants. Such is the price of adopting the thoroughgoing historicist and culturalist outlook that Freud summarizes above; and for some of us, that price will simply be too high. "Humans," as Michael Bérubé writes, "may not want to become fully secular in the sense that they take full responsibility for having created the moral and political frameworks under which they live."[16] Should that happen, should our descendants decide that historical agency and human autonomy are not worth the loss of metaphysical consolation and the comforts of certainty, they will gradually slide back to some version of the pre-Enlightenment view of humanity's place in the universe—one in which pious submission to nonhuman forces trumps human self-assertion, and the quest for certainty replaces the desire for novelty. So much the worse for them.

What these hypothetical descendants will lose, should they go down that path, is not only the sense of themselves as self-legislating beings. Theirs will also be a less tolerant, less free society than our partially secular one. For members of that society will be much more prone to take seriously the bad idea that life is a question or problem to which there is a single solution. A society organized around such a mindset will be both less cognizant of the apparently inexhaustible range of human plasticity and more inclined to persecute those who fail to meet its normative standards, because it will tend to regard those standards not as cultural creations but as prescriptions issued by some divine or pseudo-divine authority. Such a society will continue to have intellectuals, of course, but they will typically resemble Goldman more than Uncle Lazar, Descartes more than Cervantes, former Pope Ratzinger more than current Pope Francis. This is because a community that cannot come to terms with its own mortality will tend to produce metaphysically minded intellectuals who spend their lives looking for ways to transcend rather than improve their time and place.

By contrast, should our descendants realize the Enlightenment's hopes by wholly relinquishing the idea that there is something beyond culture to which we are held accountable, they will be better able to see themselves as authors of their worlds and more reconciled to their transiency. While deprived of the metaphysical consolation that comforted the lives of their predecessors, they will likely have a deeper and more compelling sense of

---

16. Michael Bérubé, "The Return of Realism and the Future of Contingency," in *Rhetorical Occasions: Essays on Humans and the Humanities* (Chapel Hill: University of North Carolina Press, 2006), 35–53, 51.

human solidarity. For, as Rorty writes, "our identification with our community—our society, our political tradition, our intellectual heritage—is heightened when we see this community as *ours* rather than *nature's*, *shaped* rather than *found*, one among many which men have made."[17] The notion of solidarity that this passage invokes is premised neither on access to a nonhuman source of power nor on the assumption of a common human nature or essence, but on the recognition of a shared vulnerability. Fostering such an awareness is, I believe, the chief moral contribution of the literary tradition that begins with Edgeworth and Scott and reaches its consummation in the twentieth-century novel of cultural extinction.

Our Tribal Humanities

Having outlined what I take to be the general moral upshot of the novel of cultural extinction, I would like to conclude by bringing the discussion closer to home: to the institutional and cultural formation that we call the humanities at this perilous moment in its history. In this final section, I want to raise briefly the question of what we humanist intellectuals might still have to learn from the thoroughgoing culturalism and historicism that we find in *The Age of Innocence*, for example, or from the withering critique of the idea of salvation through cognitive mastery that we saw in *Past Continuous*.

This question, I recognize, may strike some of my readers as either redundant or misdirected. If any sector of contemporary society can be said to have embraced the culturalist and historicist outlook, these readers will point out, it is the interpretive humanities (a fuzzy category that includes not only literary scholars but also Geertzian anthropologists, philosophical pragmatists, Foucauldian cultural critics, and others). "We Are All Heracliteans Now," writes Bérubé in this vein, "[all ready to affirm that] nothing is timeless or universal about human knowledge."[18] On one level, Bérubé is surely right: the interpretive humanities are typically the most culturalist and historicist corner of the university and thus of modern society. Their

---

17. Richard Rorty, *Consequences of Pragmatism* (Minneapolis: University of Minnesota Press, 1982), 166.
18. Michael Bérubé, "Value and Values," in *The Humanities, Higher Education, and Academic Freedom Three Necessary Arguments*, ed. Michael Bérubé and Jennifer Ruth (New York: Palgrave Macmillan, 2015), 30.

disciplines' intellectual roots in Hegel, Marx, Nietzsche, Freud, Boas, Derrida, and Foucault; the massive intellectual effort they have exerted over the last few decades under the imperative to "always historicize!"; and the volatile history of the field since the 1970s, with its rapid succession of theoretical paradigms and intellectual heroes, have made it difficult—even for the most Parmenidean among us—to explicitly deny the situatedness of knowledge or the historicity of institutions.[19]

Still, mental attitudes like *denying, affirming, believing,* or *knowing* are not unitary and indivisible; each allows for a range of ways of holding beliefs as well as for varying strengths of commitment to them. To borrow a distinction from Cardinal Newman, there is a difference between *notional* and *real* assent: between affirming a proposition in the abstract and fully internalizing that proposition into one's worldview in a way that fundamentally changes one's self-image. "And so generally," writes Newman, "great truths, practical or ethical, float on the surface of society, admitted by all, valued by few . . . until changed circumstances, accident, or the continual pressure of their advocates, force them upon its attention."[20] The proposition that our most fundamental sense-making categories (moral, theoretical, commonsensical) are fragile and transient, I want to suggest, is one of the "great truths" that float on the surface of our mental universe, and which we have yet to fully work into our self-image. In spite of the intensive deconstruction of Enlightenment universalism and debunking of old-school humanist essentialism, our intellectual culture, as numerous prominent insiders have pointed out in recent years,[21] is still metaphysical,

---

19. Frederic Jameson, *The Political Unconscious: Narrative as a Socially Symbolic Act* (Ithaca, NY: Cornell University Press, 1981), 9.

20. Newman, John Henry, *A Grammar of Assent* (London: Gilbert and Rivington, 1870), 74.

21. See, for instance, Daniel Dennett's observation that "the essentialist urge is still with us"; Rorty's reference to "our own familiar, and still metaphysical, liberal culture"; Michael Bérubé's assertion that "the vast majority" of people today still believe "that something *else*—God, natural law, objective moral certitudes—must serve as the basis for both social deliberation and beliefs about social reality"; Susan Hegeman's discussion of the persistence of the popular belief in "the asymmetry between the West and the rest, by which the West exists in the universal truth of modernity"; or Rita Felski's claim, that "in retrospect, much of the grand theory of the last three decades now looks like the last gasp of an Enlightenment tradition of *rois philosophes* persuaded that the realm of speculative thought would absolve them of the shameful ordinariness of a messy, mundane, error-prone existence." See Dennett, *Darwin's Dangerous Idea: Evolution and the*

still touched by the Platonist desire for the objective, the intrinsic, and the imperishable.

Today, this desire is once again on the ascendant. The sense that "critique," as one of its eminent practitioners put it, has "run out of steam"[22] coupled with the varied institutional and social pressures dubbed "the crisis of the humanities" have thrown the profession into paroxysms of soul-searching. Across the humanities, as Susan Hegeman observes, we are witnessing "a renewal of interest in aesthetics, ethics, and even theology . . . often combined, especially in the humanities, with methodological polemics against historicism, 'content analysis,' and 'culturalism.' "[23] Terms and research topics once thought to be quaint survivals from bygone disciplinary eras—the true, the beautiful, the good—are again assuming center stage under the duly prefixed headings of "new formalism," "new aestheticism," or "new ethics."[24] Meanwhile, in other quarters, we find scholars attempting to revamp literary studies by incorporating the methods and insights of neuroscience, evolutionary biology, and big-data technology. And though I do not want to impute a single motivation to these heterogeneous bodies of work, let alone spurn the often-suggestive explorations conducted under these banners, I do want to suggest that at least part of the energy driving these disciplinary developments stems from a desire to roll back the culturalist and historicist turn and recoup the objectivist and universalist modes of thought that it sought to retire.

This broad and uncoordinated project of recovery is closely linked to the urgently felt need to justify humanistic studies as an intellectual and cultural enterprise. The crisis of the humanities may be a "perennial" feature

---

Meaning of Life (New York: Simon & Schuster, 1995), 39; Rorty, *Contingency, Irony, and Solidarity* (Cambridge: Cambridge University Press, 1989), 87; Bérubé, "The Return of Realism and the Future of Contingency" in *Rhetorical Occasions* (Chapel Hill: University of North Carolina Press, 2006), 35–53, 36; Hegeman, *The Cultural Return* (Berkeley: University of California Press, 2012), 107; Felski, *Uses of Literature*, 13.

22. Bruno Latour, "Why Has Critique Run Out of Steam? From Matters of Fact to Matters of Concern," *Critical Inquiry* 30, no. 2 (2004): 225–248.

23. Hegeman, The Cultural Return, 4.

24. For a critical survey of the new formalism, see Levinson Marjorie, "What Is New Formalism?" *PMLA* 122, no. 2 (2007): 558–569. For a review of "the new ethical defense of literary value" see Dorothy J. Hale, "Aesthetics and the New Ethics: Theorizing the Novel in the Twenty-First Century," *PMLA* 124, no. 3 (2009): 896–905.

of the self-understanding of the profession, as some have argued,[25] but hardly anyone today would care to deny its pressing realities. Dwindling budgets, disappearance of tenure-track positions, decreasing enrollments, exploitation of adjunct faculty, the loss of public esteem—these factors all contribute to the prevalent sense that, if we humanists are to survive, we must come up with ways to justify our intellectual projects to a society that seems less keen than ever to fund them. Doing so effectively, many feel, demands that we ground the kind of work we do in some unimpeachable universal and objective rationale, of the kind that might lend an aura of necessity and inevitability to our vocation. The various disciplinary developments listed above represent one symptom of this wish for legitimation; the current backlash against historicism and culturalism is another. What both have in common is the unstated desire to recover the vision of the humanities as a privileged intellectual arena in which intrinsic values and abiding truths are discovered, assessed, and transmitted.

Against this backdrop, I would like to turn to a passage from an op-ed by Nina Handler titled "Facing My Own Extinction" published in *The Chronicle of Higher Education* in 2017: "I am a college English instructor. This is a bad time for my species—and a bad time for the study of English. In academe, we are witnessing an extinction of fields of study once thought essential. . . . I can see the future and know that I won't exist in it. I don't know if I am capable of survival in this new environment. Social Darwinists would say it's adapt or die, but I don't know how to adapt to a society that doesn't want what I hold dear."[26] What I like most about this passage—even while I doubt its premise: that the humanities are facing imminent extinction—is its description of the humanist intellectual as a member of a "species," rather than, say, as a custodian of timeless wisdom, a creator of knowledge, or a producer of democratic citizens. Handler, I am sure, would not deny that the humanities do offer their students a kind of wisdom or that they may contribute to the well-being of society. But I find her choice to avoid these shopworn self-descriptions in favor of a defiant assertion of the value of the humanities *for people like her*, both refreshing and timely. For, by describing the humanities in this way, as a

---

25. Geoffrey Galt Harpham, "Beneath and beyond the 'Crisis in the Humanities,'" *New Literary History* 36, no. 1 (2005): 21–36, 21.

26. Nina Handler, "Facing My Own Extinction," *Chronicle of Higher Education*, December 7, 2017, www.chronicle.com/article/Facing-My-Own-Extinction/241988.

site of real but relative value, she wholly circumvents what Simon During has called the "sermonic" tone that characterizes much of the literature in defense of the humanities.[27]

One becomes sermonic when one insists that what we in the humanities do is crucial for the health of society as a whole. We might call this the vital-organ defense, as its characteristic gesture is to present the potential demise of the humanities on the model of heart or lung failure, the kind of breakdown that endangers the social body entire. This familiar rhetorical strategy appears in several variations. Martha Nussbaum, arguably the most prominent campaigner on behalf of the liberal-arts curriculum, claims that the ongoing marginalization of the humanities in America and elsewhere "[threatens] the very life of democracy itself."[28] Anthony Kronman argues in a somewhat Heideggerian fashion that "only the humanities [can counteract the] forgetfulness of humanity" caused by the technological and scientific culture of modernity.[29] A more recent case in point is Peter Brooks's introduction to a collected volume titled *The Humanities and Public Life* (2014). Brooks opens this text with the following rallying cry to the profession: "we who practice the interpretative humanities need to be less modest and to stake a claim to the public importance of our task."[30] That claim, argues Brooks, should hinge on the ethical dimension of close reading, a practice he describes as "[submitting] what we want the text to mean to the constraints of the lexicon, the historical horizon, and the text as a whole."[31] The more close readers a society has, so runs his argument, the more immune it is to political demagogues, unprincipled advertisers, and other sophists.

The particular sophism that Brooks has in mind is the notorious Torture Memos, drafted and signed in 2002 during the Bush administration. To recall, these documents sought to provide legal justification for the use of so-called "enhanced interrogation techniques" by the CIA as part of the United States' War on Terror. To demonstrate that the US legal code

---

27. Simon During, "Stop Defending the Humanities," *Public Books*, March 1, 2014, www.publicbooks.org/stop-defending-the-humanities.

28. Martha Nussbaum, *Not for Profit: Why Democracy Needs the Humanities* (Princeton, NJ: Princeton University Press, 2010), 142.

29. Anthony T. Kronman, *Education's End: Why Our Colleges and Universities have Given Up on the Meaning of Life* (New Haven, CT: Yale University Press, 2007), 239.

30. Peter Brooks and Hilary Jewett, eds., *The Humanities and Public Life* (New York: Fordham University Press, 2014), 2.

31. Brooks, *The Humanities and Public Life*, 3.

allows for the use of torture required the legal advisors who drafted the memos to engage in what Brooks describes as "the most twisted, ingenious, perverse, and unethical interpretation."[32] Now, being myself a citizen of a country with a sordid history of legitimizing torture by all manner of legal shenanigans, I can readily identify with Brooks's outrage. What caused me to shift uncomfortably in my seat as I read his introduction was not his moral indignation but the lesson he draws from this ugly historical episode: namely, that had Bush's lawyers been schooled in the art of close reading, America might have been spared the indignity of the Torture Memos. "No one trained in the rigorous analysis of poetry," he writes, "could possibly engage in such bad-faith interpretation."[33]

One need not deny that the humanities can produce more sophisticated readers to see how misconceived this is. For one thing, it is unclear what a degree in English or French has over a course of study in, say, sociology or law when it comes to the production of astute readers; for another, the assumption that such readers would refrain from engaging in bad-faith interpretation (or worse) flies in the face of all we know about human behavior. And last, Brooks seems to be implying that we who have been trained in what he calls "the rigorous analysis of poetry" converge on some agreed-upon method for distinguishing acceptable from bad-faith interpretations.[34] But we have evolved no such method. Nor, I dare say, is any forthcoming.

Let me state my position more bluntly still. I think we are wrong to claim that democracy needs us. It does not—certainly not in anything like the way it needs an independent judiciary or brave watchdog journalists. Moreover, as far as I can tell, there is no special skill called "critical thinking" that only a course of study in medieval history or philosophical metaethics can impart. Of course, were it shown that arguments to this effect have been successful in forestalling budget cuts or in generating additional tenure-track positions in our departments, I would be all in favor of using them. But I suspect that the people we are trying to impress with this rhetoric find it as unconvincing as I do. After all, we've been reproducing it with considerable regularity for nearly two decades to little noticeable effect.

To be clear, like Nussbaum, Kronman, and Brooks I too value the humanities. I value the kinds of intellectual work they make possible; the

---

32. Brooks, 1.
33. Brooks, 3.
34. Brooks, 1.

human achievements they preserve, curate, and make accessible; and, yes, also the ethical relations—primarily those between teachers and students—that they sponsor. Further, I hold that if these incommensurable goods were to disappear, their loss would not only be ours. The extinction of the humanities would reduce the university to a shell of its former self while impacting society beyond its gates in many foreseeable and unforeseeable ways. We may not be essential to the well-being of humanity or democracy, but that does not mean that our disappearance would leave the world as it was.

Yet, with that said, I worry that arguments of the form fund-us-or-face-the-apocalyptic-consequences, however gratifying they may be to our collective self-image, are not only unconvincing but may actually be counterproductive. And so I take issue with Brooks's recommendation, that we be "less modest" in our claims for the humanities. On the contrary, what may be needed at this juncture is *more* modesty. This does not mean that we should become unassuming about the singular goods that the humanities provide, only that we stop arguing for the universal value of those goods. That is, we need to find ways of recommending the Socratic life, without asserting—as Socrates does—that the unexamined life is not worth living.

To overcome Socrates's tendentious account of what is highest and noblest about human beings is to accept that the vocation that he bequeathed to us, his intellectual heirs, is neither inevitable nor exemplary, but is merely one cultural form of life among others. To see the humanities in this parochial way, as a cultural tribe or species—not unlike Wharton's Old New York or Shabtai's Little Tel Aviv—is to recognize what During calls "the limits of their defensibility."[35] It is to recognize that a person has to be (at least minimally) one of us before she can be expected to feel the value of the humanities or to view their potential demise as catastrophic. This recognition, in turn, would recommend that we stop trying to convince others of our indispensability, and concentrate instead on trying to make our work more visible, relevant, and accessible to society at large, in an effort to draw more students into our world. Ultimately, the more people can be brought to share our peculiar obsessions, to see as we see and love what we love, the better our chances for survival.

I recognize that all this sounds as if I'm about to present a novel marketing strategy for the humanities, one that would be effective without being sermonic. Such a strategy is indeed urgently needed, and I think one

---

35. Simon During, "Stop Defending the Humanities."

of the reasons that we keep rehashing the vital-organ defense is that we have not tried to develop an alternative vocabulary capable of asserting the value and distinctiveness of what we do without resorting to hyperbole or self-aggrandizing. But this much-needed alternative is not my topic here. Instead, I want to spend the remainder of this final section discussing what I take to be our deep-seated resistance to thinking of ourselves in the culturalist and historicist terms that During and Handler outline. Our failure to produce non-universalist justifications for the humanities, I claim, is not due to an oversight; there are deeper reasons for why we have been reluctant to see ourselves as members of a cultural species or tribe.

Partly, the resistance is pragmatic and stems from the felt pressures of justification. What we want, after all, is to make the strongest case we can for ourselves, and that aim seems to demand that we appeal to some broadly shared human need that only a vibrant humanities can fulfill. This is what Nussbaum does when she claims that the humanities are crucial because they create "people who are able to see other human beings as full people, with thoughts and feelings of their own that deserve respect and empathy."[36] The disappearance of the humanities, Nussbaum appears to be saying, would leave the world with a severe deficit of social virtue. This is an extraordinary claim that leads one to wonder how the human race survived prior to the establishment of the modern research university. But even many who doubt that the humanities play a crucial part in the promotion of liberal tolerance and sympathy may nevertheless insist that defending them requires making *some* such argument. If the humanities do not make us more empathetic, then they must make us more resistant to political demagogues; or, if not that, then they must deal in matters of perennial human concern. Self-preservation demands that we adopt some version of this line of argument, it is said, even if we don't fully stand behind it. For to admit that the humanities are a self-contained and self-referential cultural world would be to grant that their value is largely internal to the practices and institutions that comprise it. And to concede *that* would be to fatally compromise our capacity to defend them.

I don't think this is so. In my view, those who believe that the only way to protect the humanities is to cite a general utility or invoke the pieties of nineteenth-century humanism are overestimating the suasive force of this universalist vocabulary. The fact that we are prone to such overestimations

---

36. Nussbaum, *Not for Profit*, 143.

says more about the peculiar nature of academic discourse than about the potential efficacy of alternative approaches. As Barbara Hernnstein Smith observes in a related context, "the power, richness, subtlety, flexibility, and communicative effectiveness of *a nonobjectivist idiom* . . . are characteristically underestimated by those who have never learned to speak it or tried to use it in interactions with [others]."[37] A non-objectivist, non-universalist defense of the humanities might consist, for instance, of accessible illustrations and demonstrations of what humanist scholarship at its best is like, rather than by argument or jeremiad.

Another reason that we humanists have been reluctant, on the whole, to view ourselves in culturalist terms, as participants in a form of life, is that this view offends our mildly narcissistic but wholly necessary individualism. To regard ourselves as members of a tribe or species, with everything that these terms imply, is to suggest that we are more externally determined and less autonomous and self-directing than we perhaps care to admit. Let me stress that what I'm calling our desire for autonomy and individuality is not a private psychological disposition; it is hardwired into the institutional world of humanist scholarship. Consider: the articles and books we write, in contrast with the articles produced by our colleagues in the hard and soft sciences, are rarely co-authored. We typically write, as we read, alone. The texts that we produce through these countless hours of lonely toil—for which "research" always seems the wrong word—also stand in different relation to our social and professional identities than do the texts produced by our scientist colleagues. As Foucault pointed out, the "author function" in humanist discourse is much closer to what one finds in the literary sphere than in the scientific world.[38] When reading both literary and humanist discourse we seek out the distinct voice, the characteristic cadences and individual thought-style of an author. We construct a certain personality and locate that personality within a multilayered social, political, and historical frame of reference that extends far beyond the specific topic and purview of the study or narrative we are reading. The overlapping spheres of humanist and literary writing are crowded social clubs, bristling with ego and drama—a far cry from the more sanitized (though no less vicious) preserves of sci-

---

37. Barbara Hernnstein Smith, *Contingencies of Value: Alternative Perspectives for Critical Theory* (Cambridge, MA: Harvard University Press, 1988), 158.

38. See Michel Foucault, "What Is an Author?" In *The Foucault Reader*, ed. Paul Rabinow, trans. Josue V. Harari (New York: Pantheon, 1984), 101–120.

ence. Similarly, while a scientist can hope to have her name immortalized as an asteroid or pathology, the highest honor, for both humanist and literary authors, is to become an adjective: to be spoken of as one speaks of a Foucauldian view, a Yeatsian metaphor, or a Marxist critique. This conception of authorship has no equivalent in scientific discourse. Indeed, even when we import a practice from the sciences, we refurbish it to the ends of individual, rather than collective, achievement. Our version of the research group, for instance, is much more like a creative-writing workshop than a collaborative scientific project.

The constant one-upmanship, the relentless hairsplitting and the narcissism of small differences that characterize the world of the humanities often appears absurd to outsiders. And indeed, scores of satirists of the academic life, from Kingsley Amis to David Lodge and Don DeLillo, have mined the comic potential of these peculiarities to its fullest. But absurd or not, these features of our intellectual form of life are absolutely necessary for keeping the enterprise moving. The constant faultfinding and dissatisfaction with the work of those who came before us, as Harold Bloom famously argued, are so many attempts at self-assertion and self-creation.[39] The anxiety that drives the creative person, regardless of whether she is a literary or academic writer, is of dying in the knowledge that she had failed to leave her distinctive mark, failed to make some difference in the way people see, think, or feel.

At the same time, the high premium that the institutional culture of the humanities places on distinctiveness and originality generates the instinctive aversion—typical of our kind—to being lumped together with our peers. What we want is autonomy, not membership; to sing a new song, not recite the words of others. If we are uncomfortable with the culturalist view of the humanities, then, it is because it emphasizes everything that is contextual, shared, and heteronomous about our identities, everything, that is, that we need to repress in order to invent our selves and our languages anew. It reminds us that even those rare individuals who successfully recreate themselves or make a truly original contribution to the conversation remain no more than variations on familiar cultural types. To think in these culturalist terms is to see that even the most idiosyncratic and rebellious minds—the Virginia Woolfs, Oscar Wildes, and Ludwig Wittgensteins of our world—remained for all their trailblazing originality unmistakably the children of their milieus, subject to their assumptions and constrained by

---

39. See Harold Bloom, *The Anxiety of Influence* (Oxford: Oxford University Press, 1973).

(most of their) prejudices. They left their marks, to be sure; but even their achievements were no more than scratches on the massive edifice of cultural uniformity. (But of course, if they had not rebelled against the beliefs and values of their respective cultural worlds, they would not have become Woolf, or Wilde, or Wittgenstein.)

Let me conclude by touching briefly on one more source of resistance to the culturalist view of the humanities. Put simply: to acknowledge that the humanities are neither a privileged intellectual arena in which intrinsic values and timeless truths are discovered and transmitted, nor a vital social organ necessary for the functioning of society, is to face up to the contingency, precarity, and transience of our private and collective identities. This awareness is one many of us work hard to repress even when things are going well. But when the prospect of extinction looms large, we often actively try to deny it. A typical response when a person finds herself consumed by the strangling consciousness of her mortality and vulnerability is to turn to God for comfort. In the intellectual culture of the humanities, the need for metaphysical consolation takes the form of an insistence that, despite everything we've come to believe about the historicity of value and the social construction of reality, enduring essences and intrinsic values *must* somehow be real.

Ultimately, only time will tell whether Handler is right and the humanities are currently tipping into extinction. But she is certainly right that it is vain to try to adapt to a society that doesn't want what we hold dear. As she puts it, "You can adapt only so much before the changes are significant enough that the species itself dies out. The woolly mammoth and the mastodon look a lot like today's elephants, but they are different things." If the humanities are indeed going the way of the mammoth, let us at least remain true to our woolly selves.

Binyamina, 2019

Works Cited

Abu-Lughod, Lila. "Writing against Culture." In *Recapturing Anthropology: Working in the Present*, edited by Richard G. Fox, 137–162. Santa Fe, NM: School of American Research Press, 1991.
Allen, Walter. *The English Novel: A Short Critical History*. Harmondsworth: Penguin, 1986.
Alter, Robert. *Hebrew and Modernism*. Bloomington: Indiana University Press, 1994.
Anderson, Benedict. *Imagined Communities: Reflections on the Origin and Spread of Nationalism*. Rev. ed. London: Verso, 2006.
Appadurai, Arjun. "Putting Hierarchy in its Place." *Cultural Anthropology* 3, no. 1 (Feb. 1988): 36–49.
Aran, Gideon. *Kukism: shorshei gush emunim, tarbut hamitnakhalim, teologia zionit, meshikhiyut bezmanenu*. Jerusalem: Carmel, 2013.
Armstrong, Nancy. *How Novels Think: The Limits of Individualism from 1719–1900*. New York: Columbia University Press, 2005.
Auerbach, Erich. *Mimesis: The Representation of Reality in Western Literature*, translated by Willard R. Trask. Princeton, NJ: Princeton University Press, 2003.
Augustine. *Homilies on the Gospel of John 1–40*. Edited by Allen D. Fitzgerald. Translated by Edmund Hill. New York: New City Press, 2009.
Austin, Mary. "Regionalism in American Fiction." *English Journal* 21, no. 2 (Feb. 1932): 97–107.
Bagehot, Walter. "The Novels of George Eliot, *National Review* (1860)." In *The Victorian Art of Fiction: Nineteenth-Century Essays on the Novel*, edited by Rohan Maitzen, 171–188. Toronto: Broadview Press, 2009.
Bakhtin, Mikhail. *Problems in Dostoevsky's Poetics*. Edited and translated by Caryl Emerson. Minneapolis: University of Minnesota Press, 1984.
Barnard, F.M. *Herder on Nationality, Humanity, and Freedom*. Montreal: McGill-Queen's University Press, 2003.
———. *Herder on Social and Political Culture*. Cambridge: Cambridge University Press, 1969.

Barthes, Roland. *The Pleasure of the Text*. Translated by Richard Miller. New York: Hill & Wang, 1975.
Bauman, Zygmunt. *Culture as Praxis*. London: Sage, 1999.
Becker, Ernest. *The Denial of Death*. New York: Simon & Schuster, 1973.
Bellamy, Liz. "Regionalism and Nationalism: Maria Edgeworth, Walter Scott and the Definition of Britishness." In *The Regional Novel in Britain and Ireland: 1800–1990*, edited by K.D.M. Snell. Cambridge: Cambridge University Press, 1998.
Benedict, Ruth. *Patterns of Culture*. New York: The New American Library, 1934.
Benhabib, Seyla. *The Claims of Culture: Equality and Diversity in the Global Era*. Princeton, NJ: Princeton University Press, 2002.
Bentley, Nancy. *The Ethnography of Manners: Hawthorne, James, Wharton*. Cambridge: Cambridge University Press, 1995.
Berger, Peter, and Thomas Luckmann. *The Social Construction of Reality: A Treatise in the Sociology of Knowledge*. London: Penguin, 1991.
———. *The Sacred Canopy: Elements of a Sociological Theory of Religion*. Garden City, NJ: Doubleday, 1967.
Berlin, Isaiah. *The Hedgehog and the Fox*. London: Weidenfeld & Nicolson, 1953.
———. *Three Critics of the Enlightenment: Vico, Hamann, Herder*. 2nd ed. Princeton, NJ: Princeton University Press, 2013.
———. "Two Concepts of Liberty." In *Liberty*, edited by Henry Hardy, 166–217. Oxford: Oxford University Press. 2013.
Bérubé, Michael. *Rhetorical Occasions: Essays on Humans and the Humanities*, 35–53. Chapel Hill: University of North Carolina Press, 2006.
———, with Jennifer Ruth. *The Humanities, Higher Education, and Academic Freedom Three Necessary Arguments*. New York: Palgrave Macmillan, 2015.
Bhabha, Homi K. "DissemiNation: Time, Narrative, and the Margins of the Modern Nation." In *Nation and Narration*, edited by Homi K. Bhabha, 291–332. London: Routledge, 1990.
Biddle, Francis. *Justice Holmes, Natural Law, and the Supreme Court*. New York: Macmillan, 1961.
Bienert, Michael. *Joseph Roth in Berlin: Ein Lesebuch für Spaziergänger*. Berlin: Kiepenheuer & Witsch, 1997.
Bloom, Harold. *The Anxiety of Influence*. Oxford: Oxford University Press, 1973.
Blumenberg, Hans. *Shipwreck with Spectator: Paradigm of a Metaphor for Existence*. Translated by Steven Rendall. Cambridge, MA: MIT Press, 1997.
Brodhead, Richard. *Cultures of Letters*. Chicago: University of Chicago Press, 1993.
Bronson, David. *Joseph Roth: Eine Biographie*. Köln: Kiepnheuer& Witsch, 1981.
Brooks, Cleanth. "The Heresy of Paraphrase." In *The Well Wrought Urn*. New York: Harcourt, 1947.
Brooks, Peter, and Hilary Jewett eds. *The Humanities and Public Life*. New York: Fordham University Press, 2014.

Brown, Bill. *Other Things*. Chicago: University of Chicago Press, 2015.
Brown, David. *Walter Scott and the Historical Imagination*. London: Routledge, 1979.
Brumann, Christoph. "Writing for Culture: Why a Successful Concept Should Not Be Discarded." *Current Anthropology* 40, suppl. 1 (Feb. 1999): S1–S27.
Bunzl, Matti. "Anthropology Beyond Crisis: Toward an Intellectual History of the Extended Present." *Anthropology and Humanism* 30, no. 2 (December 2005): 187–195.
———. "The Quest for Anthropological Relevance: Borgesian Maps and Epistemological Pitfalls."*American Anthropologist* 110, no. 1 (March 2008): 53–60.
Burke, Edmund. *Reflections on the French Revolution*. London: J. M. Dent & Sons, 1951.
Butler, Marilyn. "Introduction." In *Castle Rackrent and Ennui*, edited by Marilyn Butler. London: Penguin, 1992.
Buzard, James. *Disorienting Fiction: The Autoethnographic Work of Nineteenth-Century British Novels*. Princeton, NJ: Princeton University Press, 2005.
Clifford, James. *The Predicament of Culture*. Cambridge, MA: Harvard University Press, 1988.
———. "On Ethnographic Allegory." In *Writing Culture: The Poetics and Politics of Ethnography*, edited by James Clifford and George Marcus. Berkeley: University of California Press, 1986.
Conrad, Joseph. "Preface" to *The Nigger of the "Narcissus"* (1897), in *The Nigger of the "Narcissus" and the End of the Tether*. New York: Dell Publishing, 1960.
———. *Heart of Darkness*. Edited by Paul B. Armstrong. New York: W. W. Norton, 2006.
Culler, Jonathan. "Omniscience." *Narrative* 12, no. 1 (Jan. 2004): 22–34.
de Saussure, Ferdinand. *Course in General Linguistics*. Translated by Wade Baskin. New York: McGraw-Hill, 1959.
Dennett, Daniel. *Darwin's Dangerous Idea: Evolution and the Meaning of Life*. New York: Simon & Schuster, 1995.
Derrida, Jacques. *Writing and Difference*. Translated by Alan Bass. Chicago: University of Chicago Press, 1978.
Dewey, John. *Reconstruction in Philosophy*. Mineola, NY: Dover, 2004.
———. *The Quest for Certainty*. Vol. 4 of *John Dewey: The Later Works, 1925–1953*, edited by Jo Ann Boydston. Carbondale: Southern Illinois University Press, 2008.
Dimock, Wai Chee. "A Theory of Resonance." *PMLA* 112, no. 5 (Oct. 1997): 1060–1071.
Donovan, Josephine. *European Local-Color Literature: National Tales, Dorfgeschichten, Romans Champetres*. New York: Continuum, 2010.
Duncan, Ian. *Scott's Shadow: The Novel in Romantic Edinburgh*. Princeton, NJ: Princeton University Press, 2016.
During, Simon. "Stop Defending the Humanities." *Public Books*, March 1, 2014. www.publicbooks.org/stop-defending-the-humanities.

Eagleton, Terry. *Sweet Violence*. Malden, MA: Blackwell, 2003.
———. *The English Novel: An Introduction*. Malden, MA: Blackwell, 2005.
Edgeworth, Maria. "Essay on Irish Bulls." In *Tales and Novels*. London: Henry G. Bohn, 1874.
———. *Castle Rackrent and Ennui*. Edited by Marilyn Butler. London: Penguin, 1992.
Edwards, Brian T. "The Well-Built Wall of Culture." *The Age of Innocence*. Edited by Candace Waid, 482–506. New York: W. W. Norton, 2003.
Eliade, Mircea. *Cosmos and History: The Myth of the Eternal Return*. Translated by Willard R. Trask. New York: Harper, 1954.
Eliot, George. *Adam Bede*. Edited by Carol A. Martin. Oxford: Oxford University Press, 2008.
———. *Essays of George Eliot*. Edited by Thomas Pinney. New York: Columbia University Press, 1963.
———. *Middlemarch*. Peterborough: Broadview Press, 2004).
Enoch, David. *Taking Morality Seriously: A Defense of Robust Realism*. Oxford: Oxford University Press, 2011.
Ermarth, Elizabeth. *Realism and Consensus in the English Novel*. Princeton, NJ: Princeton University Press, 1981.
Esty, Jed. *A Shrinking Island: Modernism and National Culture in England*. Princeton, NJ: Princeton University Press, 2004.
Ezer, Nancy. "Memelancholia shel yachid lemelancholia shel ma'amad: me'shkhol vekishalon le'Brenner le'Zikhron Devarim leshabtai." *Dapim lemechkar besifrut* 13 (2001–2002): 23–30.
Febvre, Lucien. "Civilisation: Evolution of a Word and a Group of Ideas." In *Classical Readings in Culture and Civilisation*, edited by John Rundell and Stephen Mennell. London: Routledge, 1998.
Felski, Rita. *Uses of Literature*. Malden, MA: Blackwell, 2008.
Ferris, Ina. " 'On the Borders of Oblivion': Scott's Historical Novel and the Modern Time of the Remnant." *Modern Language Quarterly* 70, no. 4 (Dec. 2009): 473–494.
———. *The Romantic National Rale and the Question of Ireland*. Cambridge: Cambridge University Press, 2004.
Fisher, Philip. *Still the New World*. Cambridge, MA: Harvard University Press, 1999.
Foucault, Michel. "What Is an Author?" In *The Foucault Reader*, edited by Paul Rabinow. Translated by Josue V. Harari, 101–120. New York: Pantheon, 1984.
France, Anatole. "The Adventure of the Soul." *The Literary Life*. In *A Modern Book of Criticism*, edited and translated by Ludwig Lewisohn, 1. New York: Modern Library, 1919.
Freeman, Mary Wilkins. "Author's Preface." In *A Far-Away Melody: and Other Stories*. Edinburgh: D. Douglas, 1897.
Freud, Sigmund. "On Transience." In *The Standard Edition of the Complete Psychological Works* XIV, 305–307. Translated by James Strachey. London: Hogarth Press, 1957.

Fritzsche, Peter. *Stranded in the Present: Modern Time and the Melancholy of History.* Cambridge, MA: Harvard University Press, 2004.
Geertz, Clifford. "The Impact of the Concept of Culture on the Concept of Man." In *The Interpretation of Cultures*, 33–54. New York: Basic Books, 1973.
———. *Works and Lives: The Anthropologist as Author.* Stanford, CA: Stanford University Press, 1988.
Ginsburg, Shai. *Rhetoric and Nation: The Formation of Hebrew Culture 1880–1990.* Syracuse, NY: Syracuse University Press, 2014.
Hale, Dorothy J. "Aesthetics and the New Ethics: Theorizing the Novel in the Twenty-First Century." *PMLA* 124, no. 3 (May 2009): 896–905.
Handler, Nina. "Facing My Own Extinction." *The Chronicle of Higher Education.* December 7, 2017. www.chronicle.com/article/Facing-My-Own-Extinction/241988.
Hardy, Thomas. "General Preface to the Novels and Poems." In *Thomas Hardy's Personal Writings*, edited by Harold Orel. London: Macmillan, 1967.
Harpham, Geoffrey Galt. "Beneath and beyond the 'Crisis in the Humanities.'" *New Literary History* 36, no. 1 (Winter 2005): 21–36.
Hegeman, Susan. *The Cultural Return.* Berkeley: University of California Press, 2012.
Herbert, Christopher. *Culture and Anomie.* Chicago: University of Chicago Press, 1991.
Herder, Johann Gottfried. *Herder: Philosophical Writings.* Translated and edited by Michael N. Forster. Cambridge: Cambridge University Press, 2002.
Hernnstein Smith, Barbara. *Contingencies of Value: Alternative Perspectives for Critical Theory.* Cambridge, MA: Harvard University Press, 1988.
Hofmann, Michael. "Translator's Introduction." In *The Radetzky March*, translated by Michael Hoffman, v–xvi. London: Granta, 2002.
Hollander, Rachel. *Narrative Hospitality in Late Victorian Fiction: Novel Ethics.* New York: Routledge, 2013.
Howe, Irving. "Absalom in Israel." *New York Times Review of Books*, October 10, 1985. www.nybooks.com/articles/1985/10/10/absalom-in-israel.
———. *A Critic's Notebook.* Edited by Nicholas Howe. New York: Harcourt Brace Jovanovich, 1994.
———. *The Decline of the New.* London: Victor Gollancz, 1963.
Howells, William Dean. *The Rise of Silas Lapham.* New York: The Library of America, 1982.
Hughes, Jon. *Facing Modernity: Fragmentation, Culture and Identity in Joseph Roth's Writing in the 1920s.* London: Maney Publishing, 2006.
Hüppauf, Bernd. "Joseph Roth: *Hiob*; Der Mythos der Skeptikers." In *Joseph Roth: Werk und Wirkung*, edited by Bernd M. Kraske, 25–51. Bonn: Bouvier, 1988.
James, William. *Pragmatism: A New Name for Some Old Ways of Thinking.* Cambridge, MA: Harvard University Press, 1975.
Jameson, Frederic. *The Political Unconscious: Narrative as a Socially Symbolic Act.* Ithaca, NY: Cornell University Press, 1981.
Jewett, Sarah Orne. "Preface to *Deephaven* (1893)." In *Deephaven and Other Stories*, edited by Richard Cary. Albany, NY: New College and University Press, 1966.

Juergens, Thorsten. *Gesellschaftskritische Aspekte in Joseph Roths Romanen*. Leiden: Leiden University, 1977.

Kagan, Tzipora. "Sifrut shel shki'a ke'sifrut shel hitgalut." *Moznaim* 74, no. 6 (March 2000): 4–6.

Kalderon, Nissim. "Eize gvulot ata mesugal lesamen bamidron." In *Hargasha shel makom*, 21–42. Tel Aviv: Hakibbutz Hameuchad, 1988.

Kaplan, Amy. "Nation, Region, and Empire." In *The Columbia History of the American Novel*, edited by Emory Elliott, 240–266. New York: Columbia University Press, 1991.

———. *The Social Construction of American Realism*. Chicago: University of Chicago Press, 1988.

Kesten, Hermann. "Der Schriftsteller Joseph Roth." In *Joseph Roth—Sonderband, Text + Kritik*, edited by Heinz Ludwig Arnold, 7–9. Munich: Edition Text + Kritik, 1974/1982.

———. "Joseph Roth." *Wort in der Zeit* 9 (1959): 2–7.

Kilcher, Andreas. "The Cold Order and the Eros of Storytelling." In *Writing Jewish Culture: Paradoxes in Ethnography*, edited by Gabriella Safran and Andreas Kilcher, 68–93. Bloomington: Indiana University Press, 2016.

Kimmerling, Baruch. *The End of Ashkenazi Hegemony*. Jerusalem: Keter, 2001.

Kosellek, Reinhart. *Futures Past: On the Semnatics of Historical Time*. Translated by Keith Tribe. New York: Columbia University Press, 2004.

Kroeber, A.L., and Clyde Kluckhohn. *Culture: Critical Review of Concepts and Definitions*. Cambridge: Peabody Museum of American Archaeology and Ethnology, Harvard University, 1952.

Kronman, Anthony T. *Education's End: Why Our Colleges and Universities Have Given Up on the Meaning of Life*. New Haven, CT: Yale University Press, 2007.

Kundera, Milan. *Art of the Novel*. Translated by Linda Asher. New York: Harper & Row, 1988.

Lackey, Michael. "Modernist Anti-Philosophicalism and Virginia Woolf's Critique of Philosophy." *Journal of Modern Literature* 29, no. 4 (Summer 2006): 76–98.

Latour, Bruno. "Why Has Critique Run Out of Steam? From Matters of Fact to Matters of Concern." *Critical Inquiry* 30, no. 2 (2004): 225–248.

Lawson, Richard H. "Thematic Similarities in Edith Wharton and Thomas Mann." *Twentieth Century Literature* 23, no. 3 (Oct. 1977): 289–298.

Lear, Jonathan. *Radical Hope: Ethics in the Face of Cultural Devastation*. Cambridge, MA: Harvard University Press, 2006.

Lears, T.J. Jackson. *No Place of Grace: Antimodernism and the Transformation of American Culture 1880–1920*. Chicago: University of Chicago Press, 1983.

Leavis, F.R. *The Great Tradition: George Eliot, Henry James, Joseph Conrad*. Harmondsworth: Penguin, 1962.

Lee, Hermione. *Edith Wharton*. London: Vintage, 2008.

Levine, George. *Realism, Ethics and Secularism: Essays on Victorian Literature and Science*. Cambridge: Cambridge University Press, 2008.

———. *The Realistic Imagination: English Fiction from Frankenstein to Lady Chatterley*. Chicago: University of Chicago Press, 1981.
Lewis, R.W.B. *Edith Wharton: A Biography*. New York: Harper & Row, 1975.
Lovejoy, Arthur O. *The Great Chain of Being: A Study of the History of an Idea*. Cambridge, MA: Harvard University Press, 2001.
Lukács, Georg. *The Historical Novel*. Translated by Hannah and Stanley Mitchell. Boston: Beacon Press, 1963.
———. "The Ideology of Modernism." In *Marxist Literary Theory: A Reader*, edited by Terry Eagleton and Frew Milne. Oxford: Wiley Blackwell, 1996.
———. *The Meaning of Contemporary Realism*. Translated by John and Necke Mander. London: Merlin Press, 1962.
Malinowski, Bronislaw. *Argonauts of the Western Pacific*. London: Routledge, 1961.
Mansfield, Katherine. "Family Portraits." *Athenaeum* (Dec. 10 1920): 810–811. Reproduced in Wharton, Edith. *The Age of Innocence*. Edited by Candace Waid. New York: W. W. Norton, 2003.
Margris, Claudio. *Weit von Wo: Verlorene Welt des Ostjudentums*. Vienna: Europa Verlag, 1974.
Maxwell, Richard. "Dickens' Omniscience." *ELH* 46, no. 2 (Summer 1979): 290–313.
Mead, Margaret. *Sex and Temperament in Three Primitive Societies*. New York: Morrow, 1963.
Menand, Louis. *The Metaphysical Club*. New York: Farrar, Straus and Giroux, 2001.
Miller, Andrew H. *The Burdens of Perfection: On Ethics and Reading in Nineteenth-Century British Literature*. Ithaca, NY: Cornell University Press, 2008.
Miner, Earl. "The Making of 'The Deserted Village.'" *Huntington Library Quarterly* 22, no. 2 (Feb. 1959): 125–141.
Miron, Dan. "Hazikaron ke'idea." In *Pinkas Patuach*. Tel Aviv: Sifriyat poalim, 1979.
Moretti, Franco. *The Way of the World*. London: Verso, 2000.
Morstin, Graph. *Joseph Roth: Romane, Erzählungen, Aufsätze*. Köln: Kiepenhauer & Witsch, 1964.
Nehamas, Alexander. *The Art of Living: Socratic Reflections from Plato to Foucault*. Berkeley: University of California Press, 1998.
Nevius, Blake. *Edith Wharton: A Study of her Fiction*. Berkeley: University of California Press, 1953.
Newman, John Henry. *A Grammar of Assent*. London: Gilbert and Rivington, 1870.
Nietzsche, Friedrich. *The Gay Science*. Edited by Bernard Williams. Translated by Josefine Nauckhoff. Cambridge: Cambridge University Press, 2001.
———. *The Use and Abuse of History*. Translated by Adrian Collins. Indianapolis, IN: Bobbs-Merrill, 1957.
Nussbaum, Martha. *Not for Profit: Why Democracy Needs the Humanities*. Princeton, NJ: Princeton University Press, 2010.
———. "Tragedy and Self-sufficiency: Plato and Aristotle on Fear and Pity." In *Essays on Aristotle's Poetics*, edited by Amélie Rorty, 261–290. Princeton, NJ: Princeton University Press, 1992.

Orpaz, Yitzhak. *Hatszalyan hachiloni*. Tel Aviv: Hakibbutz Hameuchad, 1982.
Ortega y Gasset, José. "The Dehumanization of Art." In *Theory of the Novel: A Historical Approach*, edited by Michael McKeon, 294–316. Baltimore, MD: Johns Hopkins University Press, 2000.
Oz, Amos. *Under This Blazing Sun*. Translated by Nicholas de Lange. Cambridge: Cambridge University Press, 1979.
Parekh, Bhikhu. *Rethinking Multiculturalism: Cultural Diversity and Political Theory*. New York: Palgrave, 2006.
Pavel, Thomas. *The Lives of the Novel: A History*. Princeton, NJ: Princeton University Press, 2013.
Peel, Robin. *Apart from Modernism: Edith Wharton*. Cranbury, NJ: Associated University Press, 2005.
Perloff, Marjorie. *The Edge of Irony: Modernism in the Shadow of the Habsburg Empire*. Chicago: University of Chicago Press, 2016.
Pick, Daniel. *Faces of Degeneration: A European Disorder, C. 1848–1918*. Cambridge: Cambridge University Press, 1993.
Pippin, Robert B. *Henry James and the Modern Moral Life*. Cambridge: Cambridge University Press, 2000.
Pratt, Mary Louise. "Scratches on the Face of the Country; Or, What Mr. Barrow Saw in the Land of the Bushmen." *Critical Inquiry* 12, no. 1 (Autumn 1985): 119–143.
Redfield, James. "Herodotus the Tourist." *Classical Philology* 80, no. 2 (1985): 97–118.
Reich-Ranicki, Marcel. "Der Romancier Joseph Roth." In *Joseph Roth: Interpretation, Rezeption, Kritik*, edited by Michael Kessler and Fritz Hackert, 261–268. Tübingen: Stauffenburg, 1990.
Richetti, John. *The English Novel in History: 1700–1780*. London: Routledge, 1999.
Rigney, Ann. *The Afterlives of Walter Scott: Memory on the Move*. Oxford: Oxford University Press, 2012.
Ron, Moshe. "*Zikhron Devarim*: ha'mishpat." *Siman Kriaa* 16–17 (April 1983): 272–278.
Rorty, Richard. "Heidegger, Contingency, and Pragmatism." In *Essays on Heidegger and Others*, 27–49. Cambridge: Cambridge University Press, 1991.
———. "Solidarity or Objectivity." In *Objectivity, Relativism, and Truth*, 21–34. Cambridge: Cambridge University Press, 1991.
———. "Wittgenstein, Heidegger, and the Reification of Language." In *Essays on Heidegger and Others: Philosophical Papers*, 50–65. Cambridge: Cambridge University Press, 1991.
———. *Consequences of Pragmatism*. Minneapolis: University of Minnesota Press, 1982.
———. *Contingency, Irony, and Solidarity*. Cambridge: Cambridge University Press, 1989.

———. *Philosophy and the Mirror of Nature*. Princeton, NJ: Princeton University Press, 1979.
Rosenfeld, Sidney. *Understanding Joseph Roth*. Columbia: South Carolina University Press, 2001.
Rosenthal, Jesse. *Good Form: The Ethical Experience of the Victorian Novel*. Princeton, NJ: Princeton University Press, 2017.
Roskies, David G. *Against the Apocalypse: Responses to Catastrophe in Modern Jewish Culture*. Cambridge, MA: Harvard University Press, 1984.
Roth, Joseph. "The Myth of the German soul." In *The White Cities: Reports from France 1925–39*, translated by Michael Hofmann, 233–237. London: Granta, 2004.
———. *Flucht ohne Ende*. In *Romane and Erzählungen 1916–1929*. Edited by Fritz Hackert. Köln: Kiepenheuer & Fitzsch, 1989.
———. *Joseph Roth: A Life in Letters*. Translated by Michael Hofmann. London: Granta, 2012.
———. *The Radetzky March*. Translated by Michael Hofmann. London: Granta, 2002.
———. *The Wandering Jews*. Translated by Michael Hofmann. New York: W. W. Norton, 2001.
———. *The White Cities: Reports from France 1925–39*. Translated by Michael Hofmann. London: Granta, 2004.
Sahlins, Marshall. "Two or Three Things that I Know about Culture." *The Journal of the Royal Anthropological Institute* 5, no. 3 (Sept. 1999): 399–421.
———. *Islands of History*. Chicago: University of Chicago Press, 1987.
Sand, Shlomo. *Haintelktual, haemet vehakoach*. Tel Aviv: Am Oved, 2000.
Sapir, Edward. "Culture, Genuine and Spurious." In *Culture, Language, and Personality: Selected Essays*, edited by David G. Mandelbaum, 78–119. Berkeley: University of California Press, 1964.
———. "The Status of Linguistics as a Science." In *Culture, Language and Personality: Selected Essays*, edited by David G. Mandelbaum. Berkeley: University of California Press, 1949.
Scheffler, Samuel. *Death and the Afterlife*. New York: Oxford, 2013.
Schiller, Friedrich. *On the Naïve and Sentimental in Literature*. Translated by Helen Watanabe-O'Kelly. Manchester: Carcanet New Press, 1981.
Schor, Hilary M. *Curious Subjects: Women and the Trial of Realism*. New York: Oxford University Press, 2012.
Scott, Walter. *Waverley; or 'Tis Sixty Years Since*. Edited by Claire Lamont. Oxford: Oxford University Press, 2005.
Scranton, Roy. *Learning to Die in the Anthropocene: Reflections on the End of a Civilization*. San Francisco: City Lights, 2015.
Shabtai, Yaakov. *Past Continuous*. Translated by Dalya Bilu. New York: Overlook Press, 2002.
———. *Sof Davar [Past Perfect]*. Israel: Hakibbutz hameuchad, 1985.

Shaked, Gershon. "After the Fall: Nostalgia and the Treatment of Authority in the Works of Kafka and Agnon, Two Habsburgian Writers." *Partial Answers: Journal of Literature and the History of Ideas* 2, no. 1 (Jan. 2004): 81–82.

———. *Hasiporet haivrit.* Vol. 4, *1880–1980.* Tel Aviv: Hakibbutz Hameuchad, 1993.

Shaw, Harry E. *Narrating Reality: Austen, Scott, Eliot.* Ithaca, NY: Cornell University Press, 1999.

Soker-Schwager, Chana. *Mechashef hashevet memeonot haovdim: Yaakov Shabtai batarbut hayisraelit.* Tel Aviv: Hakibbutz Hameuchad, 2007.

Spenser, Malcolm. *In the Shadow of Empire: Austrian Experiences of Modernity in the Writings of Musil, Roth, and Bachmann.* Rochester, NY: Camden House, 2008.

Stafford, Fiona. *The Last of the Race.* Oxford: Clarendon, 1994.

Stewart, Susan. *On Longing: Narratives of the Miniature, the Gigantic, the Souvenir, the Collection.* Durham, NC: Duke University Press, 1993.

Stocking, George. *Victorian Anthropology.* New York: Free Press, 1987.

Taylor, Charles. "A Different Kind of Courage." *New York Review of Books*, April 26, 2007.

Thompson, E.P. *The Making of the English Working Class.* New York: Vintage Books, 1963.

Tonkin, Kati. *Joseph Roth's March into History: From the Early Novels to* Radetzkymarsch *and Die Kapuzinergruft.* Rochester, NY: Camden House, 2008.

Trilling, Lionel. "Freud: Within and Beyond Culture." In *Beyond Culture: Essays on Literature and Learning.* London: Secker & Warburg, 1955.

———. "Manners, Morals, and the Novel." *The Kenyon Review* 10, no. 1 (Winter 1948): 11–27.

Trumpener, Katie. *Bardic Nationalism.* Princeton, NJ: Princeton University Press, 1997.

Tylor, Edward B. "The Science of Culture." In *Primitive Culture: Researches into the Development of Mythology, Philosophy, Religion, Art, and Custom.* London: John Murray, 1871.

Updike, John. "Archer's Way." In *Edith Wharton's The Age of Innocence,* edited by Harold Bloom, 133–139. Philadelphia: Chelsea House, 2005.

Valéry, Paul. "Disillusionment." In *Sources of European History Since 1900,* edited by Marvin Perry, Matthew Bera, and James Krukones. Boston: Cengage, 2011.

Wagner, Roy. *The Invention of Culture.* Chicago: University of Chicago Press, 1981.

Watt, Ian. *The Rise of the Novel.* Berkeley: University of California Press, 2001.

Wharton, Edith. "Introduction to the 1936 Edition." In *Edith Wharton's* The House of Mirth*: A Casebook,* edited by Carol J. Singley, 31–37. Oxford: Oxford University Press, 2003.

———. "Tendencies in Modern Fiction." In *Edith Wharton: The Uncollected Critical Writings,* edited by Frederick Wegener, 170–174. New Jersey: Princeton University Press, 1996.

———. "The Great American Novel." *Yale Review* 16 (July 1927): 646–656. Reproduced in *Edith Wharton: The Uncollected Critical Writings,* edited by Frederick Wegener, 151–159. Princeton, NJ: Princeton University Press, 1996.

———. *A Backward Glance*. New York & London: D. Appleton-Century Company, 1934.
———. *The Age of Innocence*. Edited by Candace Waid. New York: W. W. Norton, 2003.
———. *The House of Mirth*. Edited by Elizabeth Ammons. New York: W. W. Norton, 1990.
———. *The Writing of Fiction*. New York: Touchstone, 1997.
Williams, Raymond. *Culture and Society 1780–1950*. Garden City, NY: Anchor Books, 1960.
———. *The Country and the City*. New York: Oxford University Press, 1973.
Wilson, Edmund. "Justice to Edith Wharton." In *The Wound and the Bow: Seven Studies in Literature*, 159–173. New York: Oxford University Press, 1965.
Wolff, Cynthia Griffin. *A Feast of Words: The Triumph of Edith Wharton*. New York: Oxford University Press, 1977.
Woolf, Virginia. "Modern Fiction." In *Selected Essays*, edited by David Bradshaw, 6–13. Oxford: Oxford University Press, 2008.
Wörsching, Martha. "Die Rückwärts gewandte Utopie." In *Text + Kritik: Joseph Roth*, edited by Heinz Ludwig Arnold, 90–100. Munich: Edition Text + Kritik, 1974/1982.
Zagarell, Sandra A. "Narrative of Community: The Identification of a Genre." *Signs* 13, no. 3 (Spring 1988): 498–527.
Žižek, Slavoj. *The Courage of Hopelessness: Chronicles of a Year of Acting Dangerously*. Brooklyn: Melville House, 2017.
Zuckerman, Ilana. "Shabtai, Yaakov: Hareayon ha'acharon" ["Yaakov Shabtai: The Last Interview]. *Yedioth Achronot* (Apr. 9, 1981).
Zweig, Stefan. *The World of Yesterday*. Lincoln: Nebraska University Press, 1964.

Index

Abu-Lughod, Lila, 7, 38n, 134
Achebe, Chinua, 3, 9
Act of Union (1801), 53, 57
Adams, Brooks, 79
Aeschylus, 8
Agnon, S.Y., 3, 144, 168n, 181n, 182n
Ali, Ahmed, 3, 9
Allen, Walter, 57
Alter, Robert, 156
Alterman, Nathan, 182
Amis, Kingsley, 203
Anderson, Benedict, 3, 19, 57
Appadurai, Arjun, 7, 35n, 133–34
Aquinas, Thomas, 41
Arata, Stephen, 79n
Aristophanes, 172
Aristotle, 41
Armstrong, Nancy, 19
Arnold, Matthew, 31, 32, 66, 94
Auerbach, Berthold, 20, 69
Auerbach, Erich, 12, 22, 68
Augustine, Saint, 18, 45, 187, 188
Austen, Jane, 91, 95
Austin, Mary, 82, 89n, 100
Austro-Hungary. *See* Habsburg Empire

Bagehot, Walter, 95
Bakhtin, Mikhail, 160
Bakunin, Mikhail, 48

Balzac, Honoré de, 20, 64–65, 66, 68, 91
Barnard, F.M., 43
Barth, John, 167, 170
Barthes, Roland, 182
Bauman, Zygmunt, 18
Beard, George Miller, 78
Becker, Ernest, 36
Bellamy, Liz, 56, 68
Benedict, Ruth, 36, 43, 71, 80, 83, 122, 191
Benhabib, Seyla, 135
Bentley, Nancy, 12n, 13, 80n, 83, 84–86, 91, 96, 106
Berenson, Bernard, 91
Berger, Peter, 10, 104, 115n
Bergmann, Hugo, 182n
Berlin, Isaiah, 15n, 48, 166
Bérubé, Michael, 193, 194, 195n
Bhabha, Homi, 19
Bilu, Dalya, 173n
Bloom, Harold, 203
Boas, Franz, 7n, 39, 84, 122
Borges, Jorge Luis, 170
Brentano, Bernard von, 118n
Brodhead, Richard, 21, 71
Bronson, David, 118n
Brooks, Cleanth, 186
Brooks, Peter, 198–99, 200
Brown, Bill, 128

Brumann, Christoph, 40
Buber, Martin, 182
Bulwer-Lytton, Edward, 3, 64
Bunzl, Matti, 23
Burckhardt, Jacob, 47
Burke, Edmund, 14, 15, 18, 25, 41–42, 44–6, 55, 57, 96, 122, 141–42, 153, 156
Burney, Frances, 54
Butler, Judith, 7
Buzard, James, 12n, 13, 24n, 39, 63, 64, 66, 96n, 134–35, 136

Camus, Albert, 170, 181n
Canetti, Elias, 128
Cather, Willa, 3
Catherwood, Mary Hartwell, 89n
Cervantes, Miguel de, 1, 193
Chateaubriand, François-René de, 49
Chopin, Kate, 89n
Clifford, James, 40, 52, 70
Coleridge, Samuel Taylor, 15, 47
Conrad, Joseph, 72–73, 91, 97, 112
Cooper, James Fenimore, 3, 64, 71, 76, 89n
Covid-19, 9
crisis of the humanities, 10, 25, 27, 194–204
Culler, Jonathan, 162
culture (concept), 7, 12, 14, 15, 37, 38–39, 40–41, 49, 50, 96, 125, 134, 135, 143
culturalism (discourse), 2, 12, 13–16, 17, 18, 19 20, 21, 25, 26, 27, 33–37, 39, 41, 44, 46–47, 49, 58, 61, 63, 65–67, 73, 75–76, 84, 86, 90, 93, 95, 96n, 97, 106, 114, 117, 119, 122, 126, 130, 134–36, 148, 152, 154, 156, 157, 163, 165, 185–86, 188, 190, 193, 194, 196, 197, 201–4; and the idea of "human nature," 6, 32, 34, 42, 47, 60, 61, 112, 113n, 185, 190, 191–92, 194; and secularism, 18, 37, 48; and vulnerability, 9, 11, 13, 16, 20, 29–34, 36, 37, 46, 52, 63, 70, 73, 75–76, 81, 117, 143, 171, 190, 194, 204
cultural extinction, 1, 3, 5, 17, 21, 25, 26, 50, 85, 153; narratives of, 2, 3, 5, 8, 9, 11, 13, 21, 25, 50, 51, 75, 115, 125, 156, 169, 185, 187, 189, 190, 194; association with peripherality, 21, 25, 26, 49, 51, 52, 53, 70–72, 77, 79–80, 125–26
Cummings, E.E., 110
Cuvier, George, 17

Darwin, Charles, 36, 72, 78, 93, 197
Dayan, Asi, 151
Defoe, Daniel, 52
DeLillo, Don, 203
Dennett, Daniel, 195n
Derrida, Jacques, 33, 172, 195
Descartes, René, 14, 18, 45, 193
Dewey, John, 4, 5, 26, 33, 93, 170, 171, 173, 188
Dickens, Charles, 20, 65, 66, 67–68, 70n, 93, 95, 97, 161
Diderot, Denis, 54
Dilthey, Wilhelm, 84
Dimock, Wai Chee, 22
Dollenmayer, David, 145n
Donovan, Josephine, 68, 69–70
Dos Passos, John, 110
Dostoevsky, Fyodor, 1, 92, 160
Dreiser, Theodore, 81, 105
Dual Monarchy. See Habsburg Empire
Duncan, Ian, 12n, 64, 65n
During, Simon, 27, 198, 200, 201

Eagleton, Terry, 7n, 8, 24, 67, 189

Edgeworth, Maria, 2, 21, 25, 50, 52–58, 59, 77, 82, 124, 125, 154, 187, 194; narratorial technique, 55–58; role in the rise of regionalism and realism, 64–70 Works: *Castle Rackrent*, 13, 53–58, 70; "An Essay on Irish Bulls," 54
Edgeworth, Richard Lovell, 54
Edwards, Brian T., 99
Ehrhardt, Julia, 100n
elegiac realism. *See under* realism (genre)
Eliade, Mircea, 17n, 77, 78n
Eliot, George, 2, 19, 64, 66, 67, 70n, 91, 93, 95, 97, 155, 157, 162, 172, 187
Eliot, T.S., 90
Elliot, Michael, 12n, 13, 24n
Enoch, David, 191, 192
Ermarth, Elizabeth, 163
Esty, Jed, 72, 73, 96
Euripides, 9, 105
Evans, Brad, 12n, 13, 24n
Evans-Pritchard, E.E., 71, 122, 133

Fabian, Johannes, 134
Faulkner, William, 27, 151, 152
Febvre, Lucien, 48, 50
Felski, Rita, 187, 190, 195n
Ferguson, Adam, 44, 60
Ferris, Ina, 54, 89
Fetterley, Judith, 68
Fielding, Henry, 52, 54
Fisher, Philip, 79
Fitzgerald, F. Scott, 88, 110
Flaubert, Gustave, 65, 68, 111
Fontane, Theodor, 3, 71
Foucault, Michel, 84, 112, 183, 194, 195, 202, 203
France, Anatole, 121
Frazer, James, 76

Freeman, Mary Wilkins, 81, 69
French Revolution [also 1789], 14, 16–17, 19, 20, 41, 47, 48, 49, 50, 52, 58, 67–68, 77, 128, 153
Freud, Sigmund, 72, 80, 88, 93, 111, 188, 189, 191, 193, 195
Fritzsche, Peter, 17, 48
Fullerton, Morton, 87

Gaskell, Elizabeth, 68
Geertz, Clifford, 15, 46, 136–37, 194
Ginsburg, Shai, 163
Gitai, Amos, 151
Goethe, Johann Wolfgang von, 102, 109n, 114
Gogol, Nikolai Vasilievich, 151
Goldsmith, Oliver, 2, 50–53, 70
Grass, Günter, 148
Graves, Robert, 110
Gray, Thomas, 50–51, 52, 70, 89
Great War, 2, 25, 72, 75–77, 79, 85, 91, 92, 93, 101, 108, 110, 147
Greenslade, William, 79n
Grossman, David, 26

Habsburg Empire, 2, 4, 25, 73, 110, 115, 117, 127, 128, 129, 130, 135, 138, 143, 144, 185, 190
Hackert, Fritz, 116n
Hale, Dorothy J., 196n
Handler, Nina, 197, 201, 204
Hardy, Thomas, 2, 3, 69, 80, 81, 97, 190, 195, 196
Hastings, Warren, 42
Hegel, G.W.F., 46, 84, 102, 104, 164, 169, 183, 195
Hegeman, Susan, 7, 12n, 16, 24n, 38
Heidegger, Martin, 5, 43, 78n, 171, 172
Helvétius, Claude Adrien, 43
Hemingway, Ernest, 110, 156, 181n

Herbert, Christopher, 122, 123, 157
Herder, Johann Gottfried, 14, 15, 18, 25, 41, 42–47, 49, 57, 60, 84, 96, 122
Herodotus, 15, 40
historicism (discourse), 12, 13, 16–19, 20, 22, 27, 65, 95, 105, 106, 108, 183, 185, 194, 196, 197
Hofmann, Michael, 113, 115
Hofmannsthal, Hugo von, 109n
Hollander, Rachel, 94
Holmes, Oliver Wendell, 4, 5, 179–80
Home, Henry (Lord Kames), 44
Howe, Irving, 22, 27, 88, 143, 149, 152, 155, 160, 162
Howells, William Dean, 23, 81, 97
Hughes, Jon, 116
Hume, David, 14
Hüppauf, Bernd, 116n

Irish Rebellion (1798), 53, 57
Irving, Washington, 68, 89n

Jacobite Rebellion (1745–46), 58, 59, 60
James, Henry, 20, 23, 81, 83, 92, 98, 110, 156
James, William, 4, 5, 186, 187
Jameson, Fredric, 19, 129
Jewett, Sarah Orne, 20, 69, 81, 155
Johnson, Samuel, 14, 45
Joyce, James, 90, 91, 112, 113n, 151
Juergens, Thorsten, 116

Kafka, Franz, 1, 91, 144
Kagan, Tzipora, 167, 169
Kalderon, Nissim, 167
Kant, Immanuel, 14, 15, 32, 34, 41
Kaplan, Amy, 21, 66, 67, 77
Katznelson, Berl, 182n
Keller, Gottfried, 109n
Kepler, Johannes, 174

Keret, Etgar, 26
Kesten, Hermann, 114, 115
Kilcher, Andreas, 26, 119, 126
Kimmerling, Baruch, 149–50
Kluckhohn, Clyde, 38
Kraus, Karl, 128
Kroeber, A.L., 38
Kronman, Anthony, 198, 199
Kundera, Milan, 20, 133

Lackey, Michael, 172
Lampedusa, Tomasi di, 3, 9
Lawson, Richard, 109
Le Bon, Gustave, 79
Lear, Jonathan, 29–37, 190
Lears, T.J. Jackson, 78
Leavis, F.R., 2, 94
Lee, Hermione, 81
Leibovitch, Yeshayahu, 167, 182n
Levine, George, 20, 95
Levinson, Marjorie, 196n
Lewis, R.W.B., 88n
Lewis, Sinclair, 82
Locke, John, 14, 15, 41
Lodge, David, 203
Lovejoy, Arthur O., 14, 45n
Luckmann, Thomas, 10, 115
Lukács, Georg, 3, 12, 16, 19, 22, 66, 113n

Macpherson, James, 50, 51, 52, 70, 76, 89
Magris, Claudio, 127n
Malinowski, Bronislaw, 62, 71, 80, 83, 120, 122, 123, 136
Mann, Thomas, 1, 109n, 148, 151, 170
Mansfield, Katherine, 100
Marchand, Wolf R., 116n
Massinger, Philip, 2
Maturin, Charles, 58
Maxwell, Richard, 161

Index

Mead, George Herbert, 115n
Mead, Margaret, 6
Menand, Louis, 4, 5, 10, 179, 180
metropolitan realism. *See* realism (genre)
Michaels, Walter Benn, 7
Miller, Andrew, 94
Milton, John, 51
Miner, Earl, 51
Miron, Dan, 150n, 151, 162, 169, 170, 183n
Montesquieu, Charles-Louis de Secondat, Baron de, 41, 43, 44n
More, Thomas, 2
Moretti, Franco, 19, 67, 91, 103
Murfree, Mary Noailles, 89n
Musil, Robert, 91, 128, 167, 170

Nehamas, Alexander, 108
Neue Sachlichkeit [New Objectivity], 25, 111, 116, 136
Nevius, Blake, 87n
Newman, John Henry (Cardinal), 195
Nietzsche, Friedrich, 26, 33, 78n, 93, 109n, 167, 195
Nievo, Ippolito, 3
Nordau, Max, 79
Norris, Frank, 105
Nussbaum, Martha, 9, 198, 199, 201

"Old New York," 4, 80, 84, 88, 99, 100–1, 103, 107, 115, 127, 128, 139, 149, 185, 190, 200
Orpaz, Yitzhak, 181n
Ortega y Gasset, José, 75, 92, 93
Orwell, George, 68
Owenson, Sidney (Lady Morgan), 58
Oz, Amos, 1–2, 26, 168n

Parekh, Bhikhu, 42, 44n
Parsons, Talcott, 46
Pater, Walter, 121

Pavel, Thomas, 47
Peel, Robin, 108n
Peirce, Charles M., 4, 5
Perloff, Marjorie, 127–28, 131
Pick, Daniel, 79n
Pinter, Harold, 151
Plato, 15, 33, 43, 106, 134, 172, 187, 188, 196
Plenty Coups, 35
Poe, Edgar Allan, 131
Pound, Ezra, 92
Pratt, Mary Louise, 134
Proust, Marcel, 92, 159
Pryse, Marjorie, 68

realism (genre), 3, 4, 11, 12, 13, 19–21, 24n, 37, 50, 54, 56, 64 70, 77, 81–82, 83, 84, 86, 91, 92–98, 101, 108, 112, 128, 153–54, 160, 163, 187, 188–89; elegiac, 21, 53, 58, 63, 65, 116, 120, 143, 183
regionalism (genre), 3, 20–21, 25, 50, 52, 64, 68–71, 77, 81–83, 89, 91, 100, 154, 155n, 169
Reifenberg, Benno, 118, 119
Reich-Ranicki, Marcel, 128n
Remarque, Erich Maria, 110
Richardson, Samuel, 52, 54
Richetti, John, 65n
Rigney, Ann, 64
Rilke, Rainer Maria, 109n, 114
Ron, Moshe, 157n, 160, 161
Rorty, Richard, 5, 9, 33–34, 103, 141, 171, 172, 191, 192, 194, 195
Rosaldo, Renato, 109n, 114
Rosenfeld, Sidney, 110n
Rosenthal, Jesse, 94
Roskies, David G., 123n
Roth, Joseph, 2–6, 8, 23–24, 25, 26, 27, 53, 73, 109–145, 147–48, 152, 185, 189, 190, 192; children in, 141–43; depiction of Emperor Franz

Roth, Joseph *(continued)*
  Joseph in, 144–45; engagement with the *Neue Sachlickeit* [New Objectivity], 25, 111, 116, 117, 136; ephemeralization of the center, 26; and ethnoliterature, 25–26, 117, 119–27; the self in, 6–8, 114–15 132–33, 140–41; work as journalist, 111, 117–20, 123–24; Works: *Die Büste des Kaisers*, 131n; "Enough with the 'New Objectivity!,'" 136–37; *Flight without End*, 110, 113, 114, 126; *Job*, 25, 116, 117, 126, 129; "The Myth of the German Soul," 115; *The Radetzky March*, 4, 5, 9, 21, 25–26, 117, 119, 120, 126, 127–45, 148, 153, 183, 185; *The Rebellion*, 110; *Hotel Savoy*, 110; *The Wandering Jews*, 123–26, 134; *The White Cities*, 119, 120, 121, 123
Roth, Philip, 147

Sadeh, Pinhas, 182n
Sahlins, Marshall, 38, 39, 48
Said, Edward, 66, 134
Sand, George, 20, 69
Sand, Shlomo, 183
Sapir, Edward, 61, 124
Sartre, Jean-Paul, 167
Saussure, Ferdinand de, 43, 156
Scheffler, Samuel, 3
Schiller, Friedrich, 121
Schnitzler, Arthur, 109n, 151n
Scholem, Gershom, 182n
Schopenhauer, Arthur, 109n
Schor, Hilary, 20–21
Scott, Walter, 2, 21, 23, 25, 50, 52, 55, 76, 77, 80, 82, 89, 125, 154, 183, 185, 190, 194; narratorial technique, 58; role in the rise of regionalism and realism, 64–70; Works: *Waverley*, 11, 13, 58–64, 96, 133
Scranton, Roy, 11
Shabtai, Edna, 151n
Shabtai, Yaakov, 2–6, 8, 21, 23–24, 25, 26–7, 53, 73, 147, 152–56, 166, 167–72, 181–83, 185, 186, 189, 190, 192; "anti-philosophicalism" in, 26, 171–74, 177, 184; ephemeralization of the center, 26, 148–49; narrator in, 158, 160–65, 174, 178; prose style, 156–59; the self in, 6–8, 112–13; Works: *Past Continuous* [*Zikhron devarim*], 4, 9, 11, 21, 23, 26–27, 147, 148, 149, 155, 167–84, 185, 194; reception of, 150–52, 167–69, 181–84; *Past Perfect* [*Sof davar*], 151n; *Uncle Peretz Takes Off*, 150–51
Shaked, Gershon, 144, 162, 169, 176
Shamir, Moshe, 182n
Shaw, Harry E., 63
Shelley, Percy Bysshe, 51
Smith, Adam, 44, 54, 60
Smith, Barbara Hernnstein, 202
Socrates, 200
Soker-Schwager, Chana, 163, 165, 169, 183
Sophocles, 8
Southey, Robert, 47
Spencer, Herbert, 122
Spengler, Oswald, 72, 169
Spenser, Malcolm, 129n
Spinoza, Baruch, 14
Stafford, Fiona, 17n, 67n
Steiner, George, 22
Stendhal (Marie-Henri Beyle), 68, 91
Stevenson, Robert Lewis, 151
Stewart, Susan, 51
Stowe, Harriet Beecher, 69; Works: *Uncle Tom's Cabin*, 82

Sültenmeyer, Ingeborg, 116n

Taylor, Charles, 6
"Little Tel Aviv" [*Tel Aviv ha'ktana*], 4, 26, 149, 150, 155, 157, 162, 165, 169, 174, 190, 200
Thackeray, William Makepeace, 66
Theocritus, 51
Thomson, William (Lord Kelvin), 78
Thompson, E.P., 143
Tolstoy, Leo, 1, 65, 92
Tonkin, Kati, 116, 117
Trilling, Lionel, 22, 94, 95, 121, 143
Trollope, Anthony, 95
Trumpener, Katie, 12n, 13, 24, 58n
Turgenev, Ivan, 20, 65, 66, 70n
Tylor, E.B., 76, 122, 156

Updike, John, 86

Vargas Llosa, Mario, 3
Valéry, Paul, 25, 76–77, 79
Veblen, Thorsten, 72, 80
Vico, Giambattista, 14, 41
Viebig, Clara, 109n
Voltaire, 14, 43, 172

Wampole, Christy, 18n
Waugh, Evelyn, 3
Weber, Max, 80
Wellek René, 22
Wendel, Hermann, 127
Wharton, Edith, 2–6, 8, 9, 21, 23–24, 25, 26, 27, 53, 73, 79–108, 109–14, 115, 118, 126, 128–29, 132, 140, 147–49, 152, 160, 166, 185, 189, 192; anthropological vocabulary in, 80–81, 83–84; as regionalist writer, 25, 81–82, 89; the self in, 6–8, 112–14, 115n, 132–33, 135, 140; Works: *The Age of Innocence*, 4, 9, 21, 25, 75, 79, 80–81, 83–86, 91–92, 98–108, 111, 126, 135, 141, 148, 153–54, 185, 194; *A Backward Glance*, 4n; *The Custom of the Country*, 111; *Ethan Frome*, 81, 89; "The Great American Novel," 112–13; *The House of Mirth*, 82, 85, 105, 106, 111, 187; *A Mother's Recompense*, 107n; *The Reef*, 111; "Tendencies in Modern Fiction," 113n; *The Writing of Fiction*, 91, 97, 111
Wharton, Teddy, 87
Wilde, Oscar, 121, 203, 204
Williams, Raymond, 2, 15n, 19, 45
Wilson, Edmund, 108
Wittgenstein, Ludwig, 43, 171, 172, 204
Wolff, Cynthia Griffin, 90n, 102
Woolf, Virginia, 90, 93, 112, 114, 151n, 159, 172, 203, 204
Wordsworth, William, 15, 17
World War I. *See* Great War
Wörsching, Martha, 116

Ya'ari, Meir, 182n
Yehoshua, A.B., 168n
Yizhar, S., 182n

Zagarell, Sandra, 154–55
Zencey, Eric, 78n
Zionism, 4, 125, 148, 149, 158, 161, 166, 167, 182; Zionist Labor Party [MAPAI], 26, 150, 165
Žižek, Slavoj, 6
Zweig, Stefan, 25, 75, 76, 127n

www.ingramcontent.com/pod-product-compliance
Lightning Source LLC
Chambersburg PA
CBHW020652230426
43665CB00008B/412